The Prism of Grammar

The Prism of Grammar

How Child Language Illuminates Humanism

Tom Roeper

A Bradford Book
The MIT Press
Cambridge, Massachusetts
London, England

MIT Press books may be purchased at special quantity discounts for business or sales
promotional use. For information, please e-mail special_sales@mitpress.mit.edu or
write to Special Sales Department, The MIT Press, 55 Hayward Street, Cambridge,
MA 02142.

This book was set in Stone Serif and Stone Sans on 3B2 by Asco Typesetters, Hong
Kong, and was printed and bound in the United States.

Library of Congress Cataloging-in-Publication Data

Roeper, Thomas.
The prism of grammar : how child language illuminates humanism / Tom Roeper.
    p. cm.
"A Bradford book."
ISBN-13: 978-0-262-18252-2 (alk. paper)
1. Grammar, Comparative and general. 2. Language acquisition. 3. Language and
languages—Variation. I. Title.
P151.R725   2007
401′.93—dc22   2006047210

10 9 8 7 6 5 4 3 2 1

Contents

Foreword

Samuel Jay Keyser

In his book *The Third Chimpanzee*, Jared Diamond suggests that what distinguishes our species, *Homo sapiens*, from other members of the tree of human evolution is innovation. Neanderthal man, he argues, provides an instructive comparison. Here is what he says. The earliest examples of complete Neanderthal skeletons date to about 130,000 years ago. They may be even older. The latest skeletons date to about 40,000 years ago. During that entire 90,000-year period, there was absolutely no change in Neanderthal culture as reflected in its artifacts. The tools of the earliest Neanderthals are identical to the tools of the latest:

Today we take cultural differences among people inhabiting different areas for granted. Every human population alive today has its characteristic house style, implements, and art.... No such cultural variation is apparent for Neanderthals, whose tools look much the same whether they come from France or Russia. (p. 43)

He then describes the cultural changes of Cro-Magnon man, the earliest known European example of *Homo sapiens*. The changes are staggering. Earliest tools evolved and were refined. Art, even superb art—for example, the Lascaux cave drawings—suddenly appeared. And in the thousand years that passed from the earliest to the latest Lascaux cave drawings, drawing and coloring techniques clearly got better and better. In other words, about 40,000 years ago there was a revolution. A creature suddenly appeared on the savannahs of Africa capable of constant and volatile change. Sound familiar? This is how Diamond describes it:

These variations of culture in time and space are totally unlike the unchanging monolithic Neanderthal culture. They constitute the most important innovation that came with our rise to humanity: namely, the capacity for innovation itself. To us today, who can't picture a world in which Nigerians and Latvians in 1991 have virtually the same possessions as each other and as Romans in 50 B.C., innovation is utterly natural. To Neanderthals, it was evidently unthinkable. (p. 50)

If Diamond is right to think that innovation is the sine qua non of being a human being, then perhaps human language is the engine of that innovation. This, at any rate, lies at the heart of the book you are about to read. Roeper writes:

A major theme of this book is that systematic creativity is what is special about every human being.... To get perspective on grammar, we start with a grammar-style vision of human nature itself.

Going well beyond Diamond, Roeper's thesis is that grammar is everything:

Every human thought and action is built by grammarlike rules. It may seem odd or bold to assert that grammar is a model for how everything in the mind works. My argument goes further:

The body is just an extension of the mind.

The body is designed to express the mind—the opposite of the common view that the body is real and the mind an illusion. The mind as pervasive is what we see when we adjust our focus to a microscopic level.

This bold vision takes very seriously the view expressed almost half a century ago by Noam Chomsky that language offers an essential insight into what it means to be human. For Roeper, the capacity for language and being human are interchangeable.

What happened in our dim and distant past that led to us? I suppose an answer to that question depends on how far back you go. But, of course, the farther back you go, the less you can know. That is one of the paradoxes of human history. A good place to start is roughly 2 million years ago in Africa when—as a result of geological changes that began 50 million years earlier—a lush, tropical landscape was replaced by one that was semi-arid, the vast African savannahs. One of the consequences of that change was that numerous hominids living in the tropical forests of Africa died out. Two survived because they were able to adapt to their new environment. One of those two was our ancestor.

Neanderthal man and *Homo sapiens* were the descendants of those African savannah survivors. But what precisely happened 40,000 years ago that left Neanderthal man in the dust? To persist in that metaphor, what lifted humankind up out of the dust of the primate world into the loftier realm of innovation? Language is what happened.

Roeper is at pains to show what language means in all its multifoliate nature. What made language happen? Here is an interesting speculation, one that Roeper is clearly attuned to. What happened may well have been a genetic fluke, a chance modification, a one-off change in the wiring of the brain that made it possible to think recursively. In Roeper's words:

An essential feature of all grammars is a concept at once elementary and mathematically profound: *put something inside itself.*

The ability to function recursively gave the brain a capacity it didn't have before, the capacity to produce words, phrases, and sentences that have no upper bound just as, indeed, it can with numbers. Both can figuratively if not literally go on forever.

It seems probable that this genetic moment had nothing to do with brain size. After all, Neanderthal man's brain was 10 percent larger than ours. Rather, it had to do with brain architecture: the way the wetware of the brain was wired, or, more accurately, rewired. One day a hominid was born whose brain was slightly different. Suddenly it had the capacity to produce words like *lion hunter*, and *lion hunter hunter*, and *lion hunter hunter hunter*, and on and on and on, each word being the input to the same rule that produced the word it came from. It is hard to know why the brain could suddenly perform this mental gymnastic, but perform it it did and does. Mutations have occurred throughout the history of life on Earth. This one was special. It gave rise to history and, therefore, to us.

While it is hard to fathom what exactly happened, it is not hard to accept that something biologically unprecedented did happen. After all, every so often a genius walks among us, someone whose vision opens vistas that the rest of us have never seen, someone like Michelangelo, or Bach, or Einstein, or Louis Armstrong—someone whose mental hard-wiring enables him or her to do things differently. The first hominid who could think recursively would certainly have been a genius among his or her peers. That creature could do what no one else on the planet could do.

Barbara Wallraff begins her book *Word Fugitives* this way:

Imagine being the first person ever to say anything. What fun it would be to fill in the world with words: *tree, dog, wolf, fire, husband, wife, kiddies.*

I have often thought about what life must have been like for the first human being, the one who could say things none of his peers could say. I have always thought life for that first person would have been a living hell. He—or she—could do what no one else could do. How could he possibly share that ability with his peers? My wife, Nancy Kelly, recalls an event from her childhood. She was four years old, and she was with her older sister and a friend. Out of the blue, it occurred to her that she could think. She meant that literally. She suddenly realized that there were thoughts in her head and that she was in charge of them. She could make her thoughts appear and disappear. She could make them move around, give way, line up, roll over, just as if they were circus animals. She was their trainer. Instantly, she wanted to know if her older sister had thoughts as well. She stared hard, trying to penetrate her sister's mind. When she realized she couldn't, she did what any four-year-old would do. She threw a tantrum. That is how I imagine the first speaker reacting to the knowledge that she could speak.

It is frustrating for all of us. But speaking is the only way we will ever begin to know what others are thinking and, of course, what we are thinking ourselves. It is a remarkable fact that the majority of the time when we are using our innate language ability, we are using it to talk to ourselves. Now, of course, this incredible gift of language is something we all take for granted. But thanks to Roeper's book, each of its readers will be able to touch a bit of that wonder. Each reader will understand what it means to be able to speak a language and that every child born into this world is an incarnation of that first speaker, the one who realized for the first time that he could speak.

Preface

This book rests on three pillars: the formal principles that guide children in the astonishing feat of acquiring their first language; the subtle nature of dialectal variation; and the social, educational, and philosophical implications of human grammar. Naturalistic observation, academic experiments, and a personal outlook all come into play.

One might ask, why put grammar, philosophy, social implications, and experiments all in one book? Whitehead once said that one should have a "devotion to abstraction and a passion for detail." In that spirit, it is precisely my goal to make connections among philosophy, empirical detail, and social implications. My purpose is to show how philosophically deep questions, and a child's basic dignity, are connected to what children say, even to the first word they speak and to what we adults think of as cute expressions. One child said, for example, "My mind is very angry, and so am I." She assumed two levels of mind, perhaps a body and a soul, and underscored the reality of the soul for a six-year-old. Beyond philosophy, I will urge that we all recognize the social significance of abstract theories.

Every act we humans undertake requires us to summon our whole being and personality in order to choose what to do. How does a person, not just a brain, decide to eat or sigh or think of love (or do all at once)? How is the mind organized so that it can integrate diverse information to make such decisions? One thesis of this book is that our grammar "machine" can be a model for all dimensions of mind and personality. Though each module of mind has its own makeup, still we generate emotions, art, athletic moves, friendship—everything our minds and bodies create—with combinatory principles similar to those we find in grammar.

What we say is like a visible DNA, a slender angle on ourselves that projects both an image of shared human nature and an intricate map of individuality. The words that tumble out of our mouths—even a child's first words—show that we each command abstract, unconscious "mathematical" principles, instantaneous creativity, and a unique personal gestalt that we share when we speak and that others can recognize. I will argue that we each have a unique formula that determines our actions. One reason why we should have respect for each other is that none of us can quite grasp that formula within another person. Intuitively, most people sense that each person has dignity beyond the judgment of others.

One way to gain respect for ourselves and for children is to look straight at the challenge of language acquisition: how do children acquire every nuance of meaning and every odd piece of grammar their native language contains? As we will see, everything about the human mind gets into the act.

Gratitude

Sometimes I feel I would like to thank everyone I ever met or heard. Almost everyone makes an indelible impression in the first words one hears from them.

When asked if her mother would come home for dinner, a six-year-old girl I met in Mississippi as a civil rights worker responded, "Sometimes she do...and sometimes she don't." Her words gave her some philosophical equanimity to cope with daily uncertainty. Henry Kissinger revealed much about himself when he said (in an interview, as I recall), "In diplomacy you have to lie even when you tell the truth." The human mind—highlighted in such simple phrases—is the most challenging scientific quarry anyone ever tried to hunt down. This book aims—with what degree of success, I can't be sure—to connect the mathematical structures behind grammar to the whole human being that radiates every time we speak.

Colleagues

Many people deserve many thanks for what I have gained from them—from nuggets of linguistic insight to their inspiring academic spirit. Much has found its way into this book in ways I do not fully grasp myself.

First, my closest colleagues: Jill de Villiers and Harry Seymour have shared the adventure of language acquisition—and its pursuit in the African-American English and Specific Language Impairment Projects—for more than twenty-five years. They have not written a single word of this book, but I feel that a little of their spirit lingers behind every one that I wrote (even a few they may not agree with).

Most of the ideas in this book originated directly or indirectly with Noam Chomsky (though I may have given a few of them a stronger twist than he would have). I want to thank him here especially for his concern for the human dimensions of linguistics, his example, and his support for this project.

Jay Keyser has been a friend, collaborator, and supporter for many years and has been kind enough to write a foreword for this book. It has been my privilege to be close enough to him to see his unseen magnanimity. In unknown and unheralded ways, as administrator, editor, and colleague, he has made hundreds of contributions to the well-being of the field of linguistics, and I want to take this occasion to thank him for all of us. His generosity helped create the world from which this book comes.

Collaborators and projects beyond the Pioneer Valley have created a kind of international electricity that has given rise to many of the ideas in this book. Jürgen Weissenborn started our serious crosslinguistic research and supported the writing of this book; he always sees that academic work has a moral dimension. Others have gradually joined in a variety of projects that have left their mark on this book: William Snyder, Frank Wijnen, Kathy Hirsch-Pasek, Teun Hoekstra, Zvi Penner, Sonja Eisenbeiss, Barbara Schmiedtova, Ayumi Matsuo, Satoshi Akiyama, Laura Wagner, Rosemary Tracey, Natalia Gagarina, Dagmar Bittner, and Uli Sauerland.

Students in language acquisition courses at the University of Massachusetts quickly became colleagues and shared the adventure of making linguistic theory connect to language acquisition. This book tries to recreate the excitement we shared in watching new intellectual angles and experiments come into view. Those who worked directly on acquisition are (in rough historical order) Susan Tavakolian, Ed Matthei, Larry Solan, Helen Goodluck, Stan Kulikowski, Marianne Phinney, Janet Randall, Xiaoli Li, Toya Wyatt, David Lebeaux, Bill Philip, Janice Jackson, D'jaris Coles, Linda Bland-Steward, Eliane Ramos, Tamar El-kasey, Ana Pérez-Leroux, Cesar Alegre, Bart Hollebrandse, Lamya Abdulkarim, Tim Bryant, Lourdes Mallis, Deanna Moore, Olivia Alvarez, Val Johnson, Kristen Asplin, Miren Hodgson, Anna Verbuk, Helen Stickney, and Tanja Heizmann. Post-doctoral students Ken Drozd and Robin Schafer became involved as well.

Other students who did acquisition research alongside theoretical work were also influential: Greg Carlson, Mats Rooth, Dan Finer, Taisuke Nishigauchi, Deng Xiaoping, Michiko Terada, Mari Takahashi, Bernadette Plunkett, Bernard Rohrbacher, Satoshi Tomioka, Min-joo Kim, Marcin Morzycki, Michael Terry, Uri Strauss, Anne Vainikka, Elena Benedicto, and Michael Dickey.

Beyond UMass, I have been privileged to serve on a number of dissertation or Habilitation committees, which are invariably enlightening: Yukio

Otsu, Jennifer Hsu, Theo Marinis, Charles Yang, Heiner Drenhaus, Maaike Verrips, Angeliek van Hout, Charlotte Koster, Tanya Kupisch, Lucienne Rasetti, Natascha Müller, Petra Schulz, Dany Adone, Doreen Bryant, and Liane Jeschull.

Faculty—present, former, and visiting—engaged in acquisition work that provides specific background for research reported here are Edwin Williams, Kyle Johnson, Hagit Borer, Lisa Matthewson, Angelika Kratzer, Chris Potts, and Peggy Speas. The sections on African-American English are deeply indebted to Lisa Green and her pioneering work. Other faculty members provided a helpful angle on many occasions: Lyn Frazier, with whom I co-teach an introduction to psycholinguistics, Lisa Selkirk, John Kingston, John McCarthy, Ellen Woolford, Joe Pater, Roger Higgins, Emmon Bach, Barbara Partee, Don Freeman, Rajesh Bhatt, and David Pesetsky.

Visitors to the Department of Linguistics and the Acquisition Center have brought many new perspectives to bear: Jürgen Meisel, Dana Mc-Daniel, Viviane Déprez, Luigi Rizzi, Tim Stowell, Juan Uriagereka, Marcus Bader, Krysten Syrett, Magda Oiry, Eric-Jan Smits, Merce Coll, Meike Weverink, Francesca Foppolo, Catherine van den Doel, Satoshi Akiyama, Laura Wagner, Alan Munn, Kazuko Yatsushiro, Young-Wha Kim, and Orin Percus.

Chuck Clifton, Gary Marcus, and Carolyn Mervis in the Department of Psychology; philosophers Gary Matthews, Robert Sleigh, and François Recanati; my good friends, physicists David Griffiths, Herb Bernstein, and John Machta; and biologists Peter Klopfer and Karen Searcy gave me perspectives on issues that lie outside my usual academic realm. An old personal friend, Tom Rossen, chimed in too, reminding me of the value of the irreverence we all championed at Reed College.

Acquisition History

This book is built upon the modern field of generative language acquisition studies (although it does not recount its history in any way). Therefore, I would like to thank a number of colleagues who have played a pivotal role in its evolution: Ken Wexler (with whom I edited *Language Acquisition* for many years), Lila Gleitman, Nina Hyams, Jürgen Meisel, Robert Berwick, Stephen Crain, Melissa Bowerman, Barbara Lust, Celia Jacubowicz, Andrew Radford, Harald Clahsen, and Virginia Valian. I would also like to thank others in allied fields: Larry Leonard, Mabel Rice, Heather van der Lely,

Bonnie Schwartz, Lydia White, Wolfgang Klein, and many others beyond my ken who have made it a vibrant, growing, and thrilling enterprise. I hope this book will add to the new avenues for all of us and the coming generation to explore.

Projects and Places

The African-American English Project at UMass has led to the development of a real application of linguistic work to problems of Specific Language Impairment: the Diagnostic Evaluation of Language Variation (by Harry Seymour, Jill de Villiers, and Tom Roeper). This project brought together many students and half the faculty from the Departments of Linguistics and Communication Disorders, and benefited from major contributions by Peter de Villiers at Smith College and essential contributions at all levels by Barbara Pearson. The staff of the Psychological Corporation in Texas— Lois Ciolli, Carol Waryas, Gay Lamey, and Pat Zurich—and the president, Aurelio Perfetti, were all very supportive. This work led to the primary argument in chapter 8 on the absence of "variables" in child language and in language disorders and to much of the extensive discussion of African-American English in chapters 9–11.

Many of the ideas in this book have been developed into software programs available from Laureate Learning Systems in Burlington, Vermont, which gave me insight into how to make experiments, and the explorations included here, smooth and precise. I have appreciated collaborating with Mary Wilson, Bernard Fox, and Jeffrey Pascoe.

The Max Planck Institute for Psycholinguistics in Nijmegen has hosted me a number of times; many collaborations have originated there. MIT in Cambridge, NIAS in Holland, the Zentrum für Allgemeine Sprachwissenschaft in Berlin, the Graduierten Kolleg in Potsdam, the Multilingualism Project in Hamburg and the University of Frankfurt, and the Project on Bare Nouns at the University of Toronto gave me many useful contacts and experiences. Applied projects in Mannheim and Groningen have provided rich and promising connections as well.

Writing

Laura Holland, my wife, writes about art and education with graceful economy, elegance, and precision of emotion—a style I cannot equal. It is nonetheless often an inspiration. Peter Elbow, whose books make him the guru of writing, read the first draft and gave me just the kind of personal response and broad advice I needed. Barbara Pearson was the perfect engaged reader, offering helpful comments and corrections from the most abstract to the most particular. She helped guide the manuscript through the modern publication process that is so heavily intertwined with computer formatting. Laura, Peter, and Barbara all helped me dodge the jargon that shimmers in society's favorite phrases about children.

Tom Stone at the MIT Press encouraged me to let my own voice be heard and was enthusiastic about supporting a general-interest book that seeks to weave together open-ended abstractions with hands-on particulars. Anne Mark cast her meticulous eye over the vast whole and over every detail. She saw connections among ideas that led to reorganizing many sections. Her delicate hand often made phrases that stumble and mixed metaphors (like this one) turn into easy rivers of prose.

Many undergraduates, who were the first readers of various chapters, contributed the looks on their faces for me to ponder as well as numerous helpful responses.

Finally, a remark Wayne O'Neil made when I was a graduate student has lingered in my mind. Criticizing someone else's writing, he said, "He should try to write like a human being." All I can say is, I've tried.

Spirit

For the writing style of this book, I owe some abstract debts as well. First, I wanted—in the spirit of Douglas Hofstadter's *Gödel, Escher, Bach*—to write a book that is at once light and serious, that mixes depth and delight, that is open to abstract and unresolved philosophical issues but concrete enough to offer parents, teachers, and children immediate experience with grammar. Steven Pinker's books were an inspiration along these lines as well. Second, I wanted to write a book whose readers find themselves as tantalized by what we do not know as they may be by what we have already found out. Malcolm Gladwell and Antonio Damasio have written books that provided some clues. Third, I sought to create a book that reflects constantly on the ethical and moral implications of how we talk about and treat children. Howard Gardner's perspectives led in this direction. Finally, I wanted to find a rhetoric that speaks to both the expert and the amateur, in the hope that we can, together, take small steps toward more responsible terms and concepts for translating imperfect ideas into language policies and for talking about and to children. I'd like to think that this idea reflects a common goal in the academic world.

My Greatest Debt

My greatest debt is to my two children, Maria and Tim. The debt is not primarily for the quotations I cite here and there, but for who they are. Each of them has the good will, good cheer, and energy—in their individual ways—to bring out the best in others. They reaffirm in my mind the positive view of human nature that underlies this book. In my collection of unusual relative clauses, I recently found this example from Maria, at age three and a half, which reflects her spirit: "I love everybody, even that I don't know."

Goals and Grand Perspectives

1 Setting the Stage: Animating Ideas, Ambitious Goals, and Ardent Commitments

Why a Prism?

Every sentence enters our ears as just a stream of sound. Instantly an inner grammar analyzes it—as a prism divides light—and links different strings of information to different domains of mind (or "modules").[1] Memory, vision, emotions, and intentions are all alerted by the contents of a sentence. The same kind of division happens *inside* grammar: a sound system, a vocabulary, a structure-builder, reference determination, pronoun analysis, and a host of hidden rules are all alerted and galvanized, much as the whole body goes to work to catch a baseball.

The plan here is to take that stream of speech apart, reverse course, and follow the sound back to see how the speaker's mind puts language meaning together, all in just milliseconds—so quickly, in fact, that a real mechanism must be present. I will do my best to disassemble the deeper structure of grammar with a minimum of technical language. Most of the fine grain of grammar (child and adult) remains largely unseen and uncharted territory. We will get as close as we can to the edge of what linguists currently know about grammar, where you will see tantalizing opportunities to study your own intuitions and explore the grammar of children you know. To do that, I will outline the challenge facing children whose task is learning their first language. This challenge reveals, over and over, the intricacy of adult language. As children progress, adult expressions provide endless puzzles for them to solve. The puzzles lead to "mistakes," which often elicit smiles or laughs from adults. Looking at those mistakes closely will, I believe, turn casual amusement into profound respect. The image of the child we come to witness reveals free will in thought, good will in conversation, and self-respect—a person whose recognizable dignity we should bear in mind.[2]

The language crafted by grammar then becomes a laser into life. It gives glimpses of the microscopic structure of human nature amid the great blur of human affairs. One singular commitment of mine is to confront the great issues of the age, the "good" and the "evil" of linguistics and of life. Most new discoveries have positive or negative social consequences that should not be hidden beneath the mantle of "scientific objectivity." Scientists must realize and accept that their work—their partial insights—has an instant impact on society. Just like doctors, who need to use the best knowledge available in choosing medicines, citizens need to use whatever knowledge is available to make linguistic decisions in their daily lives. For example, should my child have a reading tutor or will she catch up on her own? Should I correct my four-year-old's spelling? It is impossible to postpone the social relevance of ideas. As soon as Einstein proposed relativity as a theory of physics, it had social implications. People soon asked, is all morality relative too?

The structure of society is instantly implicated as well. Very often, scientific studies are tinged with social overtones that favor one group of people. A *New York Times* article quoted a geneticist on race: "Scientists got us into this problem in the first place, with its measurements of skulls and emphasis on racial differences. Scientists should now get us out of it."[3] Yet, as the philosopher Simon Blackburn has argued, "Contemporary culture is not very good on responsibility."[4] Maybe we can see our way to some improvements. Scientists should acknowledge that abstract ideas have social implications, try to clarify what they are, and lay them out for public debate. My credo is simply that all knowledge entails responsibility.

Here's one idea that carries responsibility: Knowledge of how language works is part of what we need to eliminate or reduce our quick, prejudicial social judgments about accents and tiny grammatical differences. From my perspective, human society must fight language prejudice as we fight racial prejudice. If we grasp in detail the scientific arguments showing that every language and every dialect, like African-American English (sometimes called Ebonics), is systematic, comprehensible, and legitimate, that knowledge will help achieve an egalitarian society.

This view of the role of knowledge entails the philosophy of democracy: the consequences of science are for society, not just scientists, to determine. Language policy should be consistent with insights from linguistic research, but it must also flow from a society's values. We must all help to shape social policies that reflect what research reveals.

Not every reader will agree with the views I have derived from my work in language acquisition. I hope to engage your opinions and values. We will often fence with common sense in this book. For instance, common sense says that pointing to the world around us and fulfilling desires within that world is what prods the child to communicate and thus provides the vehicle of instruction in language. But common sense can err. Science is most profound and successful when it departs from common sense.

Modern linguistics argues that the social and physical environment is necessary to language learning, but it is little more than a crude crutch upon which is perched a wonderful and delicate kind of mental growth, quite free of the physical world. A child's language reveals how much the "real" world is a world of imagination, and how much a child's words are about ideas and not about things. Montesquieu once said that the present is nothing but the past colliding with the future. Language is where the practical needs of communication collide with the philosophical disposition of human beings. Every utterance entails an "attitude" toward the world. Children do not simply refer to things. Indeed, they make their own philosophical observations, like the five-year-old who said, "Everything is like another thing because everything is something," exhibiting a philosophical distance far above the demands of everyday life. Another child was heard to say, "Don't uncomfortable the cat," producing an imaginative imperative from her own perspective by giving a power to English grammar that it does not have, but grammars of other languages do have—that is, making an adjective, *uncomfortable*, work like a verb.[5]

Linguistic theory, for which this book is an advocate, argues that grammar, just like vision, is fundamentally innate. As a wealth of detail will show, there is no real alternative to the assumption that principles of grammar are inborn, especially where grammar *coordinates* information from other parts of mind. That is, guided by genetic structure, a child uses her innate knowledge of what human grammar must be like in the act of identifying the words and the special structures of one *particular* grammar. As the book progresses, I will try to give an intuitive representation of the fundamental formal principles of this innate human grammar.

Ethics

We have much to learn from medical ethics. A few decades ago, all knowledge was kept in the hands of doctors. Patients were not told if they would die, nor did they make decisions about risky operations. Now we see it as a patient's right to know that he will likely die, to know that an operation has a 20 percent failure rate, to try experimental drugs if he wishes to take the chance, and to know their side effects.

The growth of mental ability is no different. Parents have a right to know and participate in how their children gain and use language. And linguists have an obligation to make them as informed as possible. It is important to combat overprofessionalization, the idea that only professionals are competent to explore and judge child language. (A healthy antidote is a paper by the linguist Wayne O'Neil generously titled "Linguistics for Everyone.")[6] In reality, although they are not completely reliable, parental anecdotes about what children say are a good starting point for research. Likewise, the most statistically sophisticated research in language acquisition can be unreliable if it is based on what turns out to be an erroneous view of grammar. All evidence should be taken seriously and all evidence should be viewed critically, whether it comes from parents or experts.

Public involvement in questions like these helps prevent the spread of misinformation and helps keep important questions alive that researchers may not see. It was the public who revealed that medical research was biased against minorities and women. Research into language disorders needs public involvement as well. Working out the implications of linguistic research for mathematics and literacy, for example, would benefit from the insights of teachers. In that respect, this book belongs in the tradition of the Institute for Science in Society, run by the physicist Herb Bernstein at Hampshire College, which maintains that there should be democratic involvement in both choosing research directions and defining scientific concepts.

Some Unusual Orientations behind This Book

Chapter Design

The part II chapters on acquisition (plus web-based extensions)[7] share a common design. They take a commonsense look at how linguistic structures work, outline methods acquisition researchers have used to get inside those structures, highlight surprising examples that motivate modern research, and explore the literary and human dimensions of grammar. To remain true to the child's acquisition challenge, it is important to examine the outer reaches of grammar that every competent speaker of a language masters. This approach provides a taste of what each structure is like even if some details seem opaque. Each chapter starts out from a simple perspective, so I encourage you to just move on if you are so inclined.

Part III shifts from universals in grammar to where grammars vary. African-American English is enmeshed in the fabric of American life—it remains both celebrated and reviled. This part examines both what is familiar and what may feel strange about African-American English and explores how it may affect children.

Part IV takes a second look at the image of mind behind grammar, at deeper questions of how creativity in language connects to issues of free will, and finally at the moral implications of how our study of children undermines or enhances their dignity. At bottom lies the question of how intellectuals who study human behavior exercise their responsibilities.

Novel Examples: A Method to Disassemble a Mechanism

Just as having a heart does not mean that one knows how it works, so the fact that we speak English does not mean that we know what it is. Linguists continually discover new facts about grammar that reshape their view of the mechanisms it employs. For instance, this contrast was not appreciated until fairly recently:[8]

John wanted someone to wash the dishes, and *so I did* (= wash the dishes).

does not mean the same as

John wanted someone to wash the dishes and *so did I* (= want someone to wash the dishes).

How does a child learn that a simple difference in inversion leads to a totally different interpretation? Is this remote adult stuff beyond the ken of any schoolchild? Recall from the preface the six-year-old who said, "My mind is very angry and so am I." Notably, the child did not say, "...and so I am"! However much linguists must still ponder how to explain this piece of grammar, the six-year-old has already got it right. In most sciences, it is the extremes that provide the most insight; and so it is in linguistics, where the outer edges of grammar give the sharpest insight into the properties of grammar and mind, and provide the deepest challenges to the child.

Discussions with philosophers, psychologists, teachers, and parents all reveal that we often do not share a common vision of what grammar is. How could we, if current linguistic analyses are constantly deepening— going, so to speak, from linguistic molecules, to atoms, to quarks? Each discovery both affirms and alters our insights. It is easy to misconceive grammar fundamentally, if we do not see the abstract features and the new perspectives just coming into view. For that reason, as the discussion proceeds I will always try to keep the endpoint in sight: it is the final state of the adult grammar where complexity forces hidden principles out into the open.

Explorations

Unusual Sentences Reveal the Most   Sharp contrasts in meaning linked to subtle contrasts in grammar offer the best means to get a real grip on what grammar does. My first goal in writing this book is to bring grammar to life for everyone, by opening a window on what is unusual in grammar and in the language of children. Wherever possible throughout the book, therefore, specific "explorations" are suggested—mixing, I hope, depth and delight—as an informal way to glimpse a child's grammar. The explorations are often fun for adults as well, whether monolingual, bilingual, or in the process of learning English. (My college students do them with friends.) Equally important is the fact that storylike contexts are clearer for adults than isolated judgments of grammaticality.

The explorations can generally be done with household objects or as part of a dinner conversation. The most important discussion in the book surrounds this simple question, which one can ask any child at dinner:

"Who is eating what?"

Adults know that this question requires *pairs* as answers: "Daddy is eating bread, Mommy is eating salad, and I am eating beans." More technically, a competent English speaker knows that *who* and *what* call for a potentially infinite list and that the answer must be given pairwise.

This kind of double question plays a crucial role in the communication disorders test, the Diagnostic Evaluation of Language Variation, that Harry Seymour, Jill de Villiers, and I (along with many colleagues) have developed.[9] It took more than twenty years of research in linguistic theory and language acquisition to discover the centrality of such questions to language competence and language disorders—like discovering a tiny but powerful enzyme.

Issues related to questions pop up everywhere. Plurals, for example, also involve sets. Adult English speakers know that the answer to the question

Do dogs have tails?

should be "Yes," and that the answer to the question

Does every dog have tails?

should be "No." Do children understand these two ways that plurals work? Just ask a child, "Does a dog have tails?"—you may well be surprised to find the answer is "Yes." The explorations in chapter 8 address these questions and discuss where this difference comes from and why it can be a conundrum for a child.

Most of the language acquisition work done at the University of Massachusetts has been built around stories and pictures, as is common in language acquisition studies. As I was writing this book, it became clear to me that in many cases, it is easier to manipulate real objects than to understand stories or pictures. So I believe a number of the explorations outlined here can be turned into experiments that will reveal children's knowledge of various structures, knowledge that has eluded researchers using standard methods.

Deliberately, I say very little about ages in this book. It is important not to convert the explorations into tests that may give parent and child a sense of failure. They should be closer to informal math games or Piagetian conservation games, which parents and teachers often play with children. Children learn gradually and at different rates. For instance, most children learn to skip rope in elementary school. Parents can enjoy teaching their children how to skip rope. They do not need to know whether the average child learns to skip rope at the age of six or the age of eight. We enjoy playing math games with children, but we do not need to know exactly when a child can first do subtraction. Language games should be the same.

A major goal of the explorations is not so much to see what a child has already mastered as it is to make us, as adults, aware of how very much children have to master in order to become mature speakers of a language. We should be careful not to draw conclusions too hastily if a child does not answer an exploration question as we adults would expect. There could be any number of reasons for a "wrong" (nonadult) answer: the exploration is misleading in some way; the child does not want to pay attention; the child's grammar has not developed to the point the exploration is probing; the child is trying to use a grammar different from English (this claim will become clear later in the book); the child has not mastered all the grammatical features of a particular word (like *who*); the child has not phonologically identified the structure of a word, or has understood the wrong version of a homophone (such as *there/they're/their*), or has misunderstood a word she doesn't know (for example, *same*) as a word she does know (*some*). The fact is that when a child gives a nonadult answer, we really do not know why. It is only when the child does give the target answer that we know something: the child has mastered the relevant grammatical construction.

If a child has difficulty with an exploration, just drop it (say, "That was a silly question"), wait six months, and perhaps try again. Many of the explorations in this book will be possible with two-and-a-half-year-olds, while others might be best suited to seven-year-olds, and most fall in between. Determining exactly where they fall is not a goal of this book.

Common Sense   All of the explorations circle around the notion of common sense. It is partly how common sense itself works that we need to decipher in order to build an image of the mind that the child brings not only to language but also to life. But more often the proposals made here treat common sense like the enemy of understanding. Much of science succeeds by making the obvious seem strange (as when it asks about gravity, why do things fall down instead of up?). The diversity of grammars means that what is common sense to adults may not start out as common sense to a child. To grasp the child's task, we must undo our own common sense.

Topics

In writing this book, I have omitted most of the usual language acquisition topics (such as the role of phonology in acquisition, complex questions, and missing tense). Rather than exploring what has already been done, I seek to develop a new range of questions. One reason for this is that it is important for everyone, especially language professionals, to see the full scope of the acquisition problem, so it is important to bring in as many dimensions as possible. In medicine, similarly, doctors cannot discuss only the diseases they understand well. To have a sense of what "good health" means, it is equally important to keep in mind both the well-understood terrain and the still underexplored aspects of human physiology.

It is also important to expand the acquisition agenda. My colleague Angelika Kratzer notes that philosophy made a serious mistake for half a century in looking primarily at the quantifier *every* and not at other quantifiers like *most*. Roger Brown, a pioneer in the study of child language, points out that linguists also need to guard against that possibility, by not looking at too few structures in acquisition. So I hope to open up new avenues of research by stepping into new domains.[10]

The last reason for choosing the particular topics I have included is simply one of personal preference: moving abstract linguistic discussions into new experimental domains intrigues my imagination more than rethinking old experiments.

Style

Choosing a Human Rhetoric This book is written informally for two reasons. One reason is to have a human rhetoric for a very human domain. We all respond to what children say first as human beings, not grammarians.

The second reason is more serious. Colleagues sometimes urge professionals not to mix morals with intellectual discussion. One should keep the science clean. Others lament the absence of intellectuals who publicly interpret their results in a larger framework. In my view, every scholar should, at least once, discuss what light his or her field sheds on the world at large. I find that an informal style helps me to avoid claiming undue authority for views that are partly personal in origin.

Archeological Style and the Edifice of Ideas A few reflections on the intellectual style of the book. The edifice of ideas depends upon the edifice of evidence. Yet they are quite different in character. The ideas are driven by the goal of finding simple, tightly coherent abstractions. The evidence is culled from everywhere and resembles archeology more than experimentation. Some evidence is minimal and perhaps weak, while other evidence is extremely robust. Seeing the larger edifice is really building a house of hypotheses. First we need to see where the crucial joints in the house lie; then we can go out and devise new experiments to bolster the rickety pieces.

An archeologist studying Rome considers accidental trinkets, the Coliseum, and carbon dating all together. Similarly, the examples given here range from single anecdotes to conclusions based on results from studying more than a thousand children. While some pieces of evidence are much stronger than others, the evolving theory—whether of Roman history or of language acquisition—itself changes the strength of the data.

I downplay the strength and weakness of various pieces of data given in the book, partly to try to show the larger abstract edifice, and partly because much "strong" evidence is in fact misleading. Oceans of data supported the misguided ideas that children "learn by repetition" and that what is measured by an IQ test defines a single concept called "intelligence."

Two properties of the data presented here lend cogency to the arguments in this book. First, it is *depth of detail in explanation*, not huge numbers, that is persuasive. To take an example from chapter 8 on plurals, it is the phonological impact of the "outside plural" (as when we say not **lowlives* but *lowlifes*, where the plural attaches outside the compound *lowlife*) that is probably the strongest "proof" that a whole phrase is present in the formation of the plural, not just the word *life*.

Second, *diversity of evidence* adds considerable weight. Four quite independent pillars will jointly support the theory of plurals constructed in chapter 8: naturalistic anecdotes, experimental evidence, independent facts from phonology, and theoretical necessity. Again, the fact that numbers are strong in one domain and scanty in another is of little significance. The method I adopt here is just the method of linguistic theory, where the overall logic is more important than the strength of individual judgments.

A mechanical model means that we really believe that a particular feature—like a screw (or an O-ring on a spaceship)—could be missing. If our logic leads to that insight, however evanescent the evidence, we take it seriously. In fact, we do not have a scientific description of what any single thought is. We cannot actually say how our minds add $2 + 2$. Should we not be wary of tests that claim to know what IQ is? The best assumption is that all data should be treated with both respect and suspicion, whether they are anecdotal or statistically robust. A truly explanatory theory will be inherently convincing. The data which showed Galileo that the earth circles the sun were unusually fragmentary.[11] Yet when he imagined the missing links, the conclusion was compelling.

The same archeological perspective on data is true for the study of grammar itself. Some intuitive judgments are rock solid and others are very flimsy. So far, no construction has bottomed out. New subtleties of meaning keep emerging. We cannot be sure what the bedrock features are—as if we look through ever more powerful microscopes. We are well advised to take data and ideas from all quarters seriously. That includes not only grammatical intuitions, acquisition, and disorders, but also neurology, logic, epistemology, anthropology, and computer science.

"Axioms" of How Acquisition Happens

Universal Grammar

Modern linguistics is based upon the great philosophical shift initiated by Noam Chomsky, who has used language to argue that minds are real and cannot be reduced to purely physical concepts (a sophisticated topic to which we return).

Within this general view of mind and language, Universal Grammar is a hypothesis about innate mental structure—accepted by the vast majority of linguists—that makes grammar akin to vision. Universal Grammar defines an infinite but still very narrow range of options for grammar. Some properties (such as the notion of hierarchical structure) are very general and partake of broader cognitive ability, while others (such as the notions "noun" and "verb") are astonishingly precise. The abstract and the specific intermingle in strange ways that hide deep principles. Here is an example. Sometimes words can *move* inside sentences (*I will* can turn into *will I*), but sometimes they cannot. For instance, in English *Here is a hat* is grammatical, but *Is here a hat?* is ungrammatical—yet *There is a hat* can become *Is there a hat?* Why should there be a difference between *here* and *there*? No child is taught that *Is here a hat?* is not all right, and that only *Is a hat here?* is acceptable. What deep principle dictates this difference? Such grammatical subtleties may seem a bit obscure now. The ensuing chapters will, I hope, shed light that makes them obvious.

What Drives the Child to Make Grammatical Distinctions?

As you begin to glimpse the vast array of subtle distinctions that children must master, you may feel like asking, Why should they bother? Why do children pursue them all, and indeed, why have we adults not chosen simpler modes of communication? What *drives* acquisition? Linguists have by no means all the answers to this deep question, much as scientists cannot explain the dazzling variation in species—or even among human faces. But some things are fairly clear.

Much of first language learning proceeds without any motivation. The prism metaphor applies just as well to sound as it does to sight. We need no motivation to discern color, angle, or objects when we open our eyes. Our biology does this for us. Likewise, when sound streams into our ears, the inner analyzer goes to work without the bidding of any communicative goal, picking out sounds, syllables, and words.

Each new sentence we hear is a new invention, an original application of rules. It disappears from consciousness within 500 milliseconds or so. That is, we lose the verbatim version immediately. So syntax must rapidly decode each utterance and deliver a meaning, which is then what we remember. We have a memory for words but not for sentences and their syntax.[12] That makes success in acquiring syntax even more puzzling than success in deciphering words. A child learns grammar even with no time to think about it: human minds keep meaning and drop syntax within seconds, even though holding onto syntax might help learning.

The absence of time to ruminate on syntax is a strong clue from the outset that we are dealing with an innate biological program, a set of grammatical formulas that are there already, whose details can be instantly filled in during the fleeting moment the child holds onto the syntax of an incoming sentence.

Basically, the same claim holds for both syntactic and semantic subtlety—we humans are just built to break down everything that Universal Grammar can absorb. If we hear both *a hat* and *the hat*, our inner analyzer just wants to attach a difference. Furthermore, Universal Grammar says that grammars *must* have a way to distinguish something nonspecific (*a*) from something unique (*the*) (though the story of *the* is far more complex, as chapter 5 reveals). So the inner analyzer automatically tries out the idea that one of those bits of sound, *a* or *the*, could be a specific marker and one could be nonspecific. What type of situation might point out the difference to a child? Well, suppose the child hears someone say, "John and Mary both have a book," and observes that John and Mary each have a different book. That is a clue that *a* is nonspecific. If the child hears someone say, "John and Mary both have the book," and observes that, lo and behold, they are both reading the very same book, then he has a clue that *the* is linked to something definite and unique. It is important to see that context is often needed to confirm a hypothesis that Universal Grammar automatically delivers.

Why, then, does it not happen in an instant? Partly it is because a lot more options are open than the speaker of any given language realizes. For instance, it could be that uniqueness is linked to intonation, or a suffix, or indeed an infix. Faroese puts an article *inside* a word—the equivalent of saying *ele-the-phant* in English. I will argue, in fact, that the child tries out many hidden hypotheses, quickly rejecting some and silently considering others for a while. Here is one that may not last more than an hour. In many languages, articles carry gender. So when an English-learning child hears *the man*, she might decide that *the* means "the-masculine." It is good to make the richest guess first, because it will be right sometimes. In German, for example, the article *der* in the phrase *der Mann* is in fact masculine, so a child making the "*article* means 'article-plus-gender'" guess would be right. Of course, within an hour our English-learning child might hear *the girl*, which would knock out the idea that *the* carries masculine gender. Other possibilities could last longer. Suppose a child decides that

-er freely adds an agent to any noun or verb and makes up a word like *storier*, as children do. Learning that *-er* only attaches regularly to verbs that have an agent, so that *seemer* isn't possible, is harder and does not happen at once. Moreover, there are many idiomatic counterexamples like *New Yorker* and *Detroiter*. So the surface of grammar offers many false leads about where the universals are hiding. In addition, the surface of language is laden with ambiguous phonological and lexical variation that children must disentangle to see where the universals are. So the child must be on the lookout at many levels. English has *to*, *too*, and *two*—and *too* itself has two meanings, "very" as in *too big* and "also" as in *me too*. Why does English have five kinds of *there* and three forms of *that*? Every language marks propositionality somehow, but is it marked by the equivalent of the word *that, so, and, then*, by an intonation pattern, or what? The child knows he must look for a proposition marker, but there are many options across languages. Universal Grammar is very tight in its underlying principles, but broad in their varied expression. It is the surface ambiguities that can obstruct the child and make the process slower. Indeed, it seems that acquisition would be simpler if nature spared us some of these puzzles. Perhaps, as some linguists suspect, there are helpful connections we have not seen, a hidden ladder children can climb easily once they find the first rung. Why do so many grammars (English, German, French, Hebrew, Russian, to name a few) have a directional preposition that seems to be the same as the infinitive marker (in English, *to* as in *to Bill* and *to run*)? Is it a confusing ambiguity that slows down acquisition, or does understanding directional *to* somehow help the child in understanding future or intentional *to*? There might be a connection, but we need to formulate what it is before we can say that the child uses it.

Does motivation to communicate play at least a small role here? It probably does, but the process is very obscure. I might listen hard if I know that someone is saying something important—like why I cannot have any more chocolate. But let us pursue the visual metaphor again. Looking hard, even squinting, may help us isolate a detail, but it does not change the process of vision much: color, angles, distance are all computed without special effort. Motivation probably applies only at a very broad level in language too; the details all come automatically.

Could some features of first language learning be slowed down by maturational processes? This feels like an attractive option because the meaning of so many words requires maturity. The concepts designated by the words *maturity*, *puberty*, or *flirtation*, for example, do not seem to be what children are thinking about. This does not mean that the grammar itself matures, though logically it could. I expect that very little of language is subject to maturation, just as with other organs. When a baby is born, little is incomplete in hearing, seeing, and digesting, for example; and accomplishments like physical coordination mostly involve fine-tuning processes that are already in place.

Nonetheless, in chapter 8 I will suggest, very cautiously, that the notion of variable hidden in quantifier words like *every* may involve maturation or be implicated in disorders. Others have made different but possible claims about maturation.[13] At bottom, it is extremely difficult to know whether it is surface ambiguity or true immaturity that blocks recognition of a grammatical distinction.

What Nudges the Child Along?

What nudges the child along is really the unanswered question that lies behind all of linguistic research. Linguists do not know the answer.

Sometimes, however, we can locate sharp triggers that lead to grasping a distinction. For instance, how does a child know that *there* in *There is a bear* is a statement about existence and not location? Universal Grammar dictates that children are looking for existence markers. A sentence like *There is a bear here* would be a contradiction if it involved two locations. If a child hears this sentence in a situation where a bear is clearly *here*, not over there, then he has a strong clue that *there* is an expletive, a marker denoting existence.

As mentioned earlier, the explorations suggested in this book often put children in a similar contextually sharp situation that may indeed help them along even if they initially give the wrong (nonadult) answer. Even if the child is initially confused by the instruction "Put the chair here there and the one there here," she has heard a clue that she has to sort out how *here* and *there* operate in different parts of a sentence. (Despite the complexity of that instruction, informal experiments by my undergraduate students indicate that three-year-olds have no trouble computing it.) So when a visitor then asks, "When I am here, should I put my shoes there?," she can begin to realize that a "large" *here* (meaning, in this case, "in this house") is involved. As parents and teachers, we do not really know how reading ability is achieved either, so we give children lots of stimuli and lots of support (pictures and repeated use of certain words). The explorations in this book are a bit like reading readiness games that are played in kindergarten—and I propose that in fact, grammar readiness should be promoted the same way as reading readiness.

What Should We Conclude from a Child's Mistakes?

As when a child falls short of the adult target in answering an exploration question, we should not draw hasty conclusions about any of a child's apparent errors. Like the failures of a child who falls off a bike a number of times before getting his balance, the failures of a child attempting a particular grammatical construction may contain the seeds of success. Knowing that the body learns about balance with each fall, parents are not too disturbed by this type of failure. After a few falls, a parent notices some wobbly successes—the child balances a little longer before a fall. This kind of minute improvement is probably happening in grammar in an equally invisible way.

Children's errors can be a source of great insight for researchers. Often we can see that the child is trying out a grammar that is the grammar of some language other than English. Here is just one example; we will look at others later on. The child who said,

"Only I want milk,"

to mean

"I want only milk"

apparently assumed that *only* is a movable adverb, found in the grammars of many of the world's languages. In English, for example,

I always play baseball.

and

I play baseball always.

mean the same thing, so the child's grammar analyzer reasons, "Why should *only* not move around the same way?" (see chapter 8). The best assumption is that mistakes are growing mistakes, from which the child takes away some clue we cannot see.

In sum, we have peeked at a few upcoming puzzles of grammar and squared away a few background assumptions about acquisition. Now we will examine the larger gestalt of the human mind that emerges when we treat all action as if it flowed from a "grammar"—a viewpoint that contrasts sharply with traditional psychological methods and ideas about early cognition. Then we will be ready to look at a child's very first steps in acquisition. What assumptions does a child bring to his very first word? It looks like the simplest moment in acquisition, but actually remains enigmatic to this day.

2 Grammar's Gift to Our Image of Human Nature

Ordinary sentences have the creativity of poetry in them. And like poetic creativity—think of couplets, haiku, iambic pentameter—the creativity of everyday language follows delicate and pinpoint-sharp rules. What are the rules for language? Partly they are traditional "rules of grammar" that we may struggle to learn in school. But the more interesting, more powerful rules are unconscious and unlearned ones that reflect the essence of human nature.

With those rules, our words can endlessly create new worlds. As the critic R. P. Blackmur once said, "Poetry . . . adds to the stock of available reality."[1] When we speak, we can only "add to reality" by following grammatical rules lodged in the subterranean depths of the human mind. We no more learn those deep principles than we learn to have a nose.

To an eager parent or student, this first discussion may seem far afield and too abstract. I start out abstractly because one of my goals is to connect philosophical notions to tiny utterances, to see how much human intricacy a child's first words contains. We need to get the whole human being in our sights by viewing language, thought, and action through the same lens.

Seeing Creativity as Systematic

Formal linguists see themselves as giving a precise mathematical underpinning to systematic human creativity. This view of human nature as essentially creative strongly supports the "humanistic" values of the humanities. Our ultimate discovery of the partly mathematical principles behind linguistic creativity should eventually be incorporated into exact statements about how biology works to produce all kinds of human capability. One goal of modern linguistics is to capture that creativity in a way that is bone-hard, to find the skeleton of logic that orchestrates thought.

An essential feature of all grammars is a concept at once elementary and mathematically profound: *put something inside itself*. That concept underlies our grammatical capacity to put one possessive inside another: *John's friend's car's motor*. (Those with a philosophical background will recognize that this in turn derives from Bertrand Russell's notion of sets that contain themselves.) How and where do children grasp that notion, the primary basis for mental creativity? We will look at just how children cope with it in grammar, after we lay a deeper foundation.

A major theme of this book is that systematic creativity is what is special about every human being. A microcosm of each individual's knowledge—used creatively—lies beneath the ultra-conscious words we choose to utter. Our words become "ultra"-conscious because we put them into situations and they become as real as objects, "adding to reality." When a teenager says "Awesome," the situation itself is altered. To get perspective on grammar, we start with a grammar-style vision of human nature itself.

The strong claim here is this:

Every human thought and action is built by grammarlike rules.

It may seem odd or bold to assert that grammar is a model for how everything in the mind works. My argument goes further:

The body is just an extension of the mind.

The body is designed to express the mind—the opposite of the common view that the body is real and the mind an illusion.[2] The mind as pervasive is what we see when we adjust our focus to a microscopic level.

The Indivisibility of Being

Grammar is one of many abstract ideas that penetrate the minute corners of being. Like the DNA in our cells, every act we undertake reflects our whole being. Every word, every glance around a room, the length of every step we take, is modulated by a mental assessment of our whole body and our whole mind, ultimately by a total image of ourselves, an internal mosaic of *ideas* that the brain assembles. It is not your arm that lifts a glass, it is *you* that lifts a glass. And you lift it for some reason, some goal, that your whole being has decided is what you want to do at a particular moment (get drunk, satisfy thirst, make a toast, ...). The presence of mind—of free will—in even such a simple action seems so obvious that it is not worth mentioning.

Yet the existence of that mind is often denied. Listen sometime to parents' explanations for their children's behavior. Notice how often parents give "physical" explanations rather than mental ones. Suppose a child is crying over something small—like another child taking the spot he wanted at the lunch table—and his parent says he is crying "because he is tired" or "because he had too much sugar," *not* "because he feels that something is unjust." Did sugar cause an inappropriate mental sense of injustice, or was a genuine sense of injustice magnified by too much sugar? The first view denies the reality of mind; the second respects the legitimacy of mind. The difference, as it relates to how we regard and treat our children, is enormous. Preference for physical explanations reflects a deep philosophical bias in the culture of our daily lives. My claim here runs upstream against modern culture: every action is primarily a mental event.

Every sentence—like every action—both reveals and alters who we are. To be melodramatic, every step in language acquisition creates a new person. When a child first uses the word *no*, she is suddenly empowered in a new way; her potential actions (and interactions) are transformed. The first *maybe* makes uncertainty itself legitimate and the notion of possibility viable as a part of social interaction.

Let me begin, then, by sketching an image of human nature outside language (and possibly giving new twists to hot controversies in grammar and the psychology of mind along the way). I cannot settle the scientific questions, but I will at least keep a steady eye on what each theory implies for our own, actual lives. I begin with infinity—a concept that animates much of mathematics.

Infinity

Infinity stands outs everywhere in language. Yet it is only in recent decades that linguists have seen that the concept of infinity is at the heart of language.

It comes in many varieties and obeys rules of its own. Here are two easy kinds:

Repetition: John is very, very, very, very wonderful.

Adjective sequence: the large, red, awful, beloved car

And this is the slightly harder kind I mentioned:

Possessives: Bill's father's car's motor's exhaust

Each possessive or adjective modifies the last. We could keep on adding possessives or adjectives indefinitely; the pattern could go on forever. This grammatical process, which we will look at more closely later on, is called *recursion*.

Grammar encompasses other kinds of infinity. It can even be seen *inside* a sentence. The next sentence is grossly awkward, has never been said before, and yet is completely understandable:

What did John say Mary said Bill wanted Fred to get John to see?

This sentence is interesting because a *potential infinity* exists inside the link that we make, psychologically, between *what* and the seemingly missing but actually moved object of *see*. It is, after all, something *seen* that *what* refers to. But five verbs—*say, said, wanted, get, see*—occur in between. We could keep going, and—here's what's come to be seen as the important point—put an infinite number of verbs between *what* and *see*:

what [infinite sequence] origin-of-*what*

You can make up any number of these infinite sentences yourself; we all have in our minds a capacity for creating special forms of infinity. In fact, every day, each of us creates sentences from the infinite reservoir of potential sentences that have never been uttered before. And this is true not just of structure; meaning has the same property. We each say things that have never been said before, because we mean things that have never been meant before.

Infinite Emotions

Infinite properties of grammar give us hints about all kinds of infinite mental properties, such as our capacity for an infinite variety of emotions. We must have within us an emotion-builder that resembles our sentence-builder. It produces our ability to respond in unique ways to unique situations. To throw an apple at a tree on a warm day after an exam when you are in love and you have an upcoming baseball game produces a different emotion—a different mental state—than if any of those ingredients were not present. It is the essence of being human that we can build a single feeling—say, an answer to the question "How are you?"—from an utterly heterogeneous set of factors that define our experience at any given moment. When a person finally says a decisive "Yes" to a marriage proposal, a feeling is generated that captures an intricate sense of another human being together with a vision of one's personal future. Tiny differences in expression reflect tiny differences in emotion. The remark "My back hurts, but I'm OK" is not the same as "I'm OK, but my back hurts." The hurt back has different degrees of prominence in these emotional summaries.

If we have an emotion-building mechanism, then instead of the 10 or so emotions that modern psychology suggests we all share,[3] each of us may experience 100,000 emotions—and each of us may have a genuinely personal selection. Just as novel sentences mean things that were never meant before, so each of us feels emotions that no one has ever felt before. I imagine that typing this book on a computer, where revision is easy, feels much different to me than scrawling a book with pen and ink felt to authors in earlier days, when revision was much harder. To me, the task feels more like making a verbal sculpture than taking a long journey. How I write and what I write are unified in a single feeling that is both distinctly different from and roughly the same as other writers' feelings. Though humans share experiences, none of our emotions are quite the same. How does the brain accomplish this strange algebra of emotion, which involves complexity in several domains at once? Working out complex moves in chess (which a computer can mimic) involves a single domain, but how do we combine having an exam and being in love on the same day? Insight into that question would enable us to grasp the deepest nature of human intelligence, as well as the sources of human judgment, which requires comparing incommensurate information (think of resolving the question, "Which do I want more: a new car, a new computer, or a trip to Hawaii?"). We have inside us a mechanism that arrives at actual choices and involves our whole "being," but that we hardly understand.

Mind/Body Translations

Building mental states from inherently diverse emotions in milliseconds is one astonishing mental accomplishment. Equally amazing is our capacity to translate ideas into bodily actions.

How is knowledge of a tune delivered to a pianist's fingers? The pianist takes visual information from a printed page of notes, translates it into phrasing in her mind, then translates this information into precise instructions sent out to her fingertips; and her ears check the outcome in a feedback loop all the way to the tips of her fingers again. This is what must be explained: not simple mechanics of how joints work, but how incommensurate information—from paper to touch to sound—is translated into instructions that set fingers rippling over the keyboard. We have a four-way interface here: eyes, mental representation, hands, and ears; if the pianist sings, add "mouth," and if she holds notes with a pedal, add "feet." The essence of these connections must be innate. In fact, in the first minute of life a newborn can imitate gestures—say, taking an image on his retina of someone raising a hand and translating it into physical instructions to raise his own hand.[4]

We must also add "personality" here, for a seven-way interface. The pianist pours her own personality into a rendition of Mozart—and likewise, when we talk, we sprinkle our pronunciation with subtle reflections of our attitudes.

How does a vague thing like personality get translated into the timing mechanism of fingertips, or how do attitudes, even unconscious ones, regulate the mouth cavities that produce voice tones? The essence of this connection, like the others, must be innate. A full understanding of the vocal tract will include how it receives personality information. Thus, the manner in which we creatively associate information from different parts of mind to formulate a sentence is just one example of how we create a blueprint for any kind of action. (It's important to note, though, that only some of our physical systems are open to the influence of personality. Others are utterly immune to emotional states—for instance, most of vision. We could not imagine someone saying, "Whenever I lose confidence, my perception of red turns to pink.")

Let us look briefly at what language does to coordinate inherently distinct, potentially infinite kinds of information, in milliseconds. We connect a system of sound to a system of meaning via a system of syntax, and throw our whole personality into the selection of every word. If I utter the sentence "Our dear President Bush should be *much* more careful in his manipulation of the poor," I express more than a standard liberal point of view. The word *dear* is at once ironic and friendly. Choosing the honorific *President* (not saying "George") reflects social distance between people who are not acquainted. The stress on *much*, like the loudness of *ow* in measuring pain, is finely calibrated to express the abstract notion "degree of care." The term *the poor* reflects a personal assessment of sophisticated mathematical representations of well-being within a generally affluent society. Cultural factors come into play, too: a speaker of British English might be baffled by the need to accurately assess the thrust of emphatic stress on the single word *much*, because the British intonational system conveys emphasis in a slightly different style and has an "understated" use of emphasis. One could in fact fill pages, if not books, with further analysis of the microstructure of a single sentence. For our purposes, the important question is this: how, actually, does the mind integrate these influences in a fraction of a second to produce (or understand) such a sentence? Each sentence is a unique object, so the factors are not prepackaged, but selected and coordinated anew each time we speak.

The Self-Doubt of the Tennis Player

Athletics produces similar marvelous mental accomplishments. Take this story of a competitive tennis player, who recounted that with a chance for victory at Wimbledon, she "lost confidence" just before the first game. As she bounced the ball, getting ready to serve, it hit her foot and rolled away. This surprise unsettled her, she felt insecure, and she lost Wimbledon (in her account). This is really an ordinary event, but it provides quite a challenge to any theory of mind. How exactly did the tennis player's mind take this small event, let it reverberate in a web of personality, and in turn instruct tiny muscles to behave differently? How did a loss of confidence get from her mind into her left arm? Why—being conscious of the irrelevance of her tiny mistake—was she unable to control its effect on other subtle aspects of ability?

How, precisely, does the mind convey an emotion to a muscle? Surely we don't have, among the hundreds of muscles, one labeled "confident" and another labeled "not confident." Obviously the message "Don't be sure of yourself" was delivered to the tennis player's muscles differentially—but did it cause her to lose her grip on the racket, did it affect her hand-eye coordination, or both, or more? A natural retort would be, "The message sort of affects everything." But actually it almost always applies at the micro level. If someone said, "Whenever I lack self-confidence, I can't lift my left arm at all," we wouldn't believe him. We do not believe that a lack of self-confidence can completely immobilize major muscle groups. Gross motor ability is basically unaffected. But if someone said, "Whenever I lack self-confidence, my second serve tends to be a foot out," we might believe him, because "a foot out" is caused by a tiny shift in some muscle that produces a tennis serve. Implicitly, our culture has always accepted the idea that there is a connection between large mental states and microphysical states.

What Does a Juggler Juggle?

I have argued that emotions are infinite, and our emotions can be projected into our body in subtle ways. Now let us consider a difficult question: do we each have slightly different mechanisms, a slightly different formula, for linking our feelings or intentions to physical expressions?

Take a person who can juggle nine balls at once. Two ingredients are self-evident: precise tossing (and catching) and timing. But these are abilities all of us have: we can each throw a ball into the air to a fairly precise height, and we can each keep time. But most people cannot juggle. Why do these abilities not suffice to make us all jugglers? The answer is that there exists a third ability, which allows joint monitoring of two inherently different abilities. The fact that many jugglers can quickly add a fourth, fifth, and sixth ball suggests that a formula—which we cannot define, but roughly label "coordination"—is present that can easily generate more complex action.

Hidden Formulas

The juggler uses a complex system of temporal organization, an implicit awareness of the principles of calculus, and a vast array of tiny muscle properties. Now comes a serious question: do we all have that formula latently, or does the juggler command a unique formula? To answer the second part of the question: it certainly looks like the juggler has something not all of us have—and maybe each of us has something no one else has. So let's leap to the extreme and assert that every human being composes unique, unconscious formulas:

Every individual carries unique formulas that guide his or her actions.[5]

Let us leave the first part of the original question unanswered—whether, in principle, we are all capable of every kind of mental formula. Looking at what we can see, we note that our bodies have the same organs; it is reasonable to assume that our minds do as well. Where grammar is concerned, we are all in principle capable of acquiring the grammar of any language, though we actually learn only one or a few; all normally developing children have the inner formulas needed to acquire grammar, and their experience with the language around them determines which one they learn. More broadly, it seems natural to assume that maybe our unique inner formulas are the result of both an inborn architecture and our life experience. There are deep and unresolved issues here (some of which I consider when I readdress *modularity* later). One could sum it up this way: when we say, "We are all human," just how much identity does that view entail?

Talk of formulas may seem "too mathematical" to the humanist reader, but in a sense "formulas" are inevitable for at least what we can call "fast thought." A formula where all the relations are fixed is like a mechanism, and every mechanism allows instant translations. Just as a car could not run if there were no machine inside it translating gasoline into movement on wheels, so no thought or action that takes place in milliseconds could work so fast if there were no mechanism behind it. Our fast thoughts must be mechanisms in order to be fast. (We will cautiously inquire later into the mystery of "slow thought": why do we think about some things for weeks instead of seconds?) When we say that our whole being is involved in every act, what does that mean for formulas? It means there must be a superformula into which we embed other formulas. It synthesizes our "whole being" into a momentary summation of what we think, say, or do at any given moment. Thus, before we choose a word or phrase, an inherently heterogeneous emotion must be constructed. Similar sorts of inner surveys occur across different domains, and sometimes people arrive at the same covering word for diverse mental states: a person answering the question "How are you?" ("I'm OK, I guess"), a child reporting on a new pair of skates ("They work OK"), a surgeon summing up a complex operation ("It went OK"), a president glorifying five years of war ("We all did OK").

To take an example further afield: a skilled stand-up comedian can glance at an audience and somehow, from the looks on the faces she sees, select five from a hundred jokes in her head. How does she connect face-looks and certain jokes?

And still further afield: imagine an unrepentant murderer. Does he just "lack morals," or does he follow an internal formula that—although we find it both reprehensible and unfathomable—is nonetheless human and unique? Do he, the juggler, the comedian, and all of us have slightly different formulas, different sets of ingredients underlying and motivating our actions? My hypothesis is that we do.

So all individuals carry unique formulas that guide their actions. A young child is a person whose inner formulas—even before he can speak—are reflected in his every act, and who therefore deserves our respect as a complex human being.

The Mind as Search Engine

That language is a biological *mechanism* structures the core of linguistic research. Anything that operates as fast as our language generator and analyzer must, like a computer, have a sophisticated system of links. It must possess mechanical efficiency. When we create a phrase to refer, this mechanism rapidly and creatively combines attitude, aesthetics, and perceptions.

And the mechanism must operate in reverse, too. Comprehending instead of creating, our minds seem to have powerful search engines with the same creative capacity. We must rapidly locate not only individual words, but also unique combinations. Jerry Fodor uses this example: "Can you name a city that is also an animal?" Many people answer "Buffalo!" in a fraction of a second.[6] How do we search for both animals and cities at once? Certainly we do not harbor a memory folder of animal-named cities. We have to consult two different sets simultaneously. Likewise, if I ask, "Can you name something you have had for ten years, that you saw sometime today, and that is a light color?," you will probably be able to zero in on one object out of the millions in your mind. Thus, we undertake sophisticated mental computation from moment to moment in our lives, even in the act of searching memory.

Words as Novel Mental Objects

Language has aesthetic value in itself. Simply connecting a word to a burst of feeling or to a nuance in an action gives us a sense of capturing and managing our environment. If the human mind is in a way at odds with the world, if our view of the world is partly a projection of our own ideas, then we feel satisfaction whenever we perceive a subtle fit. If we can name something, like "serendipity," or even evade something, like calling aggression "protective reaction," then whatever the real-world consequences may be, we have the private satisfaction of giving something an extra aesthetic reality by naming it. A child must have a life that glitters with such delights.

A child's inventiveness is no different from our own. We can capture nonfixed references—that is, project a unique description of a fictional object—and we do it instantaneously. Compounds illustrate this ability. We can invent *elephant icebox*, and it will refer to an icebox that looks like an elephant, or that stores elephant meat, or that sounds like an elephant, or whatever. Here is another I just invented:

bird migration computer manual problems

We construct a concept to fit the phrase, even if it never occurred to us that "problems with a computer manual for bird migration" ever existed.

Human Nature and Language Acquisition

What does this model of human nature really mean for our quest to understand grammar? It means we must confess to a fundamental bafflement before we begin. Even a child's decision to utter her first single word involves a process of mental acrobatics so intricate, personal, and free that we cannot hope to fully explain it for centuries to come. With that bit of melodramatic modesty, let us nevertheless see how far we can get, how far we can unpack the mystery of language acquisition and the mind behind it.

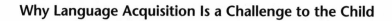

II Why Language Acquisition Is a Challenge to the Child

3 First Words: Glimpses of the Mind

Worlds within Single Words

The child, like any person, surveys the mosaic of his inner world (in milliseconds) and undertakes an action, freely, bringing together intricate physical, mental, and emotional systems. The coordination of vocal cords, lips, auditory information, and perhaps visual information is matched by the coordination of ideas, information, and motivation sketched in chapter 2. At some moment, the child's undertaking is to speak his first word—say, "Dog." The mental organization behind that action—as far as we can tell—is as mysterious as the organization behind any other action. Why speak?

The obvious answer is, to communicate. But why communicate at one moment and not another? We can discuss *what* a child says, but a real understanding of what he says would include *why* he said it, and that is a question so profound we cannot answer it. So by the child's first word science is already laid low by the wonder of mental biology.

The classic explanation of first words presupposes a kind of point-and-shoot camera. The child aims his mind at an object and shoots out a name that refers to it: "Dog." This may seem simple, but later on we will see that the seemingly simple act of "reference" is endlessly complex. We will explore reference at greater length in chapter 5, but here is one whole vista that even just one word spoken by a child—perhaps his very first word—opens to us.

Most words about things appear to obey a simple principle: refer to the whole object. Common sense reigns, it seems. It is often asserted that children organize their world with this "whole object" principle.[1] A parent says "Book." The child repeats the word, and seems to know that it refers to the whole book, not a page, not the cover, not its color.

Certain other organisms are quite different: they use smell or sound, not vision, to sense depth or danger—without ever invoking complex geometry to decide that some object should be carved out as distinct within the visual cacophony of the world. The fact that an object can be detached and moved as a unit is not a necessarily recognizable property. Monkeys seem able to communicate social relations, such as dominance, love, and protectiveness, but (leaving aside routines laboriously taught by researchers) they cannot assert simple propositions about objects, like "My arm itches."[2] Reference to objects is a rarity in nature, while symbols for social emotions are common. So, if it is true that children isolate objects, then it is really a kind of odd habit that need not resemble what other organisms do.

Appearance over Purpose

But do children really refer to whole objects? This is not so clear. What they actually do first is to refer to objects from an interesting angle, then generalize so swiftly that parents often do not see what is happening. First words seem to have a sophisticated part-whole connection: the child uses a name for one salient part to refer to a whole object or perhaps an event.[3] Appearance dominates the word-making effort.

Sound, shape, size, texture—any of these perceptual distinctions (and more) can be the "salient part" of an object the child picks out when she uses a word for that object and then generalizes it to others.

One child used *shh* to refer to a train, then boiling water, then a radiator. Only the *shh* sound is common to these objects; their visual images could not be more disparate. The purpose of the objects seems remote. Yet the child was making the connection via some creative mental set she was building.

A rooster started this sequence:

koko [cockadoodledoo] = cockerel's crowing → tunes played on the violin → tunes played on the piano → all music → merry-go-round

Observe the progression itself. The child is not just repeating sounds wildly. Instead, the progression shows the trajectory of the child's mental generalizations. No core object at all is involved, but some notion of harmonious auditory order is shared and extended.

Another child used size as the basis for generalizing:

fly = fly → specks of dirt → dust → all small insects → his own toes → crumbs of bread → a toad

Yet another picked out texture:

wau wau = dog → all animals → soft slippers → picture of old man dressed in furs

And still others used shape:

baca = large toy abacus → toast rack with parallel bars → picture of building with columns

(from a French-speaking child) nenin = breast → postmark → doughnut → the moon

cookie = novel round foods: Cheerios, cucumber → record player → music on hifi → rocking and/or rocking chair (circlelike motion)

That children focus on specific properties and create unique mental sets is especially clear from one child's use of the word *dog*:

dog = dog → cuff links → thermometer

In each object, something gleams brightly. Eyes gleam out from a background of fur on a dog. A cuff link or a thermometer catches a reflection. Here it seems that the gleam gets the reference, not the whole object. Nor is any "social" or "practical" function evident; only an aesthetic fascination is involved.

So what is our first conclusion? Children must be creating very subtle perceptual sets. The pattern is a delight to adults, but why does the child articulate them? If a child says "Shh" for boiling water, maybe she is really calling attention to an event. Maybe she wants to communicate something more about the event beyond naming it. Our adult guesses about the child's meaning here capture the core, the perceptual basis, but much more must be going on in the mind of the child who speaks. A child must follow an odd and circuitous path of adding more and more grammar before communication is really adequate. Let's see if we can watch how perceptual generalizations emerge by trying some explorations. They may well fail to elicit the "right" answer, but any answer a child gives will be instructive in some way.

Exploration 3.1
Seeing round and parallel (understanding abstract adjectives)

1. Show a child the pictures on the next page (you could also use the actual objects, or any group of objects as long as some are round):

Point to the bowl and say "Round"; and do the same with the other round objects. Now show the child these pictures (or the actual objects) and say, "Show me round":

Does the child point to or pick up the quarter, saucer, and/or doughnut?

2. Instead of pointing to the objects above and saying "Round," point to them and say a made-up word. You might point to the bowl in the first set of pictures and say "Wug," and do the same with the other round objects. Then show the child the second set of pictures and say, "Show me wug."

3. With a child who has created the type of subtle perceptual set illustrated earlier, you might try to enter the child's world and see if you and the child can share the trajectory of generalization (though with the

youngest children, one cannot expect too much). I will use the *baca* set
mentioned above (*baca* = abacus, toaster rack, building with columns) as
an example that you can adapt to your child's set.

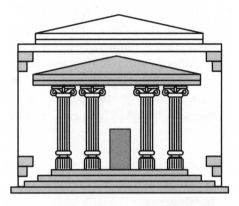

In this exploration, with a child who says "Baca" when she sees columns,
or anything with columns, I would first set out a violin, an orange, and a
hat:

Then I would say, "Show me baca." Does the child reach for the violin (the
item with the parallel strings that look like columns)?

4. Show the child any item and label one of its properties with a made-
up word. Then show her three more, one of which has the same property,
and say, "Show me _____." For example, show the child an abacus and say
"Wug." Then show her a violin, an apple, and a spoon and say, "Take
wug." Will she take the violin, the other item with parallel "columns"?

Suppose the child points to the quarter or the violin. What do we know? We know a logical and productive creativity is present, along with a real abstraction about roundness or parallelism, linked to a word. We know the child can refer to properties as well as objects, and we suspect she can compare two things and thereby treat them as a common set. In addition, we have a few inklings about the child's ability to share conceptual space with another human being.

Let us go a step further and see how children handle adjectives like *big* and *small*, which require dimensional comparison. Try setting several big and small versions of the same things in front of a child. For example:

<table>
<tr><td>

**Exploration 3.2
Seeing big
(understanding abstract
adjectives)**

</td></tr>
</table>

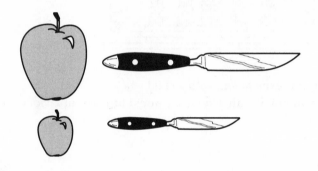

Point to each big one and say "Big." Then set out several small versions and one big version of the same thing. For example:

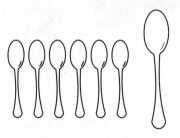

Say to the child, "Take big," or just "Big." Will the child take (or point to) the big spoon? (If you think the child might choose the big spoon simply because he or she is generally attracted to things that are big, reverse the instructions so that you end up saying, "Take small.")

Again, what do we know if a child succeeds at this task (chooses the big spoon)? We have more evidence that the child can perceive properties and sets and make comparisons. Deep abstractions are already bubbling up.

Recall the words of caution about explorations, however. If you high-jump six feet or land a space capsule on Mars, the possibility that it can be done is irrefutable. But if you fail to jump six feet or fail fifty times to land a capsule on Mars, it doesn't mean it can't be done. Myriads of things could stand in the way. Likewise, extraneous factors can hide a child's knowledge.

What should inescapably hold our attention is *success*. If a child succeeds at any of the tasks offered in this book, the feat is worth contemplation. Tremendous mental sophistication is implied by success at any of them.

Are a Child's Words Concrete or Abstract?

An interesting philosophical question lurks in these examples. Is *baca* an abstraction? The word *abstract* is deceptive. Is the roundness of the sun an abstract feature or its most concrete feature? Is circularity abstract and a chin specific? Bees use the angle of the sun to locate and communicate where honey is. Is sun-angle abstract or specific? There is no answer to these questions. All we can say is that we possess perceptual biases linked to our species. Each species must have its own theory of its world, and so what is abstract (that is, a notion broad enough to include diverse objects) may be different for a frog and a human. The real question is, what innate categories does an organism use for perception? From this perspective, all perceptual categories are specific.

A Parallel Language: "Well, gee, yes, maybe I can"

Right beside referential terms are a host of other terms that seem even vaguer, but still may give the biggest clue to the quality of children's thoughts. Tiny utterances, nonwords that have no grammatical category, can still be almost pure reflections of attitudes and feelings (that adults use too!):

uh-oh
oops
uh-huh
no
bye-bye

hi
night-night
gee whiz
upsidaisy
wow
well

These expressive words tend to occur before and after sentences, even in a big pile-up:

Can you sled down that hill?
Well, gee, yes, maybe I can.

Such words are notoriously difficult to capture in a semantic system (an entire dissertation has been written, trying to state precisely what *uh-oh* means![4]), but they are among the first ones a child uses.

The word *uh-oh* presupposes that something unexpected happened. The ability to use *uh-oh*, then, presupposes a mind that expects things. In effect, there is a presupposition about possible worlds that one must have to use *uh-oh* appropriately; that is, one must be able to imagine a world different from the actual world. I believe that any child has this ability. One hears claims that children with autism do not, and these explorations might prove useful or enlightening if pursued with them. The results, I think, should be very carefully contemplated.

Oops is definably different.[5] It entails a notion of agency. Thus, one might say,

"Uh-oh, it is going to rain,"

but it would be quite odd to say,

"*Oops, it is going to rain,"
[*in front of a sentence means it is ungrammatical.]

because *oops* implies agency, usually by a speaker, but at least by some living being. Also, *oops* seems to refer to things that just happened (past), while *uh-oh* is broader: it includes possible reference to the past, like *oops*, but also reference to the future.

Exploration 3.3 *Oops* or *uh-oh* **(understanding expressives)**	How could one tell whether a child already makes the distinction between *uh-oh* and *oops*? Tell the child a story like this:

"Billy was drinking a nice cold drink in his yard and he saw a scary dog run in. He dropped his drink on the ground and said 'Oops!' Why did he say 'Oops'?"

A child who already grasps the meaning that *oops* has in adult English will say, "Because he dropped his drink."

Now tell the child a parallel story:

"Mary was carrying cardboard boxes across the street. She saw a car coming and started to run. When she saw the car coming faster, she dropped one of the boxes. 'Uh-oh,' she said, as she ran quickly to the other side. Why did she say 'Uh-oh'?"

Here, a child who already has the adultlike meaning for *uh-oh* will say either, "Because she dropped the boxes" or "Because the car is coming." Because *uh-oh* can be used in the same situations as *oops*, it would be hard to find a story for which "Why did she say 'Uh-oh'?" can have "Because the car is coming" as an appropriate answer but not "Because she dropped the boxes." Nevertheless, if you make up several similar stories, it will be very clear from the child's answers whether he or she makes the distinction between *uh-oh* and *oops*. (You can of course also switch the questions in the two stories given here: "Why did Billy say 'Uh-oh'?" ("Because he dropped the drink" or "Because he sees a scary dog coming"); "Why did Mary say 'Oops'?" ("Because she dropped the boxes").)

What do we know when a child distinguishes between *uh-oh* and *oops*? We know that the frequent claim "Children think that 'things just happen'" is not correct and that they can verbally discriminate agency (a pivotal concept) and time (past/future). These tiny expressive words require a full mind to interpret them, just like more "conventional" words.

A Voyage of Inference

Hearing a child say a single word, how does an adult follow the path to the idea lodged in the child's mind? In general, a child's isolated words call for a tremendous amount of *inference*; that is to say, we have to use every situational clue to infer or guess what a child means. We can be utterly misguided in that inferential voyage. Any experienced parent knows how difficult it is to interpret what children seek. At the same time, small utterances can sometimes go a long way. Sara's mother hands her a toy, to which Sara says "No"; her mother then says, "She doesn't want this toy, she wants me to turn on the TV." This conclusion is surely not represented in the one syllable *no*; it is an inference from that one little word. But is the verbal version of the inference ("She doesn't want...") exactly what was in the child's mind? This is very difficult to determine, although parents are very confident of their readings.

A vast literature exists on the topic, but there are few solid, scientific conclusions. The adult ingenuity, the presumption of shared humanity, that such fanciful imagination involves always seems delightful to me. It is astonishing that across a great age divide we can share meanings with children that refer to no explicit object. It is the literature of family life, the fanciful flames that children kindle in their parents. We need no scientific blessing in our efforts to mentally maneuver our way into each other's minds. We should be clear about the fact, though, that such communication does not lie in the expressed language itself, but in something we mentally add to it.

Parental Grammar and Children's Pronouns

Perhaps this is a good moment to confront a common view: the child just speaks the way the parent speaks, and parents guide children to grammar with very simple sentences (which linguists call "motherese").[6] Trying to talk simply, parents often use short expressions. But is shorter simpler? Shorter usually means elliptical—and though elliptical speech seems simpler, it can be dauntingly obscure, as we will see.

What pronouns refer to is far from obvious. I asked some students to find out when children first hear and use *it*.[7] I expected that children start with the idea "*it* = thing." To my surprise, it turned out that children first hear *it* in sentences like *Stop it*. If the child understands the sentence, not just the emotion, then *it* = activity. There is no *object* to stop; rather, the child is being asked to stop an *activity*, so it is not clear after all that the child begins with the idea "*it* = thing." Children themselves first use *it* in expressions like *Do it*, where *it* ≠ thing. (For much more on the deceptive quirks of reference, see chapter 5.)

Indeed, isolated pronouns like *it*, *dis*, *dat*, and a location pronoun *there* are often among a child's first words. Here is a location-pointing example from the one-word stage (*1;7* is the child's age in years and months—one year, seven months):

June 1;7 (looking at a picture of a baby in a book)[8]
June: Baby. /bibi/
Mother: Uhhuh.
June: There. /dʌ/

And here are a few from the early phrase stage:

Eve 1;9 (pointing)[9]
Eve: That Eve nose . . . That Mom nose right there.

April 2;1[10]
April: Put that over there.
Mother: (moves the toys)

Adam 2;3[11]
Adam: Sit dere.

It is tempting to say that a child chooses a pronoun because he does not know the actual word. But pronouns assume *shared knowledge*. Does the child have that? Usually, shared knowledge is built up in discourse. Person A says to person B, "I have a hat," at which point A and B both know that the hat exists. Then A continues the discourse with "It is blue" (where *it* = the hat). The use of *it* assumes that both people know about the hat.

Often for children a pronoun refers to something in *visual* context instead of something in previous discourse. Now the interesting question is not whether children command all of the contextual assumptions that pronouns entail, but whether and when they know that discourse, not visual context, is crucial for determining the reference of a pronoun. For instance, if Mom says, "The dog pooped. I don't like that," the pronoun *that* does not refer either to the dog or to the poop, but to the sentence *The dog pooped*.[12]

Parents' speech is constantly elliptical, even when they are talking with very young children. Adults are likely to say "Want some?" or "More?" or "Try it?" and imagine they are being simple and clear. Just like an adult trying to work out a young child's one-word utterances, the child must use shared knowledge and a good deal of inference to figure things out.

Look at this dialogue between a mother and a two-year-old:[13]

Mother: There isn't any tapioca.
Child: Have milk.
Mother: There isn't any.
         We'll make some this afternoon.
Child: Make some.

Both *any* and *some* could refer to an unspoken *milk*; but upon reflection, *make some* seems to refer to *tapioca*. The child (and we) must figure it out— and it looks like the child may be having trouble.

A slightly older child invokes even more ellipsis:[14]

Child: I drink it all up.
         Give me some more.
         A lot.

Mother: I don't see any more.
Child: Yes you do.
Mother: Want a little milk?
            Want some?
Child: (A)n(d) shake it all up.
            A bigger one?
Mother: Mmhm.

The expressions *some, any, all, a lot, one, more, you do,* and *mmhm* all require us to mentally fill in missing syntax, finish each phrase. We will return to the fascinating vagaries of ellipsis in chapter 7 and explore how the child grasps hugely obscure words like *it*.

Seeming Egocentrism

The speech of young children raises another much-discussed question: are children egocentric? Very often a child's first words give the appearance of a conversation with himself, and indeed refer to himself—say, "Kendall" or "Me" or "Self." A whisper of a word, no eye contact, a kind of private ecstasy in having a new mental coin, a sound that fits a feeling in the mind—it seems that an interior monologue is taking place rather than an effort at communication.[15] This type of private conversation is often remarked upon and linked, unfortunately, to the yoke of egocentricity we saddle on our image of children.

Because a child's knowledge of the world is limited by experience, a whole tradition of psychology has claimed that a child's seemingly self-oriented world reflects a principled, inherent inability to grasp the perspective of others. But in another sense, if children can have wild fears and believe in imaginary characters with strange abilities, they must allow far stranger "other" minds into their world than adults do. And the presumption of egocentricity can easily blind us to children's generosity, care for others, natural sympathy, and capacity for situational teamwork. Many parents have heard a two-and-a-half-year-old say, "Don't cry, it's all right," to a one-year-old. Must we think that the child is only repeating a parental aphorism, as some might too quickly claim?

The strong form of egocentrism is inherently impossible. There would be no need to speak to someone if we assumed that others already know what we think. If people are no different from plants, then we should regularly talk to plants. In other words, the principle that *other minds exist,* whose knowledge is different from our own, is linked to whoever we are speaking with and is therefore built into the basic logic of communication itself.[16]

Nonetheless, the manner in which we establish other "perspectives" entails a whole phalanx of distinguishable abilities. Children's cognitive style might differ from adults', though one should not be hasty in drawing that conclusion. Many aspects of point of view are encoded directly into grammar and therefore must be acquired, starting with getting the use of *I*, *you*, *we*, *here*, *there* straight. In more complex situations, computing various points of view is something we all succeed and fail at in varying degrees, with situational information playing a large role.

One path into this forest lies in the intriguing domain of false belief. Children have difficulty attributing a false belief to other people, which does not mean they cannot recognize falsehood, fantasy, or the presence of other minds. We will take a look at the grammatical, cognitive, and moral aspects of this question in chapter 13.

A Case Study: The How and Why of "Hi!"

I will finish this chapter with a case study, instead of a summary, which illustrates the topics pursued here: how the use of a single word entails creativity, perceptual biases, emotional expressiveness, elliptical quality, and inferential demands.

Often, one of a child's first words is *hi* or its twin *bye*. A parent may feel, proudly, that sheer humanity radiates forth when a child first says "Hi." But saying "Hi" is also a significant mental accomplishment, since *hi* refers to no visible thing.

What do children have to know in order to use *hi*, and what does their learning path tell us about their qualities of mind? One child had a habit of saying "Hi table," "Hi hat," and probably many children do this briefly, without our noticing.[17] How exactly did this child use *hi* differently from adults? The answer starts to tell us why *hi* is complicated. It is a greeting, of course, but then, what is that? Do we greet only people? We say that we "greet the day with coffee," but we do not say "*Hi day." *Greet the day* is easily disregarded by adults as a model because it is an "idiom," but how would the child know that it is an idiom?

A child who says "Hi table" already exhibits creativity and defies the popular doctrine of learning-by-imitation. What could lead a child to say "Hi table"? He never hears anything like it—or does he? Parents now and then may talk about a highchair. Suppose the child thinks he hears "Hi chair" instead. In fact, all children do hear "high chair" (*highchair*) or "high [some object]." Now the problem has reversed itself. How does a child who hears "high chair" *avoid* the conclusion that the person speaking has just said "Hi chair" and avoid deducing further that "Hi truck" is equally appropriate? (There are some intonational differences between *hi chair* and *high chair*, but that just makes the child's task more difficult because intonational variety and creativity constitute another problem to be solved.)

Words are easy to misunderstand in this way. It is evident that children seek to find the parts of words; their mistakes in fact reveal their search to us. One child said, "Thanks for your housepitality" (apparently hypothesizing that *hos* must really be *house*), and called things "giantic" instead of "gigantic."[18] Another child said, "It's under the neath," assuming, quite logically, that if *under* takes an object (*under the table*), then a "neath" must be such an object.[19] Still another child insisted, "It's a squirm," when looking at a worm, apparently hearing the form *sq-worm*.[20] Such examples provide a miniature version of a child's mind at work: the child must get just the right rule, the right generalization about the structure of words.

Social factors also come into play in learning when to say "Hi." The exact social occasion for greeting is hard to pinpoint. *Hello* does not imply that we are acquainted with the hearer, but *hi* usually does (though perhaps that is changing). We say "Hello," not "Hi," when we first answer the phone. We may even use both ("Hello... oh, hi"), suggesting that the two words must have different meanings.[21] We do not usually say "Hi" when we move from one room to another in a house and meet a family member, though we might when we see someone for the first time that day. It is a greeting that implies a small amount of "social distance" usually created by time. How much time? We would not say "Hi" to someone after sitting next to her in silence for two hours in a dark theater. But would a child? These are all subtleties that the one-year-old who makes people smile by saying "Hi" to everyone, all day long, must in some way notice and process, on the way to the conventional, adultlike use of the word. Fine-tuning the social context of *hi* is not instantaneous.

There is a classic linguistic answer to the question of how we learn *hi*: children are innately endowed with a particular emotion, call it "greet," and they attach this emotion or idea to a word that they hear (in English, *hi*). This answer is worth pondering. The notion "attach-word-to-idea" may not be totally free; that is, perhaps there is in fact not a word for every feeling. There seem to be "ideas" or "emotions" that we experience with some clarity but that do not easily lend themselves to particular words. An adult or a child may emotionally recognize what corresponds to charm or megalomania or altruism or indifference without words to express it. It is an adult culture that has found words for them. Perhaps adults likewise experience many poignant feelings, which never will be captured in individual words. Poetry is really a kind of meaning that darts between words but is never really expressed. This is where the saying "You have to read between the lines" comes from. A complete theory of mind would reveal not just how we understand what is said, but also how we infer what is not said, what is indicated but not expressed, the state of mind of the child who chooses to speak.

4 First Phrases: Glimpses of Grammar

A lot happens in the transition from one word to two. Children learn to build structure, "merge" two words, do it again recursively, and add concepts like agency. It all starts in a shift within the one-word stage.

What Ignites Grammar?

At a particularly sweet and precious moment, a one-year-old child points to sneakers and says "Daddy." That child has revealed something probably unique to the human species.

How so? Look closely. Suddenly a word captures not an *object* but a *relation*: not sneakers, but a relation between the sneakers and their owner, specifically, a *possessive* relation (Daddy's sneakers). A new, infinite realm of communication opens. Reference itself has changed from object and event names to relationships.[1]

For each child, of course, a different verbal gem ignites this new realm of reference. A child points at a chair and says "Sweater." Why? The astute parent realizes that it is because the child left the sweater on that chair earlier, so "sweater-location" is the intended meaning. *Location* ("on chair") and *possession* ("Daddy's sneakers") are usually the first relations a child expresses, but others come quickly. A child points to the door and says "Coat."[2] This one takes some more parental puzzling, but then it is clear: you put on a coat to go out the door. The coat reflects the "manner" of going outdoors—a relation to be captured ultimately by *with* or *without* ("Don't go out without a coat!"). All at once, single words have "relational reference" (like manner-of-action) on top of direct reference (like naming), and the instrument of communication has begun to grow.

But why claim that membership in the human species shines out in this moment? Because (as far as we know) animals do not refer to objects in any creative way at all. As noted earlier, monkeys have gestures that communicate fixed social relations ("This is my lover," "Stay away from my child"), but they cannot assert simple propositions about objects ("This branch is wobbly"). Fixed social relations are just that, *fixed* in biologically innate gestures, not creative relations that can be freely invented and applied between objects and people. This infinite, expressive quality of human grammar is special and—as far as we currently know—not found naturally and without instruction elsewhere in the animal kingdom.[3]

Are we just guessing about the relations the child intends when he points and says "Daddy," "Sweater," or "Coat"? The answer is yes, a little bit. How can we prove that the child who pointed to sneakers and said "Daddy" intended a possessive relation: "Daddy's sneakers"? What if the child instead had an agent relation in mind: "Put on your shoes, Dad, let's go out and play"? It is hard to *prove* the possessive interpretation, but with a little imagination we can *support* it.

Exploration 4.1
Early relations
(understanding possessives)

We can informally test the possessive claim with this exploration using ellipsis. Put a toy next to a toy cat (as in the accompanying picture) and say to a child,

"This is the cat's toy."

Now put another toy next to a toy dog and say to the child,

"Now point to the dog's."

Does the child point to the dog or the toy? To see even more clearly whether the child understands the possessive relation, try with other animals as well (say, an elephant, a duck, a mouse), sometimes using the animal's name and sometimes using the possessive ("Now point to the elephant," "Now point to the duck's," "Now point to the mouse"). (See also the explorations on ellipsis in chapter 7.)

Exploration 4.2
Another game
(understanding elliptical possessives)

Here's another game to explore whether a child's grammar includes the possessive relation. Wander around the house and point to things. Point to something that belongs to you and identify it as yours, using a possessive. To illustrate the exploration, let's say you are the child's mother. You point to something of yours and say "Mom's." Then point to something that belongs to someone else and say who it belongs to—let's say, "Dad's." Then, crucially, point to something the child *knows is Dad's and say "Mom's."* How does the child respond? If she gives the item to you, then she understood "Mom's" as "(Give) to Mom" —a different relation from the possessive. If she says something like "No, that a hat," then she understood "Mom's" as "Mom"—not a relation, but a name. But if she frowns or says "No," then we have evidence that our guess was right: the possessive relation is already part of her grammar.

New Relations: Agent, Object, Manner

Within days, new relations tumble out of the child's mind. One day, wanting his mother to play a record, a child points to it and says "Mom"; the next day he says "'ecord"; and the next day he says "Round." He is highlighting three aspects of the same activity: *agent* ("Mom"), *object* ("record"), and *manner* ("round and round"). It is as if, through these new relations, new angles on existence are being elevated to consciousness.

How much can the child accomplish with these new "relational nouns"? A lot, but expressing grammatical relations alone does not cover everything. In fact, one of the important thrusts of modern theorizing about language is that the explicit (and efficient) *thematic relations* are really just a handful: *agent, object, possessor, experiencer, goal, instrument, manner.* Both other words and other mental operations are needed to convey complex relations. For instance, the grammatical relations do not cover actual *human* relationships. The word *détente* may reflect the relationship of the former Soviet Union to the United States, or even two-year-old Johnny's feeling toward his three-year-old sister Jennie, but none of grammar's core relations captures the notion "détente." Thematic relations only go so far.

The claim that this handful of thematic roles is special deserves a brief digression on adult grammars. Are these relations (agent, object, experiencer, and so on) just common sense? They certainly are, but they form a subset of commonsense relations. Why not have the relation "mother" or "love-object" or "edible"? The claim that relations like agent and object are special in grammar is buttressed by the fact that a set of prepositions captures them (*by* (agent), *to* (indirect object), *of* (locative), *with* (instrument), *for* (goal)), which is not true of other relations. So some of our thoughts are on the "fast track" in grammar and have special modes of expression for efficiency's sake.

Have we missed something of the human essence here? A child's personality is also richly on display. The child whose first word is *kiss* has something different on her mind than the child whose first word is *no*. Personality, of course, gets into everything. Language carries personality right along with meaning.

Now the child is ready to move on: he begins to combine words. What new power is held in the simple act of combining two words? The primary relations shoot out into endless new branches, some of which we will carefully explore. Each branch of language articulates a form of mental computation, used in language and elsewhere. Expressing mastery of each step is a further display of what it means to be human. Of course, a child is human even if she does not speak or sign at at all. Humanity is just not as vividly on display. One needs to be careful here. Absence of linguistic expression is never a guaranteed measure of any kind of absence of cognitive ability. That is another reason why one should be extraordinarily careful about attributing a cognitive deficit to any child.

Two Words to Many Words: How Children Build Phrases with the Operation Merge

The child's grammar is now on the verge of explosion. She starts to use two-word sentences that make grammatical relations explicit:

Agent-action	Baby eat	
Agent-object	Mommy eggnog	(Mommy had her eggnog)
Agent-locative	Baby highchair	(the baby is in the highchair)
Verb-object	Pick glove	(pick the glove up)
Verb-goal	Throw Daddy	(throw it to Daddy)
Possessive-object	Mommy sock	(Mommy's sock)

Is this an "anything goes" situation? Can the child combine any two relations whatsoever? Surely we cannot be confident that we have correctly labeled the relations the children intended when they said these sentences. Do children really distinguish between *goal* (as in *Throw Daddy a ball*, where *Daddy* = goal) and *object* (here, *ball*)? It is difficult to be certain. It is possible that a more abstract notion of *general object* (or *complement*) defines what the child chooses, and no distinction between direct and indirect object is part of the grammar at this point (even though the interpretations are different—the child does not heave Daddy when he says, "Throw Daddy").

What we can assert with some confidence is that a range of common relations are excluded and almost never occur:

Excluded:		
Two clauses	*Said ate	(I said I ate)
Identity	*Mommy girl	(Mommy is a girl)
Conjunction	*Fork knife	(fork and knife)[4]

Why are these forms absent? There may be multiple reasons. It is possible that some part of the child's grammar must mature before they are available. "Said ate" would require the child to put one sentence inside another; that is, the child's grammar would have to be capable of recursion (see the next section). Being able to say "Mommy girl" would require the child to grasp that *is* denotes a kind of *equivalence* ("Mommy is a girl"), which may in turn require understanding that *is* can introduce a property ("Mommy (is) tall").

The absence of conjunction, however, points at exactly how the structure is built. Now we must start to reason very carefully, and the more we look at things, the more surprising they become. It looks as if children just "combine" two words, yet we have seen that they don't make use of all the possible meanings. Why wouldn't the simplest connection be *and*? Why doesn't a child start out using lots of expressions that capture things conjoined in everyday life?

Mommy Daddy
hat coat
shoes socks
meat rice

Where should we locate this bias against conjunction? It is unlikely that the restriction is cognitive. The child certainly can put two things together elsewhere in life. Another possibility is that words are not just added: their combination invokes a particular syntactic structure that in turn invites certain meanings but not others. We are moving toward seeing a fundamental asymmetry at the core of how the human mind builds grammatical structure.

If we simply put two words together, we would produce expressions like this:

house, doll
coffee, cup

The mode of combining that produces

dollhouse
coffee cup

is fundamentally different. It creates a *modifier* relation where one element is the "main" element: a dollhouse is a house and a coffee cup is a cup. This is especially clear in a pair like *boathouse/houseboat*: a boathouse is a house, and a houseboat is a boat. This determination of primacy between words is the most basic syntactic act that distinguishes human language. It combines two things and decides which one controls or dominates the combination. Let's combine an adjective and a noun, for instance:

red, house = red-adjective + house-noun

The combination, *red house*, is still a noun. One way to represent the "pure nounness" of the whole phrase is to put brackets around it and label it as a noun: NOUN[red house]. Another way to represent the parts of the phrase and the phrase as a whole is like this:

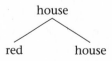

Here, the label atop the "tree" is *house*, to show which element controls the structure (*red house* denotes a type of house). Or we could (as has become customary) label the tree "branches" with syntactic categories:

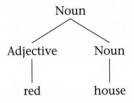

This symbolic tree shows how humans combine linguistic elements and decide which one controls: link and label. (Technically, the operation of link-and-label is called *Merge*.)[5] Importantly, linking is not *just* "linking." It is a distinctive human operation that says something more precise than "combine." The label captures the nature of the link.

Let's see how the notion of merger solves our puzzle: that children at the two-word stage do not use all the possible relations for combining words. We have seen that they do combine words in the following ways (and others), where one word controls or dominates the combination:

"Sit wall" is about sitting, not about a kind of wall.
"Pick glove" is about an action, not about a kind of glove.
"Mommy eggnog" is about possession or an action, not about a kind of eggnog.

But they do not utter what we might think of as the easiest structure: conjunction. That is, they rarely if ever use combinations like this:

knife fork   (knife and fork)
Mommy Daddy   (Mommy and Daddy)
drink food   (drink and food)
hat coat   (hat and coat)
pen paper   (pen and paper)

Cognitively, conjunction looks like the simplest way to combine words, but structurally it is not. Here is why. If a child says "Mommy Daddy," does the phrase mean "basically Mommy" or "basically Daddy"? We cannot assign a higher structure to the phrase and decide which word controls (dominates) it:

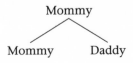

Deciding between "basically Mommy" and "basically Daddy" is a choice most families would not want to make. Now we can see that the structural claim about choosing one of the items to label the top of the tree (representing the dominance relation within the phrase) actually predicts that conjunction will not occur. Conjunction allows neither form to be the primary one. Instead, it is a hidden democratic *and*. If I say "Houseboat," you know I am basically talking about a boat:

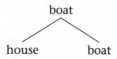

But if a child said "Mommy Daddy," the phrase would really mean "Mommy and Daddy," where and-ness is the dominating feature:

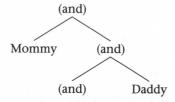

Since neither Mommy nor Daddy *is* and-ness, the core concept of the phrase is unexpressed. It no longer seems surprising that children do not start out saying "Mommy Daddy."

Simple examples, then—ones like *Mommy sock, baby highchair, *Mommy Daddy*—enable us to see right into the basic structure of language. Everything we know of children's language suggests that Universal Grammar will lead the child to always "merge"—to always build phrases where one element dominates. This is building a syntax that honors meaning (or semantics).

We can go right after this claim. The method is to create a perfect contrast like *boathouse/houseboat* and see if the child sees the difference:

Exploration 4.3
Domination or coordination
(compounds)

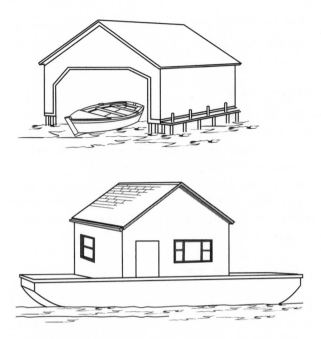

Show a child these pictures and say,

"Point to boathouse."

Which one does the child pick? That is, which word does the child take as dominant?

Now try with a made-up case that might be clearer:

Show a child these pictures and say either,

"Point to shoe-tree"

or

"Point to tree-shoe."

You can make up more yourself on the same pattern (for example, try *dollhouse, house-doll*, and *doll, house*).

In technical terms, a two-word utterance involves a form of dominance or *subordination*. In these structures, formed by the operation Merge, one word subordinates another. This seems so natural to us that it is easy to miss how profound an act of deploying mental information is involved in building such a structure. The toddler saying just two words at a time displays this feat.

Recursion: Putting Something inside Itself

The next combinatory step involves the engagement of the deep and simple property of grammar illustrated earlier: *recursion*.[6] Recursion means "Do the same operation again, and do it upon the same structure" (recall the discussion of *very, very* and multiple adjectives; and see chapter 6). It is a quintessentially simple idea—and yet its mathematical formulation is still evolving. The fact that humans carry out the Merge operation recursively, and do so in milliseconds, is fundamental evidence for claims that properties of grammar are inborn, unlearned. For example, our familiar compound *boathouse* refers to a kind of house. If we merge it with *city* to form *city boathouse*, we are still talking about a kind of *house* even though we just added another layer of structure:

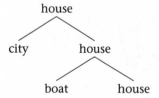

We can put an already complex form to either the right or the left of a new word to build even more structure (notice how the following two structures represent two meanings for exactly the same words):

Complex form embedded on the right

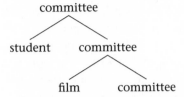

student film committee (film committee made up of students)

Complex form embedded on the left

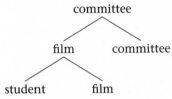

student film committee (committee for student films)

And of course we can continue: *New York student film committee* is fine and instantly understandable. We can even instantly decipher repeated identical words: *coffee-maker* and *coffee-maker-maker*.

This recursive ability—this ability to perform Merge again and again—underlies the construction of every new phrase in a sentence, when we go beyond combining nouns:

big red house
the big red house
the big red house here
Is the big red house here?

And indeed, young children produce novel compounds:[7]

| animal cup | (cup with animals) | Allison (2.33) |
| ribbon hat | (hat with ribbons on it) | Sarah (2.59) |

Predictably, recursive compounds come along as well:[8]

| Big Bird book | (book about Big Bird) | Nathaniel (2.47) |
| bunny rabbit record | (record with song about rabbits) | Shem (2.25) |

Syntax has now been launched.

The view that Merge is automatically, or innately, recursive leads to a prediction. Once the child uses Merge, the operation should be readily repeatable: the child should readily understand and produce more highly recursive forms. The child who understands *dollhouse* as two words will quickly understand *school dollhouse* or *nursery school dollhouse*. The prediction of course can be tested.

Exploration 4.4
Compound compounds
(recursive compounds)

Once a child has produced a novel compound—two nouns that definitely form a compound (*animal cup*, for example, but not *peanut*, which is one word)—we can try this exploration. The basic procedure is to expand the child's own novel compounds: add a noun at either end and see whether the child grasps the meaning of the new phrase. For example, if your child says *animal cup*, you might show her (either pictures of, or the actual objects) a house full of animal cups, a cup for animals made of plastic, and a cup with an animal house painted on it, and say,

"Show me *animal cup house*."

The prediction is that the child will have no problem understanding recursive phrases like this, where the last noun names the actual object.

Children generally have no problem with the *houseboat/boathouse* distinction, based on noun compounds. Do they understand recursive compounds created from verbs? This question is a new frontier in acquisition research. Much more complex operations are involved, beyond easy explanation, but the structures can readily be explored with older children. Show a child this picture:

Exploration 4.5
Compound compounds
(more recursive compounds)

Now say,

"This boy, Michael, is carving a block to make prints of a dog. The block will be a print-maker. Can you point to the print-maker maker?"

If the child's grammar has all the ingredients of recursion with nouns made from verbs, she should point to the boy (the print-maker maker); if it doesn't, she will probably point to the block (the print-maker).

Summary: Fundamental Knowledge in Two Words

Understanding thematic relations (such as agent, possessor, location) and using the operation Merge (to build essential linguistic structures) allow the child to enter the two-word stage—and will be useful tools for going beyond two-word phrases. But the child at this stage now commands the most powerful tool of all for taking the structure inherent in the two-word phrase and expanding it indefinitely into longer phrases and whole sentences: recursion.

These abilities do not cover all the territory of human language. Thematic relations alone cannot express all ideas, not all structures that can be built by Merge are actually allowed in the grammar, and not all operations are freely repeatable. We have much yet to explore.

5 The Absence of Absolute Reference

Instant Abstractions

How do words and things connect? As noted in chapter 3, it seems totally obvious to many people, even inevitable, that the connection could not be anything more than a "point and shoot" verbal camera. We "point and name" and that is all it takes. This has been a commonsense truth for centuries. Nonetheless, in philosophical and linguistic circles, it is a devilish challenge to state how we actually refer to objects, not to mention situations, feelings, and ideas. The rapid stream of language and inchoate demands of life force us, every moment, to combine old words in order to pick out new references.

Often, meaning seems to come in at odd angles—for instance, through word endings (morphology). Many patterns seem halfway between structure and meaning. The most obvious example is the familiar vagaries of gender.[1] In many languages, every noun has to have an article that is linked to *formal* gender; however, the article does not necessarily express *real* gender. The German phrase *das Mädchen* ("the girl") is grammatically neuter, though the true reference is obviously feminine. What seems to have a semantic origin has been "grammaticized" to become a formal notion no longer linked to its origins. Does the child follow the same path from semantic to syntactic? Does he use feminine articles only with truly feminine nouns first? Or does the leap to a formal notion just happen instantly? It is not easy to tell if there is a first, quick stage in which children force form to match meaning. Perhaps the child does use feminine *die* with a noun denoting a female first, and within a few minutes extends it to nouns that have no real gender, only grammatical gender. We researchers can never be quick enough to know.

In any event, the leap from meaning to form seems easy for all children. And where the child goes too far, we can actually see the mechanism at work. Here is a case in point. Patrick Griffiths has reported meeting a boy who called everyone *he* (there are also children who label everyone *she*). To probe the boy's grammar further, he put out a male doll and a female doll and asked the boy to point to *she*, which he obligingly did (pointing to the female doll). Then Patrick coyly pointed to the boy's mother and asked, "How about your mother?"—to which the boy confidently replied, "He's *she*." Now let's get beyond the charm: what does this mean? Not that we've come across a child who is imposing a male perspective—rather, that we've met a child who seems to have identified an abstract notion of "person" above a gender identification for *he*. And the child must have done so with no specific evidence in English. So the child is seeking abstraction, seeking a gender-neutral pronoun for people that is defined in grammar, but not easily recognizable in a world where every person has an obvious gender.

In this chapter, we will explore the most obvious terms that orient reference:

- pronouns (*it, that*),
- pointing words (*this, that*),
- place words (*here, there*),
- words that express identity (*same*),
- words that express nonexistence (*no, not*),
- words that capture uniqueness or set membership (*a, the*), and
- words that exhaust sets (*all, every*).

Each term has individual wrinkles that are part of the repertoire of reference. The overarching idea is this:

No terms actually have absolute reference in a child's experience.

They are laden with subjectivity, abstraction, and ambiguity. The grammar of each language marks its own routes to reference, so there is much to acquire. Yet there is no reason to think that children are different from adults in their mental ability to refer, and children may be innately designed to grasp certain aspects of reference (for example, to grasp the abstractness of reference (*Milk is good*) before they see how specific reference works (*This milk is good*)).

What is, step by step, the ladder of abstraction for reference in the acquisition process? It remains dim, the sequence hard to see. The explorations in this chapter are designed to extract the latent ambiguity in each referring term. The ambiguities are slightly contrived, but they reflect ambiguities that arise every day, that silently confound children, that flummox foreigners, and that must be mastered if one is to be a full adult speaker of English.

Grammar is endlessly dazzling. Words and context become entangled in ways that children may not master until the school years. (Actually, those who study language acquisition often suspect that connections are grasped much earlier, but it is not easy to demonstrate it concretely.) Some of the explorations in this chapter will reveal the grammars of young children. Others are more advanced challenges particularly suited as games to play with older children. I present them in part to provide thought-experiments that illustrate the endpoints of grammar. One is not a mature speaker of English without mastering them. (And even these examples do not get nearly to the bottom of the intricacies that the study of reference has revealed.)

Truly New Words: How Invented Words Refer

Picking out the meaning of a new word in the first place is very hard. In fact, we should ask, must a child learn "words" first? It is not so obvious. Suppose a child first recognizes commotion and activity. At the same time, he hears a parent saying, "Look! There is singing, dancing, and eating." The child might first equate *ing* with *activity* and march into a busy room and shout "Ing!" But no one reports such a result. If we want to build a good theory of acquisition, we cannot merely observe that this does not happen—we must build a theory that explains *why* it does not happen. If children are innately equipped with the principle "Learn words in isolation before more complex structures," then the fact that no adult says "Ing" by itself—the fact that *ing* occurs only in complex structures, never in isolation—means that the child is unlikely to hypothesize that *ing* itself is a word. Two other grammar-specific principles follow from the principle of learning words first in isolation: "Learn words first, then learn affixes that alter their meanings" (which explains how inflections appear) and "If an element occurs by itself, it is a word." In sum, what children say (words) and don't say (affixes) points strongly to the idea that they have grammatical assumptions from the outset.

Lila Gleitman has developed a simple method to show what an enigma learning words can be: she just asks people to learn a new word in an action situation, which should be easier than understanding an emotion term (like *embarrass*).[2] Suppose I show you a picture of a man hitting a baseball with a bat and say, "John loves the bloothe." What does *bloothe* mean? It could mean "bat," "ball," "game," "swing," "sport," "challenge." If I use a verb, things become more obscure. If I show you a picture of a man cutting a tree with a saw and say, "John bloothes it completely," you don't know whether *bloothe* means "remove," "saw," "cut," "hate," "enjoy," or what. How we use both circumstance and syntax to triangulate meanings remains a mystery.

What's the Point of Pointing? Do Gestures Help?

Even adding gestures will not do the trick. The physical act of pointing itself can be mystifying and ambiguous. For example, young nursery school teachers sometimes point at an object in the distance, like a tree, unaware that their charges are stubbornly looking at the teacher's finger, not the tree.[3]

Pointing words (deictics) like *this, that, here, there, nearby* seem exact but in fact involve more ambiguity than pointing fingers. Still, these words pop up quickly in the language of children, as if children already knew how those ambiguities work. We will try to see if they do.

The Inevitable Subjectivity of Reference

Reference is always half subjective, half objective. Words inevitably refer to more than just physical features. Suppose I point to a book and say, "Have you read that?," using one of the words that seem designed to point to specific objects. But I do not mean literally that book, nor even one with the same print or the same cover. If I read *Moby-Dick* and you did too, you could answer "Yes," even though my copy was paperback and yours hardcover.[4] *Read that book* refers to the content of the book, not the physical paper and print. If I read *Moby-Dick* out loud mindlessly, like a parrot, then I would not have really read it either. *Read* means to read and to understand. And *understand* is unavoidably linked to slightly different understandings because each person's experience is different. Thus, we rapidly move from a definition of a book to a definition of "book" that includes reflections of our mental attitudes.

That's actually how we use the word *understand* too. We say things like "You can't really understand a storm until you've been in one in a ship at sea."[5] This equates understanding with internal sensual experience, not intellectual awareness of, say, weather maps. This one-sentence summary is a caricature of the results of a century of philosophical discussions about reference. Although those discussions are abstruse, to say the least, they contain an insight we must be aware of when we speak with children. Every object word is partly subjective, for adults as well as for children. Surprising though it may seem, no words give pure, absolute reference.

A three-year-old, even a two-year-old, visiting a friend, might easily look at a toy and say, "Oh, I have that at my house!" This demonstrates that the child's version of *that* involves *reference to an abstraction*, not an actual specific object. Were it otherwise, every parent would have to explain, "He means he has a toy just like your toy. Don't worry, that toy won't magically move from our house to his." No such instruction is needed because the child grasps this abstraction immediately. We no more need to instruct children about the abstract nature of words than we need to tell them how to make a three-dimensional reality out of a two-dimensional retinal image. One could easily imagine an organism for which referentiality is concrete and not abstract. Perhaps salmon returning to their place of birth have a brain marking that refers to that place and nothing else. Humans do not happen to be such an organism.

How to Catch the Emergence of Abstract and Variable Reference

Even the seemingly obvious word *this* displays the *abstractness* of reference: it refers to an idea of an object and not an actual object. How can we reveal the way children learn about reference with *this* (and other words)? I think the best way is to go right out and ask them pertinent questions that will draw out their knowledge. Here are some simple ones.

Suppose we just follow in the steps of the earlier example about toys. Let's say your child has a particular book, and you know your child's friend has a copy of the same book at her house. Ask your child,

> Exploration 5.1
> Thisness, hereness
> (deictic pointers without
> fixed reference)

"Does your friend have this book at her house?"

Your child might say, "Well, she has one like it," or "Yes, she does," or she might say, "That's silly! How could she? The book is right here."

Or show the child the pictures on the following page (or a parallel contrast):

> Exploration 5.2
> Doggedness
> (abstract reference
> for ordinary nouns)

Picture 1   Picture 2

Point to the dog in picture 1 and ask,

"Can you see a cat next to this dog?"

A picture of a dog can be in two places, but the same particular picture cannot be in two places, just as two copies of a book can exist in different places, but the same particular copy cannot. (If you think it can, then you have seen precisely the ambiguity in language that we are trying to talk our way around, but cannot really escape.)

If the child allows the abstract notion of a picture of a dog to equal *this dog*, then (seeing picture 2) he will notice that picture 1 allows a "Yes" answer (and similarly throughout for the book example above). If the child understands *this* to mean only *exactly what is pointed to*, then the dog in picture 1 (which you have called "this dog") is clearly not next to a cat, and the child will answer "No."

It seems unlikely that the child will say, "No, it is right there all by itself," also pointing to picture 1, but it is not impossible, particularly for a young child or perhaps a child with autism who may understand context differently. Such children might see the use of *this* for two different objects as confusing, though it is easy for adults, much like the jumping back and forth between *I* and *you* that many children stumble over. An adult asks, "Are you hungry?," and the child says, "Yes, you are hungry," accepting *you* as his name. Would the same child resolutely point to the dog in picture 1?

| Exploration 5.3 |
| Variable hereness |
| (self-referential *here*) |

An exploration using *here* also reveals the *variability* of reference. It could not be simpler. While you touch your own nose, say,

"Put your finger here."

(To be sure that the child does not simply imitate the gesture, you could have a penny on your hand, point to your nose, and say to the child, "Put the penny here.")

Will the child touch *your nose* or *her own nose*? Both responses are correct, but if the child touches her own nose, then she has construed *here* as an abstraction with a hidden capacity for variation. "Here" is not exclusively where the speaker is; it can cover the hearer's "here" too.

What the child who touches her own nose already seems to know is that there is something like an algebraic variable X hidden inside the word *here* that allows the listener to introduce a new context. This property of *here* is not an odd wrinkle of language; instead, it actually reveals the essence of grammar. To use any human grammar, then, a child must be comfortable with the variable nature of reference.

Bare Nouns and Abstract *the*-ness

Abstract reference is not rare. It is constantly present in language. The intricacy of using *a* and *the* in English is another case that shows the remarkable mental capacities and accomplishments of the language-learning child.

How *a* Turns into *the*

The use of *a* introduces a conceptual set that is unbounded. "Have you got a pencil?" someone asks, and he means any pencil we can imagine. "Thank you for the pencil," he says when you've given him one, and now his words pick out just that single, unique instrument. Once introduced, *a* turns into *the*, but it still may not pick out a unique object, as we can see. Every day, teachers say things like "I have given you each a badge with your name. Please put the badge on your shirt" or "You each have a new pencil. Please use the pencil to write your name in your workbook."

A home version might go like this. Suppose a mother and her children are eating spaghetti at dinner. The mother says,

> Exploration 5.4
> How *a* turns into *the*
> (nonspecific *the*)

"Everybody has a napkin,"

and points to her own napkin. Then she says,

"This spaghetti is messy, so can you put the napkin in your shirt?"

Now *the napkin* in fact refers to a whole set of napkins. The prediction is that each child will pick up his or her own napkin, not reach for the mother's napkin. (Note also that *the napkin* does not refer to just any of the napkins on the table, either: a child cannot reach over and take her neighbor's. *The napkin* in "Can you put the napkin in your shirt?" must be linked back to *a napkin* in "Everybody has a napkin," which referred to the mother's napkin.)

For contrast, you could try this with one child. Point at the napkin in front of you and say,

"Can you pick up this napkin and put it in your shirt?"

In this case, we would expect the child to lean over and get your napkin.

Why does *a* turn into *the*? The switch actually expresses a profound mental transformation. *A* introduces a *mental set*. The conceptual move from choice to chosen is a move from a *general* perspective to a *particular* perspective. That is, an arbitrary member of a set (*a*) turns into something very specific (*the*) (though it is still not necessarily a single physical object). Language expresses a major mental shift with tiny words. A child may have the concepts, but when learning to speak and understand, he must connect them to the tiny indicator words too.

Pedagogically, perhaps situations, not explanations, are all one needs to get *the* right. Working as a United Nations volunteer in Sarajevo, I was thrust into an English-as-a-Second-Language class where the teacher was explaining English articles to eleven-year-olds—since Serbo-Croatian has none. The teacher started with the standard explanation: "*A* marks an unspecified person, place, or thing." Asked to teach on the spot, I called on my language acquisition experiments instead: "Look," I told the children, "when something is new, use *a*, and as soon as the thing is there, *a* will magically turn into *the*. Like this: *I have a hat. The hat is red.*" Although the youngsters generally refused to do homework, I said, "Come back tomorrow with ten examples like this." They did, seemed to understand the task perfectly, and loved it, which indicated once again that children just need exposure to distinctive situations, not explanation, to learn grammar. At the right moment, this would be a good game for any child, especially for children who seem to have a language deficit.

All this exposition is needed to give a partial, nontechnical explanation of something that feels like common sense. So much exposition is needed because, indeed, common sense itself has abstract principles buried in it just as vision has principles of geometry buried in it. In both cases, the action—using language and seeing—seems utterly obvious, but the underlying principles are enormously complex to explain in words.

Let's look now at some experiments and explorations designed to bring out children's knowledge and use of *a* and *the*—that is, whether they grasp that the conceptual space an object occupies has moved from "member of a set" (expressed by *a*) to "a specific item" (expressed by *the*), which both speaker and hearer agree upon. Michael Maratsos did some clever experiments demonstrating the contrast between definite and indefinite.[6] First he asked a child to knock over one of a row of cups. Then he asked, "What did you do?" Usually the child said, "Knocked over a cup," indicating that he or she was aware that it was one of a set. Then Maratsos set more toys—say, ducks—in front of the child. He said, "Here is a row of ducks," and then, "Take a duck." After the child took a duck, he said either, "Now give me a duck" or "Now give me the duck."

"Now give me a duck" naturally invites the child to select *a new duck* and give it to you. But "Now give me the duck" calls for the child to surrender exactly the duck he just acquired, even though a whole row of ducks are present. Maratsos found that children at two years nine months readily understood "Now give me the duck" (though this result has not been consistently replicated; some children choose a new duck for *the*).

Exploration 5.5
Set → particular
(understanding definite articles and sets)

This method is easily explored with anything handy. For instance, you can set a row of pennies in front of a child and say,

"Here is a row of pennies. Take a penny."

Then request either,

"Now give me a penny"

or

"Now give me the penny."

Which will the child give you in each case—his penny or a new penny?

Exploration 5.6
Referring clearly
(indefinite articles)

Getting the child to *produce* either *a* or *the* is the most persuasive evidence that she has mastered set-introducing *a*, specific *the*, and the shift between them. Here is a game involving *a*. Show a child this picture:

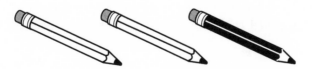

Now cover up one of the white pencils and ask,

"What am I covering up?"

Will the child answer,

"A white pencil,"

expressing recognition of a set?

<table>
<tr><td>

Exploration 5.7
The production
(producing definite articles)

</td></tr>
</table>

You can explore the $a \rightarrow the$ shift fairly simply if you present a contrast. For instance, show a child this picture:

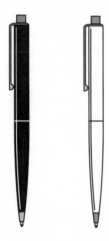

Now say,

"Here's a white pen and a black pen."

Now cover up the black pen and ask,

"Which pen did I cover up?"

A child whose grammar already includes the shift from *a* to *the* will answer,

"The black pen."

(Note that the choice of question word makes a difference. "Which pen did I cover up?" asks for a specific reference ("The black one"), while "What did I cover up?" would ask for a type answer ("A black pen").

You might try both, using a range of objects, and see if different articles emerge.)

Exploration 5.8
How much can *the* carry?
(including modifiers)

Here is another exploration involving *a* and *the* that brings up an intriguing aspect of the child's developing grammar. This can be carried out with any two objects that differ in one feature. For instance, show a child this picture of two quite different pencils:

First, say

"Look! Here's a nice black pencil,"

and touch the black pencil. Now touch the white pencil and ask,

"Am I touching the pencil?"

We expect the child to say "No" (since "a nice black pencil" introduces the set of black pencils, and you've now touched the white one). But suppose the child says "Yes." It's tempting to immediately conclude that the child doesn't "get" the *a → the* shift (or she wasn't paying attention, or she's tired, or whatever reason we might give for the "wrong" answer). But in fact, we really don't know why the child answers this way. There may be an intriguing grammatical explanation (there often is, when we look closely and deeply enough). In some languages, like the Salish languages spoken by native peoples in British Columbia,[7] if a speaker mentions one member of a set, then the speaker or hearers can refer to *other* members of the set with the *definite* determiner.

There is experimental evidence that a number of five-year-old children learning English do just that.[8] At the moment the children in the experiment were tested, they most likely knew a lot about the English article *the*, but their knowledge may still have needed some fine-tuning. Their *the* may have allowed a larger realm of reference than an adult's *the*: instead of referring just to a unique mentioned object, it allowed reference back to the *set* of objects mentioned. It is as if you were to just mention *pencil* and I could then use *the* with any pencil I subsequently referred to. Salish actually has a second definite article to refer to "unique" cases—the cases for which English uses *the*. The English-learning child must learn that English has only the "unique" definite article, and no method like the one Salish has to refer to the mentioned set—no article that an English speaker can use, after someone says "I have a pencil," to say roughly "I use *one of those* too." This subtlety is so unobtrusive that a child may not narrow his definite article down to an English-style one in a way that is obvious.

The experimental results are still preliminary, or shaky, but the underlying logic they illustrate is almost inevitable: children do not know what grammar they are learning, and they may start out with one that is off the mark—one that fits another Universal Grammar possibility, particularly in subtle ways.

Is the Part-Whole Connection Innate?

We often use *the* with no prior *a*:

I went to a restaurant. The menu was terrible.

The first sentence doesn't mention a menu, yet the second sentence refers to *the menu*. Such sentences change our easy idea that every *the* refers to an already introduced thing (or even set of things as in Salish). The use of *the* in the sequence *I went to a restaurant. The menu was terrible* represents a significant broadening of our view of how *the* refers back in a conversation. We can use *the* to refer to a subpart of an object. Adults know that the link is there if we invoke our *knowledge of the world*—of the fact that menus are found in restaurants, thus are a part of restaurants (the *part-whole relationship*). So in an abstract way, *the* in *The menu was terrible* is justified by a known object.

Jill de Villiers has developed an effective way to elicit this knowledge.[9] She tells a child this little story:

"A bird flew out of a cage. Something was left open. What was it?"

If the child says "The door," we know he comprehends the part-whole relation; and indeed, children as young as three and four give this answer. (Occasionally, though, children and adults reply "A door," so clearly all the dimensions of part-whole relations have not yet been uncovered.)

Exploration 5.9
Part-*the* and mystery part-*the*
(*the* as part-whole indicator)

You can easily use everyday objects to elicit *the* as indicator of a part-whole relation. For example, take a bottle and say,

"Here's a bottle of juice"

(or water, or milk, or whatever it is). Now take off the cap and ask,

"What did I take off?"

Will the child answer with *the* ("The top," "The cap")?

The part-whole relation, though it seems more complex than simply referring back to the whole object, may be more basic in the acquisition process. To see how this could be so, let's consider: can a
child make the connection that a named object is part
of a whole, even if the name isn't a familiar word? Imagine that we show a child this picture, saying,

Exploration 5.10
A crocodile and the zaff
(invented part-whole connections)

"Here is a crocodile. The zaff is strange, isn't it?"

Many children will—I guess—answer "Yes" and point to the hatlike object,
even though they've never heard the word *zaff* before. How is this possible?
Maybe the part-whole connection is so automatic that a child can establish
it without the use of world knowledge; maybe grammar becomes the signal
of part-whole relations for new objects. The child's cognitive system in effect says, "I'm looking at a crocodile and I've just heard two sentences of
the form 'Here is an X. The Y is strange.' The use of *the* in this construction
signals a part-whole relation; therefore, I know the speaker is pointing out a
part of the crocodile to me. I don't recognize the word *zaff* and I don't recognize that hatlike thing, so maybe they go together: maybe the unfamiliar
word is the name of the unfamiliar part."

Some children show knowledge of *the* in part-whole contexts like these
more readily than in the contexts we looked at earlier where the same object is involved ("Here is a hat. [Put on hat.] What did I put on?" "The
hat."). This shows how the acquisition path may not simply go from simple to complex. Some complex notions—like the notion of person and perhaps the part-whole relation—are already represented in the child's mind
and therefore easy to recognize and use. Most likely, as just described, the
child runs the part-whole system backward: adult *a . . . the* sequences tell the
child to induce a part-whole relation and thereby learn about the world.

A natural objection to this explanation for the child's "Yes" answer is to say, "The child picks the strange hatlike object out as the referent for *zaff* just because he's entranced by its salience." This objection can be examined by asking a slightly different question:

"Here is a crocodile. A zaff is strange, isn't it?"

In this case, we expect at least some children to ask, "What's a zaff?" If this prediction is borne out, then we have evidence that there really is an abstract part-whole relation induced by the sequence *a...the* even if the nouns are not known: the part-whole indicator *the* is missing here, and the child does not zero in on the hatlike object as the referent for the mystery word. (Of course, children may respond with as much creativity as the objects they observe. Then we will just not have found out about their knowledge of articles.)

Bare Nouns

Finally, what about the reference of "bare nouns"—nouns that have no determiner at all? Some languages—like Chinese and Russian—have no articles, so they must accomplish definite and indefinite reference differently. English-speaking children begin without articles as well. What does the two-year-old mean when she looks at a plate of cookies and says, "I want cookie"? Is "I want cookie" general (compare "I want cake"), or is the child asking for a specific cookie (compare "I want that cake")? We don't know for sure. Because I think children have ready access to abstractions, I think they start with the abstract and general meaning and learn the markers for specificity, which may vary from language to language.

There is an important corollary here. Often parents try to "simplify" their language as a way to help children. But if parents drop articles, then they deprive children of the experience they need to learn them. All the little words are in a way the essence of grammar, and children need a wide variety of circumstances and exposure to clear uses of articles in order to grasp them, since each language does them a little differently. Here is an exploration that makes this point while investigating children's grasp of bare nouns and articles-plus-nouns. Show a child this picture:

> **Exploration 5.11**
> Does *cake* mean "the cake"?
> (*the* refers to a member of a set)

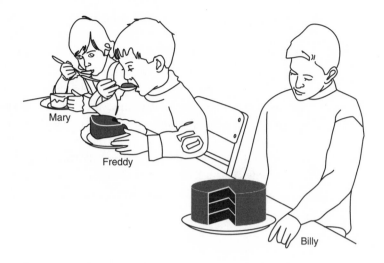

Point to Billy and say,

"Look here! Billy has a chocolate cake."

Now ask,

"Who is eating that cake and who is eating cake?"

Or you could ask the questions separately: "Who is eating that cake?" and "Who is eating cake?" An adult would answer the first question with "Freddy" and the second with "Mary and Freddy."

A very young child may well not give a comprehensible answer at all, since children below three years are typically in the nonarticle stage, or just resist artificial situations. To a child at this stage, who doesn't grasp *that*—for whom *that* is a kind of mystery word—your question may sound like "Who is eating cake and who is eating cake?" or "Who is eating zipf cake and who is eating cake?"—possibly causing the child's grammar-learning mechanism to say to itself, "It's odd that those two questions sounded the same. There must have in fact been something different about them" or "Those two sentences were the same except for one word—that word must be significant somehow." Contrastive situations like this, which make a grammatical difference salient, might provide the child with a crucial experience in grasping a point about his language—here, how to mark the difference between a general and a specific noun.

How Languages Choose to Be More Specific

What is most difficult for us adults to realize—researchers, parents, and teachers alike—is that children are trying to discover which one of a huge set of possible grammars is the one underlying their family's language. Therefore, when they use bare nouns, they may consider the language they hear around them to have a grammar that does not use articles— where definiteness is defined differently. For instance, in Russian the order of nouns can indicate definiteness. The following artificial example using English words gives a flavor of the idea; the first order indicates "dogs in general" and the second "specific dogs":

I like dogs.

Dogs I like.

Hearing someone say, "Dogs, I like," an English-speaking child could explore the possibility that English uses word order to mark definiteness and indefiniteness. She might look around for some particular dogs; finding none, she might decide that the speaker must have meant "dogs in general" and then come to a big conclusion: English only indicates definiteness with an explicit article (a conclusion that is still simplified).

That

Why does English have both the words *it* and *that*? In many situations, they cover the same ground. However, there is a dynamic difference, which the following exploration reveals.

| Exploration 5.12 |
| Cumulative *that* |
| (*that* as an extension of reference) |

You and a child are standing next to a table. On the table are a spoon and a placemat, next to each other. Say to the child,

"Put the spoon on a mat."

After the child puts the spoon on the mat, follow with this instruction:

"Now put it on the floor."

In this situation, we expect the child to put the *spoon* on the floor. However, suppose you say instead,

"Now put that on the floor."

Here, we expect the child to put *the spoon and the mat* on the floor. In other words, *that* picks out the object created by cumulative actions. If you say,

"Now put it on the floor," some people will put the spoon on the floor and some people will put the spoon + mat on the floor; but if you say, "Now put THAT on the floor," the only possible response is to put the spoon + mat on the floor. (Note that you cannot achieve this effect with the odd request "Now put IT on the floor.")

Linguists have not yet determined at what age children know this special property of *that*. It is one of the sophisticated features of language that could lead to a misunderstanding between parent and child and that may be a domain where a child with a language deficiency who is inattentive to context might err. Imagine that a father says to a child,

"Put some salt on the potatoes and then put that on the dinner table,"

whereupon the child puts the salt on the potatoes and then puts the salt on the table. The child may have understood *that* to be ambiguous, like *it*. That is, the child may have understood his father to say,

"Put the salt on the potatoes and then put it [= the salt] on the dinner table,"

in which case he would have done the right thing according to his own understanding. As noted, *it* may be ambiguous in a situation like this, even for adults, but *that* is not—*that* has the accumulated reference (potatoes with salt on them), nothing else.

Suppose the father then says,

"Why did you do that? Didn't I just tell you to put the potatoes on the table?"

No, actually he said to put "that" on the table. Since the specific words and syntax that we use are fleeting, the father's memory system has already reconstructed *that = salt + potatoes* and therefore no longer retains the information that he used the word *that*. Adults may not realize they have not actually said what they think they have said.

The real test of grammar comes when children understand meanings that go against context and common sense, as in this exploration. Say to a child,

| Exploration 5.13 |
| Can a child cope with nonsense? |
| (*that* and nonsense) |

"Put the noodles in the sink and then put them on the table."

This clearly asks the child to put the noodles on the table. Now say,

"Put the noodles in the sink and then put that on the table."

Does the child laugh and say, "I can't put the sink on the table!"? If she does, her grammar is solid as a rock. If she just puts the noodles on the table, she will have rejected some parental nonsense in favor of her own common sense (an ability she may need to use elsewhere). Even if she just looks up and frowns for a moment after hearing *that*, she is indicating that *that* seemed wrong.

There is a very serious point here. Grammar is fundamentally autonomous. We really control grammar when we understand a statement that distorts or challenges the environment, as when we deftly handle jokes that spar with reality.

Exploration 5.14
Some of some
(how quantifiers combine)

Is the behavior of *that* an isolated oddity? Not at all. It reflects a kind of "situational" recursion that is also found with the word *some*. The potential for reapplying *some* is part of how we use it. Consider this simple exploration. Hand a child a bowl of potato chips and say,

"Take some chips from this bowl and go sit near your mother in the living room."

Schematically speaking, when the child complies, he is taking chips B from bowl A. Next, say this to the child:

"Now give some to your mother."

The child might do any of three things: (1) go back and take more chips from bowl A for his mother, (2) give all of chips B (= *some* from your first request) to his mother, or (3) recompute and give part of chips B (= C) to his mother (the adultlike response). Again, we see here a subtle difference between pronouns and quantifiers like *some*: *some* is not just a pronoun but a word that reapplies each time it is used.

There Are Five Kinds of *There*: How Can a Child See Which Is Which?

Reference goes from word to thing, but it may also go back to earlier words via pronouns. Take this not too implausible conversation:

Mother: Put your hat in the closet up in your room . . .
    [Child does it and comes downstairs]
Mother: . . . and put your coat there too.
    [Child throws coat *on the floor*]
Mother: Hey, didn't I tell you to put your coat up in your closet?

Well, no, actually she said "there." As we saw in discussing *that*, the mother could be unconscious of the grammar she used—it disappears so quickly—and might not know that she used an ambiguous pronoun (*there*)

instead of naming the place again. The locative *there* requires the hearer to reconstruct an entire link from the discourse: *there = in the closet up in your room*. But of course it might also be just a contextual pointer: *there = that spot right there in front of us*.

The child learning English experiences at least five distinct uses of *there*, which Robin Schafer and I have explored:[10]

1. "There!"   Expression of satisfaction (just tied shoes)
2. "There, there."   Words of comfort
3. "There is an elephant."   Presentational (or pointing) *there* (links to nonlinguistic context)
4. "There are no elephants."   Existential *there*
5. "(We went to the zoo.)   Locative discourse link (links to some ear-
An elephant was there."   lier locative in the linguistic context)

The child must solve two puzzles here. Somehow, the language that he hears around him must express, say, the notions "presentational" and "existential"; he must pick out the words or inflections that express these notions. And for English, there is the added complication that these notions (and more) are expressed by the same word. How the child finds his way through this maze engages the most sophisticated aspects of linguistic theory, and here we will just skim the surface.

Clearly, children do find their way through the maze. The naturalistic data show that very young children already produce pointing *there*, existential *there*, and locative discourse link *there*:[11]

Early examples of pointing (or presentational) *there*
a. June 1;7 (looking at a picture of a baby in a book)
June: Baby.
Mother: Uhhuh.
June: There.
b. Eve 1;9 (pointing)
Eve: That Eve nose . . . That Mom nose right there.
c. April 2;1
April: Put that over there.
Mother: (moves the toys)

Four to eleven months after the first examples of pointing *there*, an average of eight months later, the first self-generated, unambiguous examples containing existential *there* occur:

Early examples of existential *there*

a. Eve 1;11 (staring out of window)

Eve: Fraser # no more squirrels.

Mother: No more what?

Eve: There no squirrels.

    No more squirrels.

b. Eve 2;2 (mother dishes up tapioca)

Eve: There be no more.

Mother: No # this is all.

c. Peter 2;3.24

Peter: Are there any girls in this book?

d. April 2;9

April: There was an alligator.

Mother: An alligator # that's right # that was in the movie.

Here are some examples of how children first use the locative *there* linked to discourse:

Early examples of locative-discourse-link *there*

a. Eve 2;2

Eve: Went to Colorado.

Mother: Yes.

Eve: He working there.

Mother: He's working there # uhhuh.

b. Peter 2;7.13

Pat: I think you better go in the living room.

Peter: Who's eating there?

c. Naomi 2;11

Naomi: I sticked it on these wood.

    Stays on there.

d. Adam 3;0

Mother: Tonight we'll get it (= Adam's pail) out of the car.

Adam: Why Daddy put it in (th)ere?

e. Peter 3;1.21

Peter: I fell down and make the hole.

Pat: Oh.

Peter: And there was a stick (= location of the fall) and broke it really hard and it make the hole.

f. Sarah 3;5.13

Father: It's on the cabinet.

Sarah: What's my jingle bell doin(g) up there (= on the cabinet)?

g. Mark 4;2.26
Fahter: Do you want to go downstairs?
Mark: Is there a blanket down there (= downstairs)?

This evidence suggests that somehow children know in advance that all these kinds of expression belong in a grammar, so they are looking for them. What experience would help children distinguish the different uses of *there*? Most people say that children "figure it out" in time, but of course we are trying to figure out how they figure it out. However, there is another possibility: if the child has the idea of "existential" as a part of Universal Grammar, as a biological gift, then all she needs is the right piece of evidence (or a few pieces) in the speech that she hears to find how English expresses it. Here is one possible piece of evidence. It could well be just those sentences that have the flavor of contradiction to them that push child grammar forward. Suppose someone says to a child,

"There is a nice hat here,"

and at that moment there is indeed a nice hat right here in front of him. Now if the child takes both *here* and *there* to be locatives, then a contradiction is present: the hat cannot be both here and there at the same time. But the situation reveals unmistakably that the accurate locative is *here*—so *there* must be "empty" and it must be the existential the child is looking for. It is this kind of experience that I believe moves grammar forward at every step. The explorations presented here, which develop stark choices, might also create the moments where grammar advances, if the child is ready at that moment to advance.

Robin Schafer and I developed an experiment that presented exactly this kind of stark choice: specifically, it put existential and locative *there* into competition by making both possible. In one corner of a feltboard, we made a little box with a picture of a watering can in it, which we labeled "garden." We then asked children to put a picture of a dog on the feltboard, using the following introduction and either ending (a) or ending (b):

"Here is a garden. Now look, the garden has a watering can in it."
a. "And a dog is there."
b. "And there is a dog."

When the story ended with "And a dog is there," adults put the dog in the tiny garden 90 percent of the time, realizing that *there = in the garden* in this scenario. Two-year-old children put the dog in the tiny garden only 30 percent of the time (chance level); 70 percent of the time they put it elsewhere on the feltboard. The percentage of children who put the dog in the tiny garden increased gradually with age: five-year-olds put it there 80 percent of the time on hearing "And a dog is there." On hearing the other ending, "And there is a dog," adults and five-year-olds put the dog *not* in the garden but in the larger area of the feltboard 60 percent of the time. Two-year-olds again put the dog in the tiny garden 30 percent of the time and outside the garden 70 percent of the time.

The two-year-olds, then, showed no difference between the two *there*s, preferring the nonlocative interpretation for both endings to the story. This means that they took (a) to be (b) as if *there* were empty and did not indicate a location. There is something these young speakers have not realized yet. It seems the hardest thing to do is make a connection across sentences (*there = garden*). The fact that we have exposed the child, in a gamelike atmosphere, to a sharp context that may be beyond his current grammar could help him make the next step, even if we cannot see it.

Exploration 5.15
Where's *there*?
(*there* **as subject or**
reference to location)

The same exploration can be carried out informally. You will need paper, something to write with, a plate, a penny, a paperclip, and a bean. Draw a circle in one corner of the paper (or use this illustration):

Give the child a penny and say,

"Look at this page. A circle is on the corner of it. There is a penny too. Can you show me?"

Now put the bean on the edge of the plate (or use this illustration):

Give the child a paperclip and say,

"Now look at this plate. A bean is on the edge. A paperclip is there too. Can you show me?"

The prediction is that the child will more often put the penny anywhere on the page while the paperclip will go near the bean.

This little exploration might not work for a classic experimental reason: the child might just do the same thing twice. But that is why the order is important. The first scenario does not require the child to put the penny in the corner (though it wouldn't be wrong to do so), while the second really asks for the paperclip to go on the edge.

Large *Here*/Small *Here*

Words like *here* can grab a large or a small perspective—or both at once.[12] Consider the following discourse:

When we start to drive to Michigan from Massachusetts I like to sit here in back, but when we get near there I like to sit up there in front. I don't know why I like to sit here here and there there.

sit ["small" here] ["large" here]
       seat   state

The order is actually quite strict syntactically: "large" *here* appears naturally at the beginning of the sentence, while the end allows both "large" *here* and "small" *here* but prefers the latter. Imagine a visitor from Japan discussing etiquette:

There we put our shoes here.
[Japan]   [near door]

Here you put your shoes there.
[USA]   [on rack]

Exploration 5.16
Can a child's mind point four ways at once?
(complex situational reference)

You could explore whether a child understands these multiple references with questions like these, which order *here/there* as *origin* and *destination*. (This exploration was designed with seven- and eight-year-olds in mind, but some four- or five-year-olds will understand the questions as well.) Put one object near a child and another of the same type of object in a corner. Let's say you've set up two chairs, like this:

Say to the child,

"See the chair next to you and the one over there? Can you put the one there here and the one here there?"

You could extend this by ordering the events so the child must clearly understand the origin and the destination, since you are asking her to start, counterintuitively, with the further chair:

"Can you first put the one there here and then the one here there?"

The child must simultaneously coordinate four deictics (pointer words).

Because our unconscious grammar unpacks these sentences so efficiently, we hardly notice how complex the surface of language is until we look closely. Here, the child has to use her point of view from four different angles at once to fix the right geometry on the situation. Chapter 13 will revisit the intriguing topic of how point of view is built into grammar.

How to Talk about Nothing

One stunning aspect of language is the capacity we have to refer to things that do not exist with a wide array of negative terms: for example, *no, not, never, deny, without, except.* Furthermore, negation varies extensively across languages, so, although the concept may be inborn, each child must decipher how it is expressed in his or her language. Book after book has been written about how negation works in dozens of languages. Its intricacy is like fine lacework. For the barest glimpse of this intricacy, let's look at four topics in the syntax of negation: denial, the use of *no* and *not* with nouns and verbs, the use of *not* with adjectives, and double negation.[13]

Denial

Sometimes the child's first word is *no.* Parents are taken aback when a child marches out *no* constantly. Some parents associate it with the "terrible twos." We need to get beneath the emotional force of the word, to see the cognitive achievements it reflects. Children's use of *no* goes through stages involving vastly different notions of *rejection, denial,* and *nonexistence.* A famous example is *No soap,* noted by Ursula Bellugi,[14] which can mean "I don't want the soap" (rejection), "That is not soap" (denial of a proposition), and "There is no soap" (nonexistence). Each enacts a distinct attitude, a posture toward reality. To get a taste of the complexities the child needs to master, let's look briefly at denial.

Before a child can deny a proposition, he must grasp the notion of proposition in the first place. Propositions familiar from philosophy are statements like

All men are mortal.

However, any everyday assertion like this is also a proposition:

The book is on the floor.

One way of thinking about it is that a proposition is any statement that can be denied (*The book is not on the floor*).

If propositions were prompted by every observation, we would spend our lives putting observations into sentences (that is, saying things like "My foot is on the floor," "The floor is brown," "The floor meets the wall,"...). But in fact there must be a motive for speech. If I say to you, "That toy is broken," I am making a judgment about a situation that you might not know about and that might be useful. That is, I am adding a proposition about reality to our shared reality. (The concept of propositions will play an important role when we consider false belief in chapter 13.)

Exploration 5.17
Denial or existence
(the difference between
propositions and properties)

It is important to realize that children implicitly have a distinction between propositions and observations (where, informally, "noting a property" = an observation). We can get a sense of a child's early knowledge with this simple situation. Set an empty bowl in front of a child and say either,

"Is this soup?" (asking the child to respond to a propositional claim)

or

"Is there soup?" (seeking a response to an observation).

Will the child answer the first question with "No, it is a bowl" and the second with "No, it is empty"? To give these answers, the child must grasp the deep difference between an identifying proposition (*It's a bowl*) and noting a property (*It's empty*).

The thrust of simple adult remarks can be surprisingly cloudy. Suppose a child says, "Let's throw away my broken toys," and her father replies, "Here is a no good toy." Is he referring to the toy's location ("A no good toy is right here") or making a propositional judgment about it ("This toy is no good")? It is hard to tell—but note that the logical actions that follow are quite different. If "Here is a no good toy" is a judgment, the child will look at the toy carefully to see if the judgment is correct; but if "Here is a no good toy" is necessarily true, the child might grab the toy and throw it in the trash. If a child reacts too quickly to a statement, perhaps she has not grasped the force of the statement.

No Is Not *Not*

At first blush, the words *no* and *not* seem quite alike: they negate something. What complications could they possibly pose for the child learning English?

Consider these two sentences, which—when written down—differ only by the letter *t*:

John likes not dancing.

John likes no dancing.

In *John likes not dancing*, the word *dancing* is a verb. It therefore has to have a subject, and *John* is the natural choice. John is the nondancer. We also note that the verb *dancing* is negated with *not*. In *John likes no dancing*, the word *dancing* is a noun (derived from a verb) and names an activity as if it were a thing. It therefore needs no particular subject. The sentence means that John dislikes the activity itself, no matter who is doing it. The noun *dancing* is negated with *no*.

Not many years ago, people presumed that children begin with a vague generalized *no* that covers all situations and that cannot possibly be distinguished from *not*—that is, that they cannot understand the difference in structure and meaning signaled by the difference between *no* and *not* in sentences like *John likes not dancing* and *John likes no dancing*. Before investigating this distinction experimentally, I thought myself that children would only grasp it at eight or nine years. The children who participated in the experiment ranged in age from three to nine years—and remarkably, even some of the three-year-olds showed knowledge of the distinction.[15] (This experiment was in fact the first to show that preschool children grasp the refined grammatical distinctions that linguistic theory identifies.)

Exploration 5.18
No is not *not*
(understanding *-ing* as marking both a noun and a verb)

Here is one way I explored the distinction with five-year-olds. The method is easy to imitate. Ask the child you're with any question on this model that elicits a story:

"Can you tell me a story about . . ." [choose (a) or (b)]
a. " . . . Mom likes not singing."
b. " . . . Mom likes no singing."

After the child tells you that story, ask another question:

"Now can you tell me a story about . . ." [choose (d) if you chose (a) above; choose (c) if you chose (b) above]
c. " . . . Dad likes not running."
d. " . . . Dad likes no running."

For (a), I expected the five-year-olds to tell stories like "Her throat hurts so she doesn't want to sing"; for (b), stories like "The kids' noise bothers her"; for (c), stories like "He's always tired"; and for (d), stories like "It's not good to run in the house." And that's in fact what they did. In doing so, they showed knowledge of a difference between verbs and deverbal nouns ending in *-ing*. They also showed that they grasped the abstract concept of a noun: any word that can follow a noun marker like *the*, *some*, and *no*. (In this sense, they showed that they knew more than the mistaken grammar teacher who defines a noun as the name of a "person, place, or thing.")

Not Little Is Not *Not* and *Little*; *Not All* Is Not *All Not*

Negation sometimes defines reference in a two-step process. First it can modify an adjective, as in *These toys are not little*, which then becomes pronominal:

These are not little toys.

The negative sentence is now ambiguous: *not* can modify either the whole noun phrase (*little toys*) or just the adjective (*little*):

not [little toys]
not little [toys]

Exploration 5.19 *Not little* is not *not* and *little* (ambiguous negatives)

How might you find out what a child knows? You might set some plates, big toys, and little toys in front of a child, like these:

Now say,

"Show me the ones that are not little toys."

Try to keep your intonation even. Adding emphasis complicates the structure.

Suppose the child points to both the big toys and the plates. That suggests she sees both sides of the ambiguity—or took the meaning differently. If she points just to the big toys, then she has taken *not* to apply just to *little*. But experience in fact suggests the opposite:[16] children will let each modifier modify the noun by itself (*not toys*, *little toys*) before the modifiers modify each other. Similarly, as we will see in chapter 6, in an experiment carried out by Ed Matthei some children misinterpreted the phrase *second white ball* to mean "second, white ball" (that is, "the second and white ball").

> **Exploration 5.20**
> *Not all* is not *all not*
> (more ambiguity:
> negation and quantifiers)

Matthei and I found a related phenomenon involving *not all*.[17] To explore this yourself, take three plates and put nickels on one, pennies on the second, and half pennies and half nickels on the third.

Now say to a child,

"Show me the plate where the coins are not all pennies."

If the child already has the structures that make up the adult grammar of English, he will point to the plate with half pennies and half nickels. However, it turns out that children often take . . . *where the coins are not all pennies* this way:

the coins are *all not* pennies → the coins are all nickels

They apply the word *not* to *pennies* instead of just to *all*.

But why? Why would *not* apply to a word farther away in the sentence (*pennies*) instead of a word right nearby (*all*)? We do not know for sure, but one possibility is that such results reflect a resistance to a certain kind of structure. Here is a simple way to see it. Children certainly understand *The toys are not little*. It is just the phrase *the not little toys* that they stumble over. So what is the structural difference? It seems that children can carry out one Merge operation to connect *little* with *toys*, then take the object formed in that operation (*little toys*) and merge it with *not* ([*not* [*little toys*]]), building a larger tree structure one step at a time as in (A). What they avoid is (B), merging an *already complex* element (*not little*) with *toys*. Here is what it looks like spatially:

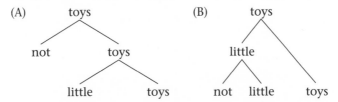

Why should there be a bias against (B)? Maybe (A) is just a biologically more natural structure. Such a claim may seem strange and improbable. I imagine that if someone had approached a person in the Middle Ages and said that not God but two invisible strands of DNA in the structure of a double helix determine all of who we are, the medieval citizen's mind would have rebelled. But nowadays the structure of DNA feels like just another piece of knowledge. We should find a structural bias in grammar no more surprising than the particularity of strands of DNA.

Whatever biology ultimately says, the core claim here is this: children can only see what reference the adult has in mind if they can build a complex structure to match it.

Double Negation: "No, I Am Not a Nothing Boy"

In the adult grammar of English, negation can explicitly interact with itself: for example, in *I cannot not go*, one *not* cancels the other out, and we understand the positive sense "I must go." Do English-learning children understand double negation the same way? There are indications that children initially see multiple negatives in a sentence as instead *agreeing* with each other, leading to one negative expression. Thus, the boy who said, "No, I am not a nothing boy,"[18] perhaps meant "No, I am a boy," and the child who says, "I don't want no hotdog," actually means "I don't want a

hotdog"—the negatives reinforce one negative assertion rather than can-
celing each other out. Reinforced negation is called *negative concord*, and it
is the system of negation found in most languages of the world, including
African-American English.

Exploration 5.21
Negating negation
(combining negatives)

Can children understand double negation as anything
but concord? Tell a child this story twice, ending once
with (a) and once with (b):

"Susan is sick on the day of her friend Dan's birthday party. Dan really
wants her to come."
a. " 'You *can't not* go,' her mother says. What does her mother want her to
do?"
b. " 'You *can not* go,' her mother says. What does her mother want her to
do?"

Using our adult-English, double-negation grammars, we would answer,
"Go to the party" for (a) and "Stay home" for (b). How will the child
answer?

Or just start a conversation and see where it goes. "You can't not
breathe," you might say to a child. "Is that true?" If the child answers,
"Yes, I always have to breathe," then she has the adult English grammar
concept that two negatives cancel each other. If she answers, "Yes, but not
for very long," then she took the double negation as one (negative concord) and understood you to mean "You can not breathe."

Exploratory work suggests that four- and five-year-old children do not
allow one negation to cancel another: they treat *You can't not go* like *You
can not go*. Is the concept of double negation truly unavailable to young
children? Considerable careful research is needed before the acquisition
path becomes clear, but we take a few steps toward that goal when we discuss African-American English (see chapter 11).

Groups and Individuals: *All* Is Not *Every*

We often refer to things in bunches. Even though different ways of referring to bunches seem the same, grammar actually separates different
kinds of bunches. *Susan ate all the raisins* and *Susan ate every raisin* seem to
mean the same thing. However, *all* can have a collective
meaning, but *every* must be distributive.[19] The following
exploration makes this clear. Show a child these pictures:

Exploration 5.22
Distributivity and collectivity
(collective and distributive
quantifiers)

 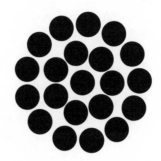

Say,

"Point to all the boxes."

Then say,

"Point to every circle."

If the child grasps the collectivity of *all* and the distributivity of *every*, he will use one or two gestures in response to "Point to all the boxes" and many in response to "Point to every circle"—or say, "I can't, too many." (Note: The objects are deliberately drawn small here, so that the child responding to the questions is tempted to make just one gesture for *all* but forced to make small, individual gestures for *every*. Treating *all* like *every* is not wrong, but treating *every* like *all* means that the child does not recognize the distributivity principle.)

Every and *each* are not quite the same either. *Every* prefers a distributive reading but allows a collective reading for a few actions, while *each* is adamantly distributive. Someone could eat a bunch of raisins in one gulp and say, "I ate every raisin," but not "I ate each raisin." This lends itself to a quick and easy exploration. First, take a pile of grapes and eat them one by one. Then ask,

Exploration 5.23
Each* is not *every
(how quantifiers differ)

"Did I eat each grape?"

We expect the child will say "Yes." Next, eat a pile of raisins in one gulp, and ask,

"Did I eat each raisin?"

Here, we expect the answer "No." Finally, eat a pile of M&Ms all in one gulp, and ask,

"Did I eat every M&M?"

This time, we expect the answer "Yes." The last two situations are essentially identical and reveal that *each* and *every* are not quite the same: *every* is allowed to refer to a group, but *each* is not.

No one knows whether children have this subtle knowledge, but it is a part of English—it is what speakers need to know before we can say they fully understand *each* and *every*.

If a child grasps the difference, she is building a connection between a set of objects and a set of gestures.

What's the Same?

In real situations, our meaning—our references—can be starkly and poignantly evident ("Oh dear, we forgot the housekeys"), but still those meanings are not in language alone, but in how our minds—not our words—make the connection to the myriad circumstances. Nothing in language gives absolute reference. Really? Let us argue with ourselves a bit: can't we create words or a construction that gives absolute reference?

How about being utterly explicit and saying *the same*, as in *They both like the same girl*? In this case, *same* seems to be getting at what we want: they both like one particular girl. But what do you think when someone says this?

They are both wearing the same dress.

Here we are no longer referring to one object: two dresses are involved. Suppose we add *exactly*:

They are both wearing exactly the same dress.

Nothing changes: two dresses are still involved. Will *literally* do it? No:

He made literally the same mistake twice.

Again, we cannot fix on a single object: two mistakes were made, not one. So *same* appears to be ambiguous: it can pick out "same object" or "same kind of object."

What do children understand *same* to mean: "literal same" or "same kind" or both? It is difficult to know. For example, there are only about ten uses of *same* in all the files from a nursery-school-age child called "Peter" in the CHILDES database. We find exchanges like this one between adult and child (where the child has something in mind not shared by the adult):

Adult: Whose Frisbee is it?

Peter: Huh.

Adult: Whose Frisbee are you looking for?

Peter: The same [!!] Frisbee.

　　　　 The same [!!] Frisbee.

Adult: The same Frisbee?

Adult2: The same Frisbee?

Peter: The same [!!] Frisbee.

At a later point, beyond three years, we find Peter's adjectival use of *same* to be more advanced:

Adult: I go where Daddy goes.

Peter: Where Daddy goes.

Adult: Yeah # the same school as your daddy goes to.

Peter: Same school as my daddy goes to.

Peter: A green.

Adult: Mmhm.

Adult2: Is it the same as that?

Peter: Uh # yep # and this one's same as that as that.

The dialogues show the obscurity of what children say. The crucial issues we are exploring are unanswerable from such data. Careful exploration will give us a sharper sense of what the child means. Here is one possible approach.

　　As noted, the word *same* is ambiguous between "literally the same" and "figuratively the same." If I say, "We both own the same car," it could mean that we have one car in common (the "token" meaning) or that we each have the same type of car (the "type" meaning). Do children see both of these senses? We can look into this with a simple exploration, much like early work of Piaget's. It is appropriate for older children, but one might try it even with a three-year-old.

Exploration 5.24 **When is *same* not the same?** (**different types of *same***)

　　The first variant of the exploration looks at whether children understand the type meaning of *same*. Show a child the following pictures, where two children have one kind of car and a third child has a different kind of car:

Ask,

"Are two children in the same car?"

If the child says "Yes," follow up with

"Which ones?"

If the child says "Yes," then she has the "same kind" meaning for *same*; if she says "No," then she understands it to refer to a specific object. (This exploration works well with ordinary household props, too. For instance, take one big fork and two identical little forks. Pick up a piece of bread with the big fork and a cracker with a little fork, and ask,

"Did I pick up both things with the same fork?"

Then pick up a bean with one little fork and a piece of banana with the other little fork, and ask,

"Did I pick up both things with the same fork?")

The second variant looks at whether children understand the token meaning. Two children are riding in one car, and another child is riding in a second car:

Ask a child this question:

"Are some children in the same car?"

If the child says "Yes," then ask, "Which ones?" If the child points to the two children riding together, then he understands the nonspecific "same car" interpretation.

Now, what happens when we combine the two situations? Here we have two children in one car, a third child in an identical car, and a fourth child in a different car:

Show a child this picture and ask,

"Which children are in the same car?"

Pointing to just the two children riding together reveals that the child sees the token meaning of *same*; pointing to the three children in the two identical cars reveals that the child sees the type meaning. For my grammar, it seems that the *token* meaning takes precedence over the *type* meaning in a case like this, so I would predict that children (if they already have the adult-grammar understanding of *same*) would point to the two children riding together. This engages something called an *implicature*: choose the strongest example of sameness. Here we begin to connect how words work with how we think about situations. Its official title is *pragmatics* of language.

John Smith and His Corpse: Even Proper Names Refer to Ideas

Skepticism about the view that there is no absolute pure reference dies hard. So let's confront the ultimate "real thing," the last bastion of seemingly pure reference: proper names. Proper nouns really do seem to refer to a concrete, utterly particular object, like a person. But is that all the meaning they carry? One form of a person is a body, which can be a corpse. Suppose I say, "The corpse of John Smith is in the gully." Now what is John Smith as distinct from his body? If John Smith were identical to his body, then we could reverse those terms: *The John Smith of the corpse is in the gully*, or even *The John Smith of John Smith is in the gully*. But those sentences are nonsense. Or suppose I say, "John Smith is important to all of us." Well, now, is John Smith just his live body, or is he in part an idea that we carry in our heads? Each of us has a slightly different idea about John Smith, and the sentence *John Smith is important to all of us* actually treats that collection of ideas as if the term *John Smith* refers to them all, something far more complex than his body alone. Our ideas may even be contradictory (I think John Smith is good-looking, you think he is homely).

So the term *John Smith* refers to something that is not clearly bounded by any physical reality. At this point, you may feel your mind reeling down a hopeless slope of abstraction. And perhaps it is. There is no easy answer to what it means to have a meaning or to refer to the world around us.

This mélange of concrete reference, implications, and subjective attitudes should add up to an immense challenge for a child: hundreds of very strange mental abstractions combine in reference to a single object, a human being. How does the child grasp them all? The fact that the child has so little difficulty strongly suggests that many concepts come prepackaged, like the concepts "person" and "another person." The concept "person" automatically includes a sense of an independent will, as well as a host of physical attributes, like height, smell, awkwardness. The concept "another person" implies both shared and distinct qualities—and crucially, it implies a different mind. Many other prepackaged concepts may be available to us as well, making acquisition of the words that refer to them much, much easier.

We live in a world of pure ideas that happen, in ways we do not fully grasp, to partially correspond to "a" real world outside ourselves. The frog has an image of the same world that is also correct but different from ours. Note that I am not asserting that all views of the world are equally valid, nor am I asserting that it is impossible to arrive at an abstract characterization of the world that is free from human bias. It seems to me that indeed it might *be* possible. That is the scientific hope. Nevertheless, it takes a vast mental effort to sift our human biases out of the scientific enterprise. Language itself never loses its human stamp, its oddities of perspective that come from the human species.

Conclusions: Mental Tools Embedded in Grammar

A number of new tools in the child's range of puzzle-solvers have emerged here. They are features of Universal Grammar that enable the child to figure out language like a complex quadratic equation. Recognition of one feature feeds recognition of another. Exactly how that happens is what students of language acquisition struggle to understand. We have a jumble of observations, but no one knows how the various referential terms influence each other's acquisition. For instance, does learning how *that* works help children learn *the*? We are still in the early phase of getting still-shots of the principles involved and laying out the questions. Building a dynamic, sequential model remains on the horizon.

We can, nonetheless, summarize the abstract principles that have been on display:

1. Children unconsciously manipulate a notion of *variable* (for instance, *here* can refer to more than one place). In chapter 8, we will see that the absence of variable reference may underlie an important kind of communicative disorder.
2. Children build what we can call *reference chains*: they make direct connections of identity across a discourse (for instance, understanding that *there* in one sentence replaces *in the closet up in your room* in a previous sentence). They must build chains to previous sentences as well as to context.
3. Universal grammar provides methods, like the $a \rightarrow the$ shift in English, to move from *general* to *particular*.
4. The child may use apparent "contradiction" as a device to isolate abstract grammatical features (for instance, the presence of locative *here* in *There is a nice hat here* may signal that *there* has an expletive function).
5. Children control grammar just when they understand sentences that *disagree* with context or reality. It is freedom from the control of our environment that marks linguistic knowledge.
6. Reference can build upon itself, composing new meanings from the same parts (*here here*, *some* of *some*, *not not*, and so on). Here we can see that we are deploying a *mechanism* to express ourselves.

The questions about reference that continue to confound philosophers are not far from those that confront children; they seem fundamental to what thinking itself is and what the mind does. What leaps out from the hubbub of grammatical detail we have looked at is a very strong claim about how minds work: in a child's experience (and indeed, in all human experience), *no term actually has absolute reference*. This claim remains a matter for lively debate among philosophers. Why is this important? The absence of absolute reference has a profound philosophical benefit on the flip side: it reflects *freedom* in our capacity to refer. It means that our environment does not control our thoughts, that language is an instrument which child and adult can use creatively to connect to ever-shifting experiences—indeed, to design new experiences. This freedom is inherent in the grammar, not something that must be learned. One might ask, could it be otherwise? It could: bees have a communication system that lacks freedom from the environment. Their communication system is a fixed method to establish location, nothing else. They can say where honey is, but not that honey makes them happy.[20]

John Donne, a religious poet, sought to deduce the truth about reality from the imaginary, much as religions seek to define reality by articles of faith about invisible divinities. His poems often started with an indefinite article ("Catch a falling star") and ended with a definite one ("The world is glorious").[21] Just as the word *if* creates a world at odds with the actual world, so the indefinite article *a* conjures up a "set of possible objects" and is part of inventing a possible world—like one where you can catch a falling star.

Renaissance poetry used *five to ten times* as many indefinite articles as modern poetry. The religious focus was otherworldly, and indefinite articles helped deliver the many images of idealized objects (like angels) and other worlds that were endlessly the topic of religious discussion.

In modern poetry, it is no accident that T. S. Eliot wrote *The Waste Land* and not *A Waste Land*. Sometime in the eighteenth century, preference for direct sensation over imagination took over poetry, and with it came the inclination to refer to a shared observed reality rather than sharing the imagination of possible worlds. Shared reality licenses the definite article *the*. Following other dominating philosophies in modern life, modern poetry often underscores the view that the concrete has extra legitimacy and the truly imaginary is suspect. Intellectually, we readily prize the actual and express suspicion about possible worlds—perhaps to our detriment.

Nonetheless, our ordinary language honors the imaginary in almost every conversation. We, child and adult, do the same as Donne in miniature, pursuing a constant interplay among a set of mental visions, of possible worlds, before we ultimately commit ourselves and our beliefs to an object we see or an action we take. It happens so swiftly in the change from *a* to *the* that we hardly notice.

6 The Heartbeat of Grammar: Recursion

Just a few weeks after they begin combining words, children seem suddenly to explode with long sentences. Two words blossom into three, four, five words, full of intriguing quirks of child grammar. Here are a few English examples from a child twenty-five months old, where two structures are connected in not quite adult fashion:[1]

I can no eat it.
I can no get it.
I want cut it the bread.
I trying hammer it.

Not only words are merged; structures, too, are laid on structures to build hierarchies (*I trying* + *hammer it*). Whole systems get locked into each other, like a motor onto a chassis and the chassis onto wheels. The same simple form of creativity we saw in compounds is at the core, pounding like a heart. The child first uses Merge to bring words together and then recursion to create new structure. Now the child is ready to break into more complex expressions.

Recursion: The Core of Linguistic Creativity

All of grammatical theory circles around the idea of recursion. It is central to Chomsky's original insights in developing "generative" grammar—a system that generates more of itself from within itself. Now Chomsky has argued, along with Marc Hauser and Tecumseh Fitch, that it is recursion that separates human language from animal communication systems:

FLN [faculty of language in the narrow sense] only includes recursion and is the only uniquely human component of the faculty of language.... [It] appears to lack any analog in animal communication ... [and allows] us to communicate an endless variety of thoughts.[2]

And I think the essence of the acquisition challenge may lie right there, too: how children are to see *where* recursion occurs in the language they hear. In this chapter, we will take a close look at what children manage to decipher.[3] Once we have seen the power of this amazing syntactic engine, we will examine (in chapters 7 and 8) how meanings are projected onto it.

Repetition and Concord

To see better what recursion is, it will help to look first at what it isn't. Repetition and concord are two "reproducing systems" for linguistic elements, but they are not usually considered to be recursion. Repetition (iteration) reproduces the whole entity (*very, very, very*); concord (a kind of agreement) marks something reproduced by recursion; and recursion reproduces something inside itself (like a sentence inside a sentence).

Repetition

Repetition iterates the same word again and again, usually to intensify meaning:

very, very, very big

I once asked a four-year-old how many times you can put *very* in front of *big*. He obligingly produced at least twenty-five *very*s.

   But even this simple intensification system shows limits and complications that the child needs to master. We can repeat words, but not phrases, or units of two words. These are fine:

very, very, very big
big, big, big house
so, so, so big house

So is this recursive form:

big strange house

But these are not:

*so very, so very, so very happy
*so big, so big, so big house
*big strange, big strange, big strange house

These examples show that the repetition property cannot apply to previously merged or recursive forms.

Moreover, not every type of word can be intensified by simple repetition. Adjectives can be, as we've just seen, but nouns and pronouns cannot:

*I bought a new car, car, car.
*I see it, it, it.

(When college students say, "I'm going home-home," they are not intensifying *home*; rather, they are differentiating two homes ("hometown," not "home dorm").) To emphasize nouns and pronouns, we use loudness instead of repetition: *I love YOU*.

There is no evidence that English-speaking children ever extend adjective intensification to nouns in sentences:

*I want that, that, that.

They are more likely to say, "I REALLY want that." Are these patterns universal? Perhaps. It is reasonable to suppose that every language allows recursive adjectives and blocks recursive nouns as intensifiers.

Concord

Concord is the term for marking the same meaning in several places across a sentence. It builds upon structures that recursion produces; but unlike recursion, it does not change meaning. Consider this sentence, where the prepositional phrases have been created by recursion:

I saw a man [$_{PP}$ in *some* place [$_{PP}$ at *some* time [$_{PP}$ for *some* reason]]].

When we negate this sentence, all of the *some*s turn to *any*s, marking the negative meaning across the sentence:

I *didn't* see a man [$_{PP}$ in *any* place [$_{PP}$ at *any* time [$_{PP}$ for *any* reason]]].

It is not completely clear what mechanism lies behind concord—but it is clearly easier for children to master than the self-embedding of recursion. As noted in chapter 5, negative concord is common in many languages and in child English as well. In fact, children spontaneously impose concord where it doesn't occur in adult English:

No, I am *not* a *nothing* boy.[4]
I do*n't* want *none neither*.

A single negative idea is expressed in two places: *I don't want none* essentially means the same thing as *I don't want some*. Again, it is interesting that children spontaneously use these forms even if they do not hear them in the speech of adults around them.

Self-embedding Recursion: Put Something inside Itself!

First let us get a broad overview of the places where recursion takes place; then we will unpack the mechanisms behind one of them: possessives. In English, words, phrases, and clauses all reproduce themselves:

Word level
Prefixation: re-re-read, anti-anti-missile missile
Adjective: big, black, strange bear
Compound: student film group festival

Phrase level
Possessive: John's friend's car's motor
Prepositional phrase: in the kitchen in the cabinet in the corner
Conjunction: and I came and I saw and I conquered
                    John and Bill and Susan

Clause level
Infinitive: John wants to start to go to sing.
Finite: Mary thinks I think you think she did it.

In categorial recursion, it is a grammatical category that is merged again and again; for instance, the category "noun" undergoes recursion to create noun compounds in English. *Self-embedding* poses a more intricate mechanical challenge than either concord or repetition and requires the composition of new meanings. Each noun in a compound *modifies* another one. The right-hand one marks the ultimate object and therefore the top node. Take, for example, *student film group catalogue file repository*:

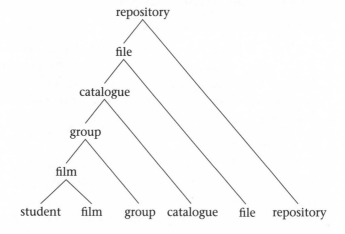

Only the last noun names what the whole object actually is (a repository), but each preceding one changes the type of object.

Self-embedding recursion with possessives requires composition of new meanings in the same way, with the final word determining the type of object:

John's friend's brother's car's motor

The child must see that it is not John's and not the friend's and not the brother's motor, but the car's.

We just keep merging—but English speakers cannot merge everywhere. Certain other languages, such as Mohawk and Bantu, allow merged verb phrases called *serial verbs*.[5] Roughly, the structure is like this (using English words):

Buy read a book. (actually, the structure is often *buy book read*)
Find love a flower.
Discover read assign a book.
Find buy eat a food.

English allows embedding one verb inside another only once. Thus, this construction is nonrecursive in English because recursive rules by definition are infinite:

Go read a book.
Come find a flower.

English speakers cannot say, "*Come see talk to me," no matter how natural the meaning might be. On the other hand, inside a verb phrase, complements can undergo recursion extensively. For example:

John looked for a book [to buy [to read [to assign to his class]]].
Mary said [that you think [that I think [that she thinks boys are awful]]].

There are other powerful limits. Though bare nouns can iterate recursively (*student film group file repository*), noun phrases cannot:

the student *the* film *the* group *the* file *the* repository

Nor can adjective + noun sequences:

good student *old* film *new* group *new* file *big* depository

Notice that there is really nothing wrong with the meanings we are trying to generate here. Why should we not have a compound made up of nouns each modified with something like *new* or *old*? We can easily express the same meaning using rightward modification of the noun:

a big depository of a new file of a new group of old films of good students

So it is the *grammar* that is blocking this level of recursion.

But why can't English speakers do recursion to the left with nouns and adjectives or definite articles? It is as if some grammars say, "Build to the left"; others (like English) say, "Build to the right"; and still others say, "Build both to the left and to the right." Such fascinating kinds of abstract variation go beyond what we can address in this book, but they also go beyond any secure scientific insights. Getting the right technical theory is what tantalizes linguists.

Children also spontaneously impose recursion. One child thought he spotted another pocket of recursion in *as . . . as*:[6]

I'm not *as* tall *as* you *as* Mom.
[meaning "Mom is closer than I am to being as tall as you"]

English allows only two instances of *as*. Hearing two, this child apparently felt, why not three? We also saw an overgeneralized *as* in the chapter 5 discussion of *same*:

Peter: Uh # yep # and this one's same as that as that.

Same . . . as does not extend to *same as . . . as* in adult English. The interesting fact is that children can *spontaneously impose recursion where the adult grammar does not allow it*. It clearly does not happen everywhere, nor does it happen often, and it seems to be initiated by some doublet, like *as . . . as*.

How Discourse Recursion Fails, and So Do Birds

Does recursion happen at the discourse level too? Parallelism with other levels (word, phrase, clause) leads us to look for it. Certainly, discourse exhibits embedding, where an exposition involves a digression after which we return to the main topic. But mechanical recursion is a machinelike property at the sentence level, so I suspect it will not be found at a higher level. Discourse may be governed by cognitive systems for putting ideas together that are inherently different from the systems that govern the word, phrase, and clause.

We can approach the question by asking what real discourse recursion would be like. We do find a parallel sort of implicit subordination with *that*:

The earth is flat. The textbook said that.

Substituting the first sentence for *that* gives

The textbook said that the earth is flat.

But will it work recursively? Let's add another level:

Mary told Bill THAT.

And yet another:

The teacher didn't believe THAT.

Even adding lots of emphasis, it is pretty difficult to reconstruct what the last sentence means.

On the other hand, if we use normal recursion, there is no problem:

The teacher did not believe that Mary told Bill that the textbook said that the earth is flat.

We humans are built to generate the syntax of recursion effortlessly— together with meaning, which gives us something to talk about. (We will find this reasoning useful when we consider false belief in chapter 13.) Discourse pronominal connections (*it*, *that*) can refer to the content of a previous sentence, but not with the same recursive power.

Nor do birds have that power. Timothy Gentner, Kimberly Fenn, Daniel Margoliash, and Howard Nusbaum have claimed that songbirds are capable of recursion and that Chomsky, Hauser, and Fitch's argument that recursion "appears to lack any analog in animal communication" is false.[7] The Gentner group's claim is based on the fact that they trained a few birds to recognize a center-embedded pattern. This pattern may be—though not necessarily—described as one sort of recursive system. It does not carry meaning for communication. Only humans link meaning to structure, step by step; and only humans can compositionally unpack what they hear. Our capacity to build recursive structures is innately linked to our ability to construct endlessly unique references (which makes life interesting).

Still, if I am claiming that the whole mind has principles similar to grammar, perhaps it is a good idea to keep looking for a deeper representation that would capture "digression" as a form of "embedding" that followed an operation of "discourse recursion." Whether or not recursion happens at the discourse level is a nice question, but we do not yet have the tools for cognitive description to make a precise claim about it, beyond pointing out, as above, that one kind of discourse recursion with emphatic *that* seems not to work. It refers to the whole dialogue, not precisely the sequence of propositions subordination articulates.

A Case Study of Recursion: Possessives

What kind of input does it take for a child to recognize recursion? We will get an idea of the acquisition path of a form of recursion special to English—possessives—by doing a kind of case study.

Recognizing Recursion and Infrequent Triggers

Vanishingly few recursive possessives occur in either adult or child English. Numbers are hard to obtain, but it would surprise me if 1 percent of possessives involve recursion. That is, there are probably 99 cases like *John's car* for every case like *John's friend's car*. The transcripts of one child's speech from two and a half to five years turned up only 35 instances of *wh* + possessive (*whose*), compared with 2,000 instances of *what*, and 12 of those occurred in just one session.[8] Recursive possessives are rarer still, but when they occur they seem to come in batches, as in conversations about kinship (for example, *John's grandparents' house is nicer than Mary's father's or your sister's*).

There is a very important implication for acquisition in general here: children's recognition of recursion cannot depend on hearing particular recursive structures frequently, because recursive structures for some types of construction are found in just a few languages and are often very infrequent in daily life—like triple possessives (*my mother's friend's daughter's car*). It must be that a few examples trigger recognition that a structure can embed itself.

We might ask, does the child need to hear a particular recursive structure to know it is possible in his language? Here crosslinguistic arguments become critical. For example, German and Swedish allow only one prenominal possessive. In German, it must be animate; in Swedish, it can also be inanimate.[9] So (again using English words), single possessives like these are possible:

Maria's house (German and Swedish)
a car's motor (Swedish)

Double possessives like this are not:

*John's car's motor (German and Swedish)

One must instead say the equivalent of *the motor of John's car* or even more baroque equivalents to get the meaning across. The occasional linguist who says two elements are possible in German will nonetheless balk at three (the equivalent of *John's friend's car's motor*). (One can only wonder how the German translation of this Monty Python sequence would go: "They've taken everything we had. And not just just from us! From our fathers, and from our father's fathers." "And from our father's father's fathers.... And from our father's father's father's fathers.")

Children learning German and Swedish do not spontaneously create recursive prenominal possessives. So hearing one prenominal possessive is not enough to suggest to the child that she could put even more in front of the noun. Therefore, it is probably the rare instances of recursive possessives in English that are themselves crucial triggers for the English-learning child. And, as we will see, English-learning children stoutly resist them at first. (As do second-language-learning adults. I was once talking with a group of foreign language professors, all of whom were nonnative speakers of English, but many of whom had lived in the United States for decades. I asked them whether they used double possessives. They all said they still found them very difficult and avoided them, quite unlike native speakers.)[10]

Now we have bumped up against the edges of our knowledge. Why exactly should recursion occur in some places, but not in others? Why should English, for example, allow recursion with prenominal possessives but not with noun phrases? And why with bare nouns but not bare verbs? We have bumped into a new acquisition problem as well: how does the child determine exactly where his language's grammar has recursion? The real power of grammar lies in these tiny creative engines, lodged in various parts of the grammar. Some are universal—so maybe the child does not have to learn them—but others have to be recognized. This may be the most profound part of the acquisition problem. Ken Hale, the famous field linguist from MIT who specialized in deciphering previously unstudied languages, commented that he always looked for the most complex parts of a new grammar first—the recursive parts—because they reveal the deepest regularities. In effect, complexity always illustrates transparent recursion, no matter how infrequently it is used in daily life.

Children's Dialogues about Possessives

The acquisition path for possessives is long and not completely visible. It starts with no actual possessive forms at all and ends eventually with the recursive forms. Here is a child at the start of the path (a child whose linguistic development was scrupulously followed to determine the emergence of possessives):[11]

Me: I want me bottle. Where me Q-car? That me car. Have me show. Me turn. Me cat. Me pen. (2;6–2;8)
You: No you train. It's you pen. It's you kite. It you house? (3;2)
Him: I want to go in him house. Him bike is broken. It's him house.
Mine: Mine banana. Mine bottle. Mine car. Mine apple. Mine pasta. (2;4)
My: My car. (3× at 2;4) My pasta. I want my key. It is my TV.
His: What's his name? (3× at 3;6)
Your: Where's your friend? It's your car? I got yours. (3;4)

This child obviously uses the notion of possession before he masters the morphology to express it. He uses *me, mine, my* (and other children say *mines*) all to express possessive. It is possible that a child who uses several forms simultaneously has slight semantic variations in mind. It is very hard to determine from the naturalistic data just what the range of possible meanings is.

These dialogues between parents and children show youngsters from three to five years grappling with recursion and vigorously resisting it:[12]

Father: Donna's dog's name is Tramp.
Mother: That's like um what's Auntie Marian's doggie's name?
          What's Auntie Marian's puppy dog's name?
          What's Auntie Marian's puppy's name?
Sarah: (unclear)
Mother: Huh.
          What's your... what's... what's *your* cousin *Arthur's mummy's* name?
Sarah: I don't...
          Your cousin?
Mother: Yeah, Arthur... Arthur... *what's his mumma's* name?
Sarah: I want pin.

Sarah clearly has difficulty with recursive *'s*. Note the form *what's*, where *is* is contracted to *'s*, which may add to the confusion in an insecure grammar, if the child thinks that *what's* is another possessive.

■ ■ ■

Mother: Sarah, what's my mummy's name?
Sarah: Nana.
Mother: And what's my daddy's name?
Sarah: Grampy.
Mother: And what's Daddy's mumma's name?
Sarah: Huh?

Here Sarah manages to answer the first two questions, but note that the first possessive in these cases is lexical *my*, which may have a slightly different structural representation from *'s*. (See the phrasal exploration 6.4 below.) When true recursive possessives get involved, there is joint bafflement: the child is baffled by the adult's question and the adult is baffled by the child's bafflement.

Mother: What's Daddy's daddy's name?
Sarah: Uh.
Mother: What's Daddy's daddy's name?
Sarah: Uh.
Mother: What is it?
         What'd I tell you?
         Arthur!
Sarah: Arthur! Dat my cousin.
Mother: Oh no, not your cousin Arthur.
         Grampy's name is Arthur.
         Daddy's daddy's name is Arthur.
Sarah: (very deliberately) No, dat my cousin.
Mother: Oh.
         What's your cousin's mumma's name?
         What's Arthur's mumma's name?
Sarah: Uh.
         Oh.
Mother: Thinking?
[Sarah nods]

Things keep going as the mother tries to probe the child's knowledge, but actually she reveals the child's incomplete grammar:

Mother: What's Pebbles' momma's name?
Sarah: Wilma.
Mother: Wilma...yeah.
         And what's Bamm-Bamm's daddy's name?
Sarah: Uh, Bamm-Bamm!
Mother: No, what's Bamm-Bamm's daddy's name?
Sarah: Fred!
Mother: No, Barney.

Here a persistent parent tries to get a child to simply repeat a double possessive:[13]

Father: How about the Dukes of Hazzard's boy's car?
Child: Yeah.
Father: What is it called?
Child: The boy's Dukes of Hazzard car.
Father: No, not the boy's Dukes of Hazzard.
          It's the Dukes of Hazzard's boy's.
          Can you say that? Dukes of Hazzard's boy's car?
Child: The boy's Dukes of Hazzard car.
Father: That's not right.
          Can you say it right?
Child: The boy's Dukes of Hazzard car.
Father: No, the Dukes of Hazzard's boy's car.
Child: The Dukes of Hazzard . . . the boy's Dukes of Hazzard car.
Father: No, say it right.
          Now say the Dukes of Hazzard.
          Say the Dukes of Hazzard's boy's.
Child: Car.
          The boy's Dukes of no the boy's Dukes of Hazzard car.
Father: No.
Child: The boy's Dukes of Hazzard car.
          No.
Father: No.
Child: The boy's Dukes of Hazzard car.
Father: No.
Child: The boy's Dukes of Hazzard car.
Father: No.
Child: The car Dukes of Hazzard boy's.
Father: The Dukes of Hazzard's boy's car.
Child: Dukes of Hazzard's boy's car.
Father: Good.

Although the child finally says the recursive possessive phrase, we cannot really be sure this is more than simple imitation. The recursive possessive may not yet be in his grammar.

This dialogue shows the strength of the child's current grammar. He persistently translates the double possessive into a single possessive (*boy's*) and a compound (*Dukes of Hazzard car*): "the boy's Dukes of Hazzard car," which achieves almost the same meaning but in a different way. At one point, the child tries to satisfy his father by changing word order rather than doing recursion: "the car Dukes of Hazzard boy's." It is clear that

Sarah and this boy really resist both the comprehension and the production of recursive possessives, as do other children.

The child confronts other mysteries of recursion around possessives. Often the noun is actually left off, as in this case:

Mother: We're goin(g) up to Donny's mother's. (= Donny's mother's house)

Or this one:[14]

Mother: Can you get it out of the bowl? 'Member, the beater's yours, the bowl's Sky's. (= the bowl is Sky's bowl)

We will go down other tortuous canyons of ellipsis later.

Finally, note the children's possessives in these two dialogues:

Mother: What was the caterpillar's name, Sarah?
Sarah: Like mine's, like mine.
        It's called . . . I don't remember.

Adding 's to *mine* is a stage many children pass through, much like saying *feetses* where the plural is doubled. The child is trying to assimilate 's to *concord*, not *self-embedding recursion*.

Child: He's Barney.
Father: Who's he?
Child: He's Fred's Flintstone's Fred's friend.[15]

Fred's should not have a possessive marker. It seems again that the child is imposing possessive concord across all of the noun phrases. Such "overgeneralizations" really reinforce our story: children pursue concord before embedding recursion. To ask why concord is more available than embedding recursion is to ask a question as profound as any about grammar. It is by studying tiny facts like these that the structure of mind will someday be laid bare.

Getting It, Finally

Do young children themselves ever use possessive recursion? Hardly ever, as far as we can tell (such searches over large databases are difficult). Just one example has surfaced in the CHILDES database:[16]

Child: What's Toto's girl's name?
        (= What's the name of the girl who owns Toto?)

Anecdotes related to me by Jill de Villiers suggest that when children acquire the recursive possessive, they love to make a game of it: "...and this is Daddy's sister's hat and this is your brother's friend's hat." (Much the same happens when children learn "tag" questions (*I can sing, can't I?*): they suddenly use them excessively. Adam, one of the original children studied by Roger Brown, used thirty-two tags in one three-hour stretch!)

What causes children to finally "get it"? We really do not know. Perhaps the elicitation techniques described below will eventually reveal more.

Pursuing the Mystery: How Possessives Emerge

When we embed possessives, we in effect put one meaning inside another, so both syntax and semantics are involved: *my brother's friend's car* and *my friend's brother's car* do not mean the same thing. So perhaps it is exactly the fact that one has to compute both a *meaning* and a *structure* that creates the challenge in acquiring recursive possessives. (I am simplifying both the semantics and the syntax here.)

Perhaps children first hypothesize this structure for recursive possessives:

my brother's and friend's car (= my brother's friend's car)
my friend's and brother's car (= my friend's brother's car)

That is, perhaps they treat the elements as conjoined, without an embedding relation (a kind of weaker recursion); perhaps they compute an additive meaning, not seeing that it is embedded.

> **Exploration 6.1**
> **Father's father's father's father**
> **(recursive possessives)**

In experimental work, Sarah Gentile found that children made just this conjoined error quite often.[17] You can easily use Gentile's method to explore whether a child's grammar has the recursive or conjoined structure for double possessives. Show the child

1. a picture of Cookie Monster,
2. a picture of Cookie Monster's sister, and
3. a picture of Cookie Monster and his sister.

Say,

"Here is Cookie Monster and his sister."

Now ask,

"Can you show me Cookie Monster's sister's picture?"

Pointing to picture 2 shows understanding of recursive possessives. Gentile found that by four years of age, 65 percent of children answered correctly;

however, three-quarters of the three-year-olds pointed to picture 3 or tried to point to more than one picture.

You could also use family photos for this exploration: if the family album has a photo of Mary and her sister, say to the child,

"Can you point to Mary's sister's foot?,"

and see whose foot the child points to.

In a study on recursive adjectives by Ed Matthei, exploring a suggestion by Carol Chomsky, precisely a preference for coordination emerged with four- to six-year-old children.[18] Matthei set some balls in a line in front of a child so that the second one and a later one in the line were both the same color. Schematically, using black-and-white representations for Matthei's colored balls, the line might look like this:

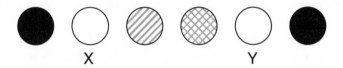

He then said to the child,

"Show me the second white ball."

Over one-third of the children (in this study and replications) chose ball X (the second and white ball), as if they preferred a conjoined version of the descriptive phrase (with a comma): *the second, white ball*.

It would be nice to make this even simpler. Suppose we tried it with a simpler adjective than *second*—say, *big*. The array of balls might look like this:

> **Exploration 6.2**
> **Big and black balls**
> **(how adjectives intersect)**

The request to the child would be

"Show me the big black balls."

How would the child understand this sentence? If she reconstructed it as a conjoined structure ("Show me the big balls and the black balls"), she would pick out all the big balls and all the black balls. But if she reconstructed it as a recursive structure, she would pick out just the balls that involved the intersection of those properties: the big black balls.

Another possibility is to see what set of balls the child picks if you explicitly use *and*:

"Show me the big and black balls."

Will the child pick those that are both big and black; those that are either big or black; or those that are either big, or black, or big and black? Each choice reflects a different kind of adjective composition.[19]

Ingredients for Mastering Possessives

How do we avoid being stumped like the parents in the dialogues above, who unknowingly are testing recursion? Repetition does not make the child grasp it—and just confronts him with repeated failure. Perhaps we just need to wait for something to mature, either inside or outside of grammar. But recursion is a basic principle of grammar, and it is present elsewhere in the grammar. It can hardly be that recursion itself matures. What, then, are the steps to the recursive possessive? Linguists haven't yet worked this out; but here is one possibility.

First, the child may realize the notion of possession inside a major category—for example, inside a pronoun like *mine*. That is what folklore suggests, since most children learn to say *mine* early on. We can explore this straightforwardly with very young children. You might put a hat on yourself and a hat on a child, and say,

> Exploration 6.3
> Nouns and possessives
> (simple possessives)

"I have a hat and you have a hat,"

followed by either

"Can you point to *me*?"

or

"Can you point to *mine*?"

(You can also extend this by asking,

"Can you point to you/yours?,"

and—with a third person in a hat—

"Can you point to him/his?")

To see the next step in the child's path to the recursive possessive, we need to make a detour and ask this perhaps odd-sounding question: can word-endings go on phrases?

Imagine a child saying—as my daughter once did, with some agitation—"There's a bike-rider with no hands." We know just what the sentence means, and enjoy a smile at how she talks. Why a smile? What is the ripple of deviance that we are aware of? For adults, the sentence requires the meaning that the person, the rider, has no hands. But the child is using *with no hands* to modify the action of biking, not the person. It is as if the child were looking past the *-er* to the verb inside and modifying that verb plus its modifier (*riding with no hands*), not putting a modifier on a person (*person with no hands*). In fact, we could represent the relation as follows, with brackets around the whole verb phrase, to which *-er* applies:

[the ride bike with no hands]-*er*

This reformulation is not just a metaphor. We can take it to be a hypothesis about how the child actually restructures the sentence mentally. Janet Randall has shown experimentally that children regularly construe *-er* as if it applied to a whole phrase: for children, *a chef with a fork* is a cook who has a fork nearby, but *a writer with a candy bar* is someone who is using the candy bar to write with.[20]

The child's phrasal *-er* has a kind of adult model: possessive *'s* is overtly phrasal in the same manner in English. *The boy on the corner's hat* refers to the boy's hat, not the corner's hat, as if the *'s* were like *-er* and modified the entire phrase rather than the last noun:

[the boy on the corner]'s hat

After the child grasps that *'s* is a possessive on a single noun, the next step in acquiring the recursive possessive may be this: when the child hears clearly contrasting cases like the following, the contrast may trigger recognition that *'s* attaches to a phrase, not a word. Then the phrases can be recursive and one can be put inside another.

the man next to you's hat
the man next to your hat

The child already knows that when the single word *you* becomes possessive, *your* is the result. Hearing a different form that's apparently also possessive, *you's*, the child assumes it must signal a different structure, so he's led to assign it a phrasal structure: *[the man next to you]'s* hat. If the child realizes that it is the man, not the hat, that is next to her, this realization should force the possessive 's to attach to the whole phrase in order to deliver that meaning. A postcard from a seven-year-old girl to a six-year-old made me realize that phrasal possessives are not so far from a child's world. It said, "Look at the one in the middle's fur."[21] So let's try just the kind of scenarios described by *[... you]'s X/your X*, to see what children do.

Exploration 6.4

**What gives us a grip on phrasal 's?
(possessives on whole phrases)**

Put a hat on a child and say, "This is your hat." Put a hat on yourself, then take the hat off the child and put it between you and the child. Schematically:

| you with hat | | hat | | child |

Now ask,

"Can you point to the person next to your hat?"

After the child replies, follow with

"Can you point to the person next to you's hat?"

If another person is present, put a hat on that person. Take your own hat off and put it between yourself and the other person. Now you have:

| you | | hat | | other person wearing hat |

Ask,

"Can you point to the person next to me's hat?"

Then ask,

"Can you point to the person next to my hat?"

(You can also work out situations for trying *person next to him's hat/person next to his hat, person next to her's hat/person next to her hat.*)

Another way to extend this exploration is to put a big hat on a small person:

| you | | hat | | small person wearing big hat |

Now ask,

"Is the person next to me's hat big?"

and

"Is the person next to my hat big?"

<table>
<tr><td>

Exploration 6.5
The man in the tree's hat
(more phrasal possessives)

</td></tr>
</table>

Here is another way to explore children's preferences that should be fun. Harry Seymour and Janice Jackson tested children's grasp of phrasal possessives by showing them two pictures—one of a man wearing a hat sitting in a tree, and one of a tree "wearing" a hat with a man in it—and requesting,

"Show me the man in the tree's hat."

Pointing to the picture on the left means that the child understands

[the man in the tree]'s hat

where the possessive is on the whole phrase, *the man in the tree*, and not just on *the tree* (*the tree's hat*). If the child just points to the hat on the tree, he has not computed the sentence correctly.[22]

So children seem to follow this path: pronominal possessive (*mine*), then recognition of an affix *'s* on a noun (*Mommy's*), then expansion of the noun to a full noun phrase (*[the person next to you]'s hat*). Once the *'s* applies to a phrase, the possessive itself can be recursive, because phrases can generate more phrases inside themselves. (More technical details are needed to make this last step precise.)[23]

Now children face another challenge, quite different from comprehension—namely, production. Can we elicit recursive possessives? It is certainly worth a try. Show the child this picture, where John and his friend each have a square hat, John's dog has a round one, and John's friend's dog has a flat one:

First say,

"John's dog has a round hat. Here's John's friend. Whose hat is round?"

The child who has reached the stage of producing recursive possessives will answer with

"John's dog's."

Now say,

"His friend has a dog too that likes John's dog. Whose hat is flat?"

Being able to answer

"John's friend's dog's"

—a three-term possessive—would be some feat! More likely the child will use some more complicated phrasing, or point and say "That dog," or describe the dog in some other way. Still, it would be interesting to repeat the exploration over a period of time and see when the recursive possessive actually occurs.

This discussion reveals a new potential question the child must answer: can any word-ending go on a phrase? Surely Universal Grammar does not allow affixes to attach just anywhere, but more languages will need to be studied to find out exactly where they are allowed. We will see in chapter 8 that plurals can attach to phrases, too.

Wrapping a Wrap-Up Up

We are trying to grasp the linguistic world through which the child must navigate. Are there pitfalls we have not seen? Does the child ever encounter evidence that might suggest a form of recursion that doesn't exist? Actually, such evidence is widespread. For example, while English has recursive prefixes, it has no recursive suffixes. Thus, *re-reread* is eminently possible but **a follow up up* is not, even though it would seem like an economical way to say "a follow-up to a follow-up"; nor can we call an outdoor workout a **workout out*. English grammar seems to exclude this possibility, and arguably all grammars do. Could the child ever hear evidence to erroneously suggest such a thing? The title of this section is a case in point. Of course, it has to be understood as "wrapping up a wrap-up" and not "wrapping a wrap-up-up."

Neither adults nor children are tripped up when they hear "We have to put the takeoff off for ten minutes" or "We had to take the cookout out of the schedule." Such constructions never actually mistrigger recursive suffixes because—although they are present every day in speech that adults and children hear—the properties of Universal Grammar guide all of us around them.

Recursion Unlimited

We have seen that the child, equipped with the biological capacity to generate recursion, must perceive just where it occurs in her language. We have found a variety of forms of recursion in English: adjectives, nouns, possessives all have their recursive loops.

How do children ultimately find their way into recursion? Linguists are just in the process of formulating the question itself—not even partway to a solution. And this question immediately raises others. Does a kind of simple repetitive recursion trigger meaning-changing embedding? Does one form of embedding make a child look around for others? Is there a semantic kind of embedding recursion as well that applies to concepts?

Does the human mind contain prisms inside prisms? These are intriguing questions we are left with; we will return to them when we look at whether recursion is needed to explain false beliefs. No answers are here, but still our image of the child is, to my mind, altered by observing the role of recursion in language and considering the larger cognitive questions that it raises—do we need recursion for mental representations of vision, bodily motion, or maybe even social relations? Could we have recursive emotions? Can I be mad at myself for being mad at John? Will it go on? Can you be mad at yourself for always being mad at yourself for losing your temper (since lots of other people lose theirs too)? What emotional algebra accomplishes that?

7 The Structure of Silence

The Ghost of Syntax in the Unspoken

Grammar carves out verbal images in the mind that are so precise they give structure to silence itself.[1] Much of what we say is so clear to us and our listeners that we do not actually have to say it. Sound like a paradox? If I say to you, "I've got peas. Want some?," I don't have to say "want some peas" because the grammar tells you what is missing ("some *peas*," not "some *anything*"). Nothing reveals so dramatically the automatic, machine-like quality of grammar than the fact that we are empowered to communicate elliptically; that is, we just leave certain things out, yet we and our listeners know exactly what we've left unspoken.

Linguists do not know just how children master various elliptical structures. Surely it doesn't happen all at once. Nevertheless, children exhibit great competence early on, in both using and understanding ellipsis. Two-year-old Sarah's ability to deal with long sequences carrying along an elliptical hole is typical; note that she never mentions the liquid here:[2]

Sarah: I drink it all up.
         Give me some more.
         A lot.
Mother: I don't see any more.

When we apply the lens of grammatical analysis, four-year-old Abe's three seemingly simple words *look how much* turn out to be a tour de force of hidden complexity:[3]

Father: She picked up most of it.
Abe (4;7): Oh yeah she left me to pick up this stuff. Dad, look how much.

Abe's words require his dad not only to reconstruct clauses after *how much*

. . . look how much [she left me to pick up this stuff]

but also to form an indirect question that adds *how much* to *of this stuff*, moves it to the front, and then deletes the original of *this stuff*:

...look *how much* of this stuff [she left me to pick up ____]

It is an unusually complex form of ellipsis that imposes question formation on the dropped material.[4]

In this chapter, we will look at some steps on the child's path through ellipsis. Even though all suggestions made here need to be more carefully explored before every acquisition step is clear, they will show the complexity of ellipsis as a grammatical construction, the interpretive feats it requires children to accomplish, and its power as a research tool—a microscope through which to examine children's language learning and Universal Grammar as a whole.

Is There Life without Ellipsis?

Life would be impossibly inefficient without ellipsis. It is our constant companion—no conversation would be bearable without it. Here is how we usually talk:

A: A guy stole an apple.
B: How?
A: Really fast when the shopkeeper wasn't looking at him.
B: When?
A: Yesterday.
B: Where?
A: Across the mall.

Without ellipsis it would go like this:

A: A guy stole an apple.
B: How did a guy steal an apple?
A: He stole an apple really fast when the shopkeeper wasn't looking at him.
B: When did he steal an apple when the shopkeeper wasn't looking at him?
A: He stole an apple yesterday when the shopkeeper wasn't looking at him.
B: Where did he steal an apple yesterday when the shopkeeper wasn't looking at him?
A: He stole an apple yesterday across the mall when the shopkeeper wasn't looking at him.

The conversation would die before we said all that. I doubt that real conversation would exist in the human species without ellipsis. Talking is just too laborious if you actually have to say everything. Ellipsis grants us a merciful efficiency.

But then how do our listeners reconstruct the silence? The grammar has to tell us exactly what has been left out.

Verbal Context Trumps Visual Context

Ellipsis

Doesn't a child need to hear an expression in full before he experiences only its elliptical absence—to hear the elliptical hole filled before it is empty, so he knows what it contains? If this were the case, parents should avoid ellipsis. The reality, though, is quite the opposite. Parents, out of human necessity and perhaps because they think "Shorter is easier," use ellipsis all the time: "Want some?" daily replaces "Do you want some cookies?" Nevertheless, these shorter but elliptical sentences are *actually* as complex as their longer versions because the child really does have to fill in the holes. In fact, as we will see, for the language-learning child they are often more complicated to interpret. Parents do not always see the difference between helpful and harmful brevity. Here's a bit of communication failure that is not atypical:[5]

Mother: Do you want some milk or do you want some juice?
Sarah: I milk juice [?]
Mother: Huh?
Sarah: milk juice
Mother: No, you can either have one or the other. You can('t) have both.
Sarah: milk juice

The child gets the topic (milk and juice), but her speech is so elliptical that we cannot tell if she gets the idea of choice. The exasperated mother is being emphatic, using unhelpful ellipsis with the expression *one or the other . . . not both*, so that the child has to fill in *of the milk and juice*.

Such verbal gridlock is not uncommon—it even invades children's literature. Children's stories (to which we turn below) are rife with baffling ellipsis. What looks simpler is often harder, even when every sentence seems neat and short.

Hearing an elliptical sentence, how do children (and adults) fill in what's missing? Often we can reach out to *physical context*. If a child sees you carrying a bag of cookies and hears you say, "Want some?," then surely the word missing after *some* is *cookies.*

But reaching out to context doesn't always work. What if all you have to go on is previous dialogue, with no specific outside context to help? What parts do you take from previous dialogue to fill in the holes of the sentence you just heard? Is there room for error? These are tricky questions (which we will consider at length), and all of grammar gets into the act.

At first, the answer looks easy: to fill in an elliptical hole in a dialogue, just *add missing material from the previous sentence.* Let's try it:

Three lovely children brought some flowers. Do you want to see some?

It seems as though we just add *flowers* from the previous sentence:

Three lovely children brought some flowers. Do you want to see some [flowers]?

But wait—couldn't we add *lovely children* instead?

Three lovely children brought some flowers. Do you want to see some [lovely children]?

Either *flowers* or *lovely children* is possible (even though the situation does aim a bit more at flowers).

Now, what happens if we have both physical context and previous dialogue to draw on, when we need to reconstruct meaning from ellipsis? Here a specific principle comes into play:

Verbal context always trumps visual context.

Children have to realize this feature of Universal Grammar.

Exploration 7.1
Words over vision
(ellipsis interpretations:
implausible and necessary)

A little exploration illustrates this principle of words over vision. Let's say you and a child have two piles in front of you: one of fruit and one of cookies. Say to the child,

"Look, here is some fruit."

Then pick up two cookies and say,

"Did I take some?"

An adult would say "No," because the gap after *some* has to connect to the word *fruit* in the previous dialogue, not to the physical cookies that you picked up. What does the child say?

We can offer the child a sharp contrast with a nonelliptical form by just saying, in a parallel environment,

"Did I take something?"

In this case, the child should feel entitled to say "Yes"; *something* does not refer back to the previous sentence and allows the child to answer by surveying the visual context.

You could orient the dialogue directly to the child, by making him the actor. This requires making one alternative decidedly less desirable—say, a pile of nails. To make the incongruous alternatives not totally unexpected, you could start out by saying, "Sometimes I think about funny things."

Show the child two bowls: one full of nails, the other full of cookies:

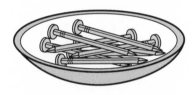

Say,

"Here's some nails. Do you want some?"

A child who says "Yes" and then takes the cookies might be seen as willful or disobedient. Actually, though, he may not realize he is in a discourse environment that requires reconstruction and therefore that he pay attention to words over context.[6] (To make things humorous, you could also say, "Here's some nails. Do you want to eat some?" The child is likely to respond, "No, that's silly, you can't eat nails!")

Exploration 7.2
Words trump context
(what fills silence?)

With an older child, you could try a more complex scenario to explore the primacy of words over context. Put two cats and two toys in one spot; nearby, put two dogs and two more toys:

Point to the first two toys and say,

"Here's the cats' toys. Now show me the dogs'."

The second sentence could of course be understood as including just a plural rather than a plural possessive:

"Now show me the dogs."

Will the child point to the dogs or to the toys next to the dogs? If she points to the toys next to the dogs, she indicates that she can fill in parts from a previous sentence, borrowing *toys* from your original statement "Here's the cats' toys"; she understands that you requested,

"Now show me the dogs' (toys)."

That is, she can make use of the whole discourse and obey the thrust of a previous sentence. If she prefers the plural interpretation (pointing to the dogs), she indicates that she prefers a reading where one does not have to borrow parts from a previous sentence. Current literature suggests that children do not (or even cannot) use discourse, so they should resolutely prefer the plural interpretation.[7] I suspect that the opposite is true, and this exploration would show it.

In sum, to fill verbal holes following *some* we must look to dialogue over context (in English at least, though perhaps not Chinese where context plays a larger role). In our fruit-and-cookies scenario, a speaker of English has to fight off the implications of context. Context alone would allow a "Yes" answer to "Here is some fruit. Did I take some?," when what you actually took was a handful of cookies. It is only obedience to the thrust of the previous sentence that tells us that *fruit* must follow *some*, not *cookies*. Because words dominate visual context in grammar, the listener is *required* to choose a verbal antecedent. Failure to know how dialogue works is a failure to really know English (or the grammar of any language).

At first, children must inevitably lean heavily on context: they have to link single words to objects or actions. In time, as we can see, grammar demands that context often be ignored. Nonetheless, children who lean too much on context may not establish the priority of words over context when they should. This would be a serious disorder if it persisted. As noted, there are suggestions in the acquisition literature that all children readily prefer context; however, several explorations below show the necessary dominance of dialogue.

Pronouns

Taking a little detour from ellipsis, we can note that pronouns display essentially the same discourse restriction: to interpret what a pronoun refers to, we must pay attention to verbal rather than visual context. A little experiment tested this idea in a way you can easily replicate.[8] Take two familiar dolls of the same gender; stand one of them up and lay the other down. Let's say Ernie is standing up and Bert is lying down. Now say to a child,

| Exploration 7.3 |
| Who's he? |
| (discourse-linked pronoun) |

"Look, Ernie is standing up. Now is he lying down?"

In adult English, the answer should be "No" because it is Bert who is lying down, not Ernie: in the listener's mind, *he* has to connect to *Ernie* in the previous sentence, ignoring the visual situation. If the connection between sentences—the verbal context—weren't the primary factor, "Yes" would also be an appropriate answer, because it is true that there is a "he" lying down that the listener can see. (In fact, with emphasis on *he* ("Is HE lying down?") the reference can shift, so be careful not to emphasize it unless you want to.) The actual experiment revealed that most three-year-old children can easily say "No" in this situation, showing that they make the verbal rather than the visual connection, though it is claimed that up to the age of six years some children do not.[9]

| Exploration 7.4 |
| Shoes or sneakers? |
| (*one* ellipsis) |

Here is a variant: Two shoes and a sneaker are on a table. Put the sneaker under the table and say to the child you're with,

"There are two shoes on the table. Did I put one under the table?"

Will the child understand *one* to mean "one shoe" and say "No"?

Filling in holes in discourse is probably much easier than actually linking up pronouns. Easier for people, that is; it might be the reverse for monkeys.

We do not know. Humans are programmed to communicate in dialogue—our lives may depend on it—so we project holes (carry out ellipsis) whenever we can. Monkeys may achieve some fairly complex language, but do their lives depend on it? Maybe they have communicative methods with just as much compressed knowledge in some other module of interaction, but it does not look like language.

Strange Canyons of Ellipsis

What looks easy is not. Ellipsis takes odd turns, creating odd patterns of holes inside sentences. When we reach back into dialogue to reconstruct an elided phrase, it is easy to snatch too much or too little from a previous sentence.

With props as simple as coins, a piece of paper, and a plate, we can explore how children handle ellipsis.

> **Exploration 7.5**
> **On the inside of empty phrases**
> **(number ellipsis)**

This exploration has two parts. Start by putting some nickels on a plate, with two of them heads up:

Then put three pennies on that plate, with none of them heads up:

Now say,

"I put three pennies on the plate. Are two heads up?"

Since you mentioned pennies, a listener who grasps the verbal-over-visual-context principle has to insert *pennies* after *two* in your question ("Are two [pennies] heads up?"), rather than *nickels*, and will say "No." But a listener who reconstructs *two things* might say "Yes." In fact, in an experiment almost identical to this (based on proposals about parsing by Lyn Frazier), Frank Wijnen, Hiske van der Meulen, and I found that children four to six years of age sometimes do say "Yes."[10]

Now let us narrow the challenge. Put three pennies on a piece of paper, with two heads up:

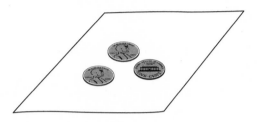

Now put three pennies on a plate, with no heads up—

—and as you are doing so, say this:

I am putting three pennies on this plate. Are two heads up?"

Adults will say "No"; following the verbal-over-visual-context principle, they reconstruct the prepositional phrase from the previous sentence (to differentiate pennies-on-paper from pennies-on-a-plate) and understand "Are two [pennies on the plate] heads up?" Wijnen, Van der Meulen, and I found that many four- to six-year-old children (but far from all) said "Yes" and pointed to things like the pennies on the paper.

Each case we have looked at so far shows that listeners have to be very complete in reconstructing information the speaker leaves out. Are there ever cases where we are required to reconstruct *less* information than is present in the dialogue? A brief look at contrast and alternatives shows that there are.

Exploration 7.6
There's where *there* is
(ellipsis, number contrast, and *there*)

Here again, an exploration will introduce and illustrate the point most clearly. Put three pennies on a plate, all heads down, and another three pennies on a piece of paper, with two heads up:

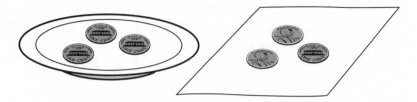

Say to a child,

"Three pennies are on the plate. Are there two heads up?"

Note the change from "Are two...?" in the previous explorations to "Are there two...?" Many adult English speakers will now answer "Yes," allowing *two* to reconstruct as *two [pennies on the paper]*.

Why? In a way, *there* operates like a *contrastive* location: *there* blocks restoring *on the plate*. In this situation, the listener may understand instead, "Three pennies are on the plate. Are there [two pennies (anywhere)] heads up?"

Now, if I say, "There are three pennies on the floor and two in the cupboard," you will end up with a contradiction if you reconstruct the entire prepositional phrase in the ellipsis gap: *"There are two [pennies on the floor] in the cupboard." The newly mentioned location (in the cupboard) blocks the previously mentioned location (on the floor).

Now suppose I say, "There are three pennies on the floor and two are on the rug." Here we have an ambiguous sentence: my "two are on the rug" could mean "two [of the three pennies on the floor] are on the rug" or "two [pennies] are on the rug" (in addition to three other pennies that are on the floor). So we may have a choice about whether to keep the prepositional phrase *on the floor* or not—in other words, whether to add *on the rug* to, or substitute it for, *on the floor*.

What governs the choice? The deciding factor seems to be whether there is an *articulated alternative*. Consider:

John put a dollar on the table and so did Bill ____.
   → Bill put a dollar on the table

John put a dollar on the table and Bill ____ on the floor.
   ⇥ *Bill put a dollar on the table on the floor
   → Bill put a dollar on the floor

If the sentence involves a *contrast*, then we substitute phrases in filling ellipsis holes instead of adding one to another. So we have to decide if the sentence includes a contrastive piece that is exempt from ellipsis. Suddenly we see a whole new dimension, contrast determination (which can have a link to intonation), that the child has to encompass. It is like adding a steering wheel to a chassis in building a car.

We are starting to see how complicated the job of filling in these verbal holes really is. It still feels "easy" and "natural," though, just as seeing appears easy and natural, because the human mind is built to make these intricate dialogue connections, just as our bodies are built to see when we open our eyes. Yet because different languages make these connections differently, there is more to the story than just this innate endowment: the child has specifics to learn, as we will see.

Illegal Holes

Are there impossible holes in language? In fact, most "potential holes," even natural ones, never occur. We cannot delete just anywhere. For example, we cannot just chop a noun away from its adjective in a sentence like this:

*I have an odd hat and you have a strange ____.

The adjective requires a noun, or at least a pronoun (*a strange one*). Taking out the noun seems even worse if recursive adjectives are involved:

*I have a big old hat and you have a new small ____.

Can we show that children know this limitation? Let's stack the deck and see if children will resist reconstructing a noun after an adjective. If they do resist, it will be a clue that their grammar, like adults', prohibits stranding an adjective without its noun.

> **Exploration 7.7**
> **Got an orange?**
> **(bare noun ellipsis)**

Making sure you keep your intonation even, first say to a child,

"John has an old red house and Bill has a new orange."

Then ask,

"What does Bill have?"

Will the child say, "A new orange" or "A new orange house"? (Or show the child pictures of an orange house and of an orange and say, "John has an old red house and Bill has a new orange. Show me what I said that Bill has.") Children might go for the house.

Comparing languages often leads to deeper linguistic insights than looking at one language by itself. Consider this sentence from German:

Ich habe ein grosses rotes Haus, und du hast ein kleines gelbes ____.
[I have a big   red house, and you have a   small yellow ____.]

Why should leaving out the final noun in this type of sentence be possible in German but not in English? The endings of the German adjectives actually carry some extra information that isn't present on English adjectives: in our example, -es marks singular number and neuter gender (matching, in this case, the number and grammatical gender of *Haus* "house"). The ending plays the role of a pronoun, as if we were to say in English "a small yellow one." It is this hidden pronoun, like *one*, that allows the ellipsis; German does not really strand adjectives after all. At an abstract level, then, both grammars follow the same restriction, but German-speaking children must hear elliptical sentences (like ...*du hast ein kleines gelbes* ____ above) before they recognize how endings work. Yet maybe Universal Grammar leads them to expect ellipsis right here.

How would Universal Grammar express this expectation? Grammar requires that we chop off natural units, not just odd pieces. A natural unit seems to be one where the main ingredient of a phrase is present:

In an elliptical construction, the *main ingredient* of the phrase (noun, verb, or adjective) must be present in some way.

So, for example, we can elide a whole noun phrase (*Mary is an excellent student and Jane is, too*), but we cannot chop out just the noun itself; something continues to *represent* the noun (**Mary is an excellent student and Jane is an excellent* ____, *too; Mary is an excellent student and Jane is an excellent one, too*). German speakers also cannot chop out just the noun itself; something—in our example, the adjective endings—continues to *represent* it. The underlying restriction is the same, but the two languages deal with it differently; the child must learn how it's done in the language around him. (We might conjecture, then, that if an English-learning child responds to "John has an old red house and Bill has a new orange. What does Bill have?" by saying "A new orange house," maybe he is trying to speak German. This is not a peculiar joke, but a deep hypothesis about language learning, as we will see.)

This idea immediately predicts, correctly, that these ellipses are impossible:

Noun: *John has a tie and Bill has a ____ too.
Adjective: *Bill is tall and Fred is very ____.

Universal Grammar does not allow a hanging modifier with the main in-gredient absent, so *a* or *very* cannot be left alone. It follows that the ending -*es* in German must represent the main ingredient, as *one* does in English.

The reader with a critical hat on should now pounce and observe that this conclusion abruptly fails when we try out verbs:

Verb: John can sing and Bill can ____ too.

If *can* modifies *sing* the way *the* modifies *hat*, then our grammar should not allow this sentence, but it does. So how do we handle such an incon-sistency?

Questions like this are touchstones in the ongoing evolution of linguistic theory. Here is one important strategy:

Keep the deep idea, and cope with the counterevidence.

In this instance, the direction of argument is quite natural: modifiers like the modals (*can, must, will, may*) and others (*have, be, do*) are *not* a part of the verb; instead, they make up their own category, *auxiliary verb*. If so, we have indeed dropped the whole verb in a sentence like *John can sing and Bill will, too*, not just part of it. We just did a judo-job on the counterevidence: it became *supportive* evidence for the idea that auxiliary verbs constitute their own category. Pursuing this line of argument would take us too far afield, but it should give you a taste of linguistic reasoning.

Two-Way Ellipsis: Backward and Forward

We have been discussing "forward" holes, but there are "backward" holes too, even two backward holes:

John gave ____ to Mary and also ____ to Bill [a large inheritance].

(= John gave a large inheritance to Mary...)

Some languages, astonishingly, do both at once. In English, we could not say this:

John can ____ books and Bill ____ read newspapers.

(Intended meaning: "John can read books and Bill can read newspapers.")

However, just such sentences are possible in German:

Hans <u>kann</u> Bücher ____ und Fritz ____ Zeitungen <u>lesen</u>.

So both alternatives are possibilities that the child somehow has to keep abreast of.

Big Holes: Eliminating Almost Everything

So far, we have looked at dropped nouns and dropped verbs. What happens if we drop both a noun and a verb: if, in a subject-verb-object sequence, we drop the subject and the verb (replacing the latter with a sort of "pro-verb," a form of *do*)? This form of ellipsis is a favorite among linguists because it creates curious patterns of reference. If only the subject is elided, in a sentence like

A boy can sing and [a boy] can dance all day. →
A boy can sing and can dance all day.

it must be the *same* boy who both sings and dances. But upon hearing a sentence like

John saw his mother and so did Bill.

the listener has to resurrect the verb and the object:

John saw his mother and so did Bill [see his mother].

All of a sudden, with this type of ellipsis, we have ambiguity: the speaker might mean either that John and Bill saw different mothers (each one saw his own) or that they both saw John's mother. A variant, ambiguous in the same way, is

John saw his mother and Bill saw his mother too.

But notice that we can force the two-mother reading by deleting *mother*:

John saw his mother and Bill saw his ____ too.

This pairwise reading is called a "distributive" reading because objects are distributed one by one across subjects. We saw it before in sequences like *Everybody has a pencil. Please pick up the pencil*, where each person picks up the pencil that is his (we will return to this in chapter 8).

Why do we get two interpretations if we delete the whole phrase *saw his mother*, but only one (paired, two-mother) interpretation if we just delete *mother*? Such questions are the subject of active theoretical research.[11] Subtle differences like these are not taught in nursery school (or in high school either), so they most likely follow from innate principles.

Can acquisition contribute relevant ideas to the theoretical debate about coreference and ellipsis? Acquisition studies have shown that children grasp the distributive interpretation at a young age for sentences of the *so did John* variety.[12] How about the narrower case we just looked at (*and Bill saw his ___ too*)?[13] To explore this with a child, find two dolls of the same gender. Again, let's say you have Bert and Ernie. First show the child Bert and Ernie, with a ball next to Ernie. Have Ernie bounce the ball, then have Bert bounce it. Then say,

Exploration 7.8
Whose is whose?
(coreference and ellipsis)

"Ernie has a ball. Ernie bounced his ball. Did Bert bounce his?"

If the child answers, "No, Bert doesn't have a ball" or "No, he bounced Ernie's," then she grasps that *his* with ellipsis must have a distributive interpretation (in this case, she grasps that you must be asking about two balls, one for each doll: "Ernie bounced his [own] ball. Did Bert bounce his [own ball]?"). It is as if it is only deletable if it has its own physical referential object.

Yet we still must be on the lookout for strange detours on the child's acquisition path. When a child gets something complicated right, it is too easy for an acquisition scholar to assume that he got it exactly right. Surprisingly, it turns out that children impose distributivity even where adults dislike or even prohibit it. Lamya Abdulkarim explored this in various ways.[14] For example, she showed children two dolls (named Mary and John), each of which had a car. You can easily build the same scenario following these pictures, so the rest of Abdulkarim's experimental method and results are translated from *Mary* and *John* to *a girl* and *a boy* to fit the pictures:

Exploration 7.9
Are children too pushy?
(pairing)

Show a child the pictures and say,

"A girl pushed her car and so did a boy. Show me."

In Abdulkarim's experiment, four- to six-year-old children usually made the boy push his own car; they interpreted the ellipsis in the pairwise, distributive way. Then Abdulkarim varied the instructions, using *the* or even a noun designating a third person, to see how children would respond:

"The girl pushed the car, and so did the boy. Show me."

"The girl pushed the policeman's car, and so did the boy. Show me."

In each case, most children around the age of four happily made the boy push his own car, not the policeman's.

Now we might start to suspect that this "pairing" happens outside of grammar, that maybe it is a general cognitive rather than a specifically linguistic behavior. Maybe children impose a sense of orderliness everywhere. Maybe pairs just seem like fun. But in fact Abdulkarim showed that children indeed recognize a fixed reference. When she gave the instruction,

"The girl pushed her car. The boy pushed it too. Show me."

children made both people push the same car. The pronoun *it* guaranteed a single reference. We know that it's the grammar that's at work (not, say, general cognition), because only certain structures allow pairing.

A big question is hanging in the air here: why are children more liberal than adults? It's easy to grab a processing or a social reason: "They didn't really hear" or "They're just lazy." Yet suppose that in fact children's rules for recovering missing material are slightly different from adults'.

Here is an approach currently being pursued by Ayumi Matsuo and Nigel Duffield.[15] Suppose the child reconstructs only the noun and not the potentially complicated modifier that, as we have seen, can even be recursive (*the, Bill's, Bill's friend's, the most frequently seen*, etc.). This means that from the experimenter's statement "The girl pushed her car and the boy did too," the child would reconstruct this structure:

The girl pushed her car and the boy did too [push car].

If what the child reconstructed was just the bare noun, with no possessive and no article, then it could be linked to any car—in our example, either the girl's car or the boy's car or the policeman's car. It could even be linked to a spare car sitting in the experimental space but never mentioned by the experimenter.

Why would a child have a grammar like this?

Verb Noun
push car

In early stages of language development, children often say things like "Want cookie" with no article. More importantly, whole families of grammars, among them Spanish, allow bare objects. Even dialects of English like African-American English allow forms such as this:[16]

I ate hotdog.

So perhaps all children at first assume a grammar that calls for the sequence "verb + noun" before they shift to one that calls for "verb + article + noun." This is another case where children restore a little less when they interpret ellipsis than an adult would.

More clues point in this direction. Jill de Villiers notes that children up to six years of age often answer the question

"What do you need after a shower?"

with "Towel," while adults normally say "A towel."[17] Only fairly late does the child somehow acquire a special rule of English: count nouns (not mass nouns like *water*) always require an article. In projecting into silence— filling in gaps in ellipsis constructions—the child reverts to the original grammar, which allows a slightly wider range of possible references. The child who has labored to build noun phrases with complicated articles, adjectives, and agreement apparently reproduces that labor in deciding just how much gets recreated under ellipsis.[18]

Adults also use bare count nouns in everyday life. For example, we use bare count nouns in creating compounds: forms like *the dog-lover* start out as *[love dog] + er*, not *[love the dog] + er*. If *the* were included as we created a compound, we would end up with **the [the dog-lover]*.

Headlines do it too: "Man Bites Dog." And angry people go for bare nouns.[19] We say things like this, to ourselves or others:

"You fool, you idiot, you madman!"

Yet other constructions, even angry ones, continue to require an article: *What a moron!/*What moron!, I consider him a fool/*I consider him fool*.

Dialogue often drops prepositions, leaving just a bare noun:

A: When are you playing?
B: Noon.

A: Where are you going?
B: Detroit.

But it is impossible to drop the preposition here:

*I am playing noon.
*I am going Detroit.

Dialogue seems to give us license to reach back to a streamlined grammar—just the one the child starts with.

These observations about children's bare nouns lead in another direction as well. In essence, I am making the—at first sight possibly bizarre—claim that when children hear a sentence like *Mary pushed her car and John did too*, they are using English grammar when they interpret the first half of the sentence (*Mary pushed her car*) and something Spanishlike when they interpret the second half (*and so did John [push car]*). Results from an experiment by Deanna Moore can be interpreted the same way.[20] Moore showed children a picture of, for instance, John eating hotdogs in the kitchen and Bill sitting in the living room. She asked,

"John is eating hotdogs in the kitchen and Bill in the dining room. Is that right?"

Some children answered "Yes." They seemed to understand *Bill ____ in the dining room* to mean "Bill is in the dining room." In other words, they did not carry over the verb at all. This is not so far-fetched, since in many grammars (such as Russian, Hebrew, and African-American English), no *is* is needed here (as we discuss below). English drops *is* in several constructions:

John considered Bill smart.
John made Bill angry.
With Bill sick, Mary stayed home.

So the child's error is not so far off from a real grammatical option.

One might look at the claim that "the child is speaking Spanish (Russian, Hebrew, etc.)" as just an overheated metaphor—or, more wisely, as an insight into the idea that languages are not so different and that every language carries inside it the kernel of many grammars. When we face grammar variation squarely in a later chapter, even more bizarre claims about other grammars hidden in the corners of English will follow.

Ultra-microgrammar

In effect, ellipsis lays bare the ingredients of phrases. It provides us with a linguistic microscope for studying not only how human language (Universal Grammar) works, but also how individual languages work and how they vary..Might the microscope of ellipsis also reveal that individual speakers' grammars vary—or, in asking that question, are we trying to chisel grammar too far down, beyond any reasonable refinement? A look at adults suggests not. Adult speakers do vary in how much they reconstruct under ellipsis. Consider:

John broke his arm and so did Mary.

If asked to interpret *so did Mary* in this sentence, some people object and say that the sentence is not quite right or that Mary (in addition to John) broke John's arm.[21] But most people say that *so did Mary* in this sentence means that Mary broke her own arm. Why? These adults are restoring slightly less in the ellipsis, just like children, but at a more refined level. We can say that *his* incorporates three features: masculine, possessive, and reflexive (self). When speakers reconstruct *and so did Mary* to mean "and Mary broke her arm too" instead of "and Mary broke his arm too," they are reconstructing two of the three features inside *his* and ignoring one (masculine):

John broke his arm and
so did Mary [break [possessive + reflexive] arm]

If these speakers recreate an abstract "possessive" feature instead of the literal word *his*—that is, they reconstruct the concept of possession but not of gender—then their interpretation makes perfect sense. (This example also shows the legitimacy of saying that words like *his* are really little molecules made up of atoms of meaning. The features of gender (masculine/ feminine), possession, and reflexivization are independent ingredients that we can actually manipulate inside silence.)

All of this suggests that the endpoint of acquisition is a bit ragged: not every feature is reproduced in the same manner by each person. Each speaker has an individual dialect (which linguists term an *idiolect*), an individual grammar that differs from other people's grammars on points like the interpretation of our *and so did Mary* sentence. When asked repeatedly to interpret different cases of the same construction, individual adults will adhere steadily to their idiolects, as fieldwork in linguistics regularly demonstrates. No harm is done, until one starts writing—then the red pencils of grammar mavens emerge! Not every teacher will tolerate interpreting *John broke his arm and so did Mary* to mean "Mary broke her arm." Something more than right and wrong has emerged: we have gotten our grammatical blood under a microscope and can now watch which molecules are formed. We have arrived at the point where the claim that people construct individual formulas for their lives connects with language. Each of us has a different formula behind our grammar.

Disorders of Ellipsis

Bare nouns seemed curious to our acquisition team when we first observed that some children who had been diagnosed with communication disorders would answer the following question with a bare noun:

Adult: How did the woman sweep the room?
Child: Broom.

No preposition and no article. The discussion above suggests that such a disorder would affect comprehension as well. While such deviance is often described as a broad tendency to use "incomplete sentences," maybe a genuinely grammatical deficiency lies at the root of it. The child fails to move from the streamlined verb + noun grammar to the adult grammar: verb + possessive (or article) + noun. A teacher might respond with irritation when a child uses *teached* or *bringed*, yet say generously, "Oh well, I know what he means," when the child uses bare nouns in places where English requires modifiers. Yet it is really the bare noun which suggests that a child may lack the special oars for orientation in the sea of half-sentences that constitutes most conversations. We may know what she means, but does she know what we mean?

More Challenges: Rare but Real Ellipsis in Clauses

Ellipsis is everywhere in language—silence might hold a noun, verb, adjective, phrase, clause, or more. Each type of ellipsis poses a separate challenge to the child, and linguists have hardly begun to explore them. Believe it or not, we have looked only at simple cases! Here are a few more initial snapshots of ellipsis structures the child has to master, insights ellipsis gives into human language, and ways ellipsis research sheds light on the child's linguistic journey.

Linked Invisible Agents

Sometimes subjects are invisible, as in infinitives:

John started to sing.

Here, *John* is the subject of both *start* and *sing*. Children have no difficulty with this connection. Sometimes, though, if the speaker links invisible agents, children can be misled. If I say,

"To know him is to love him,"

I cannot mean

"*For Mary to know him is for Susan to love him."

Both the knower and the lover have to be the same person. This kind of connection actually occurs more commonly in phrases like *To play football is to get covered with dirt*. But do children know that the connection is grammatically fixed, even against pragmatics?

This question was explored in a little pilot experiment by Katy Carlson, which you might try out with a doll and a bowl.

Exploration 7.10
To know him is to love him (linked invisible agents)

Setting the empty bowl in front of the doll, say to a child,

"Here is a bowl of cherries. Mary ate them all up. See? The bowl has none."

Now say,

"To eat cherries is to become empty. Is that right?"

(Or you can give the child a cup of raisins and say,

"Eat 'em up!"

Then

"They were good, right? To eat raisins is to become empty. Is that right?")

The answers to these questions will reveal whether the child requires linking between invisible agents. If the child can give different subjects to *eat* and *become* ("For *me* to eat raisins is for *the bowl* to become empty"), she lacks the obligatory linking principle for invisible subjects. And indeed children initially do not seem to make this link. In the pilot experiment, half a dozen children four to five years old said things like, "Yes, he ate the cherries and the bowl got empty." By contrast, the children over six years said, "No, no—he became *full*," showing recognition that the two invisible subjects have to be linked. Other linking principles are overt, as in *John helped himself*, but are still not acquired instantly, so it is no wonder that linked invisible subjects take time.

Comparatives

Just to crawl a bit further into this tangled, mysterious, overwhelming web, consider how comparatives work.

In an informal exploration, Susan Tavakolian found that even children between eight and ten years old could provide no distinction between the structures *a bigger X than Y* and *an X bigger than Y*.[22] To explore sentences like this with an older child, show a child this picture:

> **Exploration 7.11**
> **More than more**
> **(adjectives inside and outside noun phrases)**

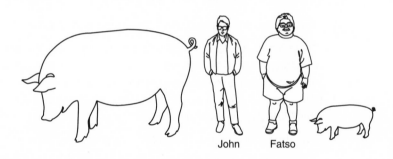

John   Fatso

Now say either,

a. "John has a bigger pig than Fatso."

or

b. "John has a pig bigger than Fatso."

Then say,

"Tell me a story about this."

Both (a) and (b) could be expanded by either *than Fatso <u>has</u>* or *than Fatso <u>is</u>*. Using the name *Fatso* should bias children toward *is*. Now, assuming that they do expand the sentence using *is*, the question is whether they reconstruct

...than Fatso is *a big pig* (a)

or

...than Fatso *is big* (b)

Only in (a), where the adjective is inside the noun phrase, must one reconstruct the whole noun phrase (*a big pig*). So the child's story should reveal whether she thinks Fatso is a pig.

The two answers follow systematic rules for reconstruction that are too technically involved to reproduce here. These sentences serve to remind us again of what the endpoint in the acquisition of English must be.[23]

Attachment

One tiny switch in words in an elliptical sentence can reveal a hidden principle. In a sentence with embedded clauses, one major question is just which clause ellipsis refers to. Look at this contrast:

John wanted someone to wash the dishes, and so did I.

John wanted someone to wash the dishes, and so I did.

The inverted form *did I* somehow forces us to take the upper clause to fill the gap (*so did I [want someone to do the dishes]*), while the lack of inversion forces us to take the lower clause (*so I did [wash the dishes]*). Since such sentences are rare, the sharp difference must follow from some principle—but what? Roughly, we might say this:

Basic distortions of order (verb before subject) occur only in the highest clauses; therefore, the speaker reconstructs the highest clause available to fill the gap after *so did I*.

This kind of principle must follow from something deeper, which linguists cannot put their fingers on yet.

Do children know this principle? An experiment by Carol Chomsky suggests that they might not.[24] She told children around five years old little stories like this:

"The cowboy scolded the horse for running away, and I would have done the same."

When she asked the children what she would do, many answered, "Run away." While adults must (who knows why) link *same* with the whole clause (...*scolded the horse for running away*), children link it only with the lower clause (...*running away*). You could easily construct parallel examples and explore them with a child.

And *and*: The Meaning of Silence

In an elliptical sentence, does the silent, dropped part mean exactly the same as the spoken part? Deletion might seem to *guarantee* perfect identity, but a careful look shows that it does not. If I say,

"A boy ate a hotdog and a boy ate a hamburger,"

there could be one boy (eating both a hotdog and a hamburger) or two boys (one eating a hotdog and one eating a hamburger). But if I drop one subject reference (one instance of *a boy*) and say,

"A boy ate a hotdog and a hamburger,"

the two-boy meaning is almost impossible: it must be the *same* boy who ate both the hotdog and the hamburger.

Have you ever really thought about the word *and*?[25] It can link at every level: across words, phrases, and sentences, and even as high as across paragraphs (*And it was the night before Christmas* ...) and as low as inside words (*pre- and postoperative*). It is among a child's first words, yet until recently no one seems to have ever asked whether children start out with the same idea behind it as adults. A student mentioned to me that if her mother said something like "We're going to town, and get gas, and go to lunch, and go to the library," her small brother would complain if they got lunch before they got gas. The mother had an unordered list in mind and the child had a temporal sequence.

Students of temporal relations have pointed out that

She got pregnant and got married.

is not the same as

She got married and got pregnant.

In this case, *and* seems to carry time with it. On the other hand, if I say,

"I ate meat and potatoes,"

I don't seem to imply that I ate them in any order. We adults get a temporal reference when we conjoin verb phrases (*got married and got pregnant*) but seem not to when we conjoin noun phrases (*ate meat and potatoes*). But does a child do the same?

Exploration 7.12
The meaning of *and*
(logical and temporal *and*)

A salt shaker and a sugar bowl are all we need to explore whether a child attaches a temporal meaning to *and* or understands it simply as a logical connector.

Point at the salt shaker, then point at the sugar bowl. Say,

"Did I point at the sugar bowl and the salt shaker?"

Adults uniformly say "Yes," but many children polled in informal experiments say "No." They seem to interpret *and* as meaning "and then" (that is, "Point at the sugar bowl *and then* the salt shaker")! (This needs to be explored in careful experiments once linguists informally get the lay of the land regarding children's understanding and use of *and*.)[26]

Why would a child want to impose an extra temporal level on a simple notion of addition? One possibility is a bias toward imposing an *event structure* on language. Life presents us with big composites that we grasp as a whole—an instance of the idea that "holistic" analysis is important—and the child may try to see the world in terms of a sequence of whole events. The notion of "and" outside of time, though it is logically simple, is experientially abstract. We experience the world in time, so to subtract time from our concept may be difficult.

Still, we should be cautious about this bit of apparent common sense. Much of memory succeeds only because we can create groups that are *not* temporally linked. The question "What restaurants do you like?" could not be answered if we had to think about eating at them all simultaneously.

And presents another wrinkle, involving time and events. *She got married and got pregnant* seems to talk about two different times and two different events. But if I say, "John bumped the wall and hurt his knee," I am describing one real-world event—yet, as an adult speaker of English, I feel that the sentence itself conceptually implies two events. In this case, it feels like the grammar fits the real-world event poorly.[27]

If children impose nonsimultaneity on *and*, do they ever do the opposite and impose simultaneity? Doreen Bryant has explored environments where some children do seem to impose simultaneity.[28] She gave children a toy elephant, dinosaur, and rabbit, along with a feather and a toy broom, and asked them to demonstrate this sentence:

The dinosaur brushed the elephant with a feather and the rabbit with a broom.

The child must copy *brush* after *and*: the dinosaur brushed the rabbit with a broom. If restoring an elided verb after *and* (*The bear brushed the dog and* ____ *the cat*) works the same way as restoring an elided subject after *and* (*The boy ate and* ____ *drank*), then the event depicted in this example is in a sense one act of brushing, which forces a simultaneous interpretation. That is the interpretation many children act out: they force the dinosaur to hold both instruments at once. Why? What imposes simultaneity for children? This is a challenging question if we accept that children can comprehend simultaneity cognitively. One angle is that when a single verb is present, a single time is present. In order to have a second time, the child must copy the verb and attach a new time to it. Adults apparently can copy the missing verb back with a tense marker (the dinosaur "brushed" with a broom) and allow that invisible tense marker to link to the world with a new time. If children do not copy both the verb and the tense marker, they will not get a second time reference. Failure to copy the tense marker looks like the failure to copy the possessive that we discussed earlier (*push car* instead of *push his car*). There are other tantalizing possibilities here.

Is there anything like this in the adult language? Consider a sentence like this:

John got drunk and Bill got mad.

We easily interpret it to mean that Bill got mad *because* John got drunk. But if we delete the second verb, we lose the "because" implication:

John got drunk and Bill mad.

Perhaps the presence of just one verb implies a single time, so no second event is caused—Bill getting mad after John got drunk. Whether children grasp this difference in causation with different *and* constructions has yet to be explored.

Clearly, children must acquire a very subtle interpretive ability with *and* (not to mention *or*!).

Literacy and Math: Is Shorter Really Easier?

Although mastery of ellipsis surely extends into the school years, the ill-informed dictum that governs much of children's literature and early readers is "Shorter is easier." Therefore, some books are governed by limits like "No sentences longer than six words." But such limits encourage ellipsis. No one counts the silent words or measures their complexity. If silent words *are* counted, and the labor of projecting structure into ellipsis *is* measured, then shorter sentences may be—in stark reality—longer than longer ones.

What follows is the most cursory review, based on an hour spent roaming the Internet for children's stories. Here is the start of one story:[29]

Once upon a time there lived a young frog.
His name was Sniffy.
Probably because he liked flowers.

The last line has just five words. Yet when we read *Probably because*, we must mentally resurrect a clause:

Probably [*he was called Sniffy*] because he liked flowers.

This is not the only option. Rather than interpreting the sentence fragment as a case of ellipsis, we might interpret it as the start of a new sentence, say,

Probably because he liked flowers, *he was always in the garden*.

In fact, then, the reader must wait until the end of the sentence to know whether or not she should reach back to an earlier sentence to determine just what *probably because* is about. Thus, our "simple" five words make a tough nut for a child to crack.

Take a look at another story:[30]

Here's Buzzy sharing a flower.
Did you save some for me?
Yumm.
You can never get too much of a good thing.
Except sometimes.
Rescued again.

Pictures help, but they do not do all the work. The child has to see that

some = some [nectar] [from flowers]
except sometimes = sometimes [you can get too much of a good thing]
rescued again = [Buzzy was] rescued again [by other bees]

The amount that has to be restored is even more than was said.

Ancient, venerable children's literature is quite the opposite, with endless repetitive sentences: think of *the cat that chased the rat that ate the cheese*. As Jill de Villiers has suggested,[31] children's rhymes and riddles may in fact have a secret point: to show the child where recursion can occur. But note: they are long and full, not cryptically short.

How about mathematics? Look at a problem on the statewide fourth-grade math test in Massachusetts:[32]

Liu is separating the figures below into groups according to their properties. There are at least three figures in each group. So far, he has made two different groups.

List at least 3 figures that could go into each group. Explain what all the figures in each group have in common.

How do we interpret the instruction *Explain what all the figures in each group have in common*?

all the figures in each group
= only the figures that are in each one of each different group?
= every figure within each separate group?
in common
= with other figures in that group?
= with each figure in all the groups?

Construing how *all* and *each* interconnect is not so obvious. Realizing that *in common* is elliptical shows that what is elided is ambiguous. The actual pictures help to partly resolve the ambiguity, but still, the child reading the sentence has to cope with these ambiguities as he reads. A careful study of ellipsis in all sorts of mathematics problems is clearly needed. In fact, I think that teachers should not only be made aware of these ambiguities, but make them the topic of classroom study and discussion. It would be interesting to see what a fourth-grade class says about "what is missing" in many of the examples above.

"Cultural" Ellipsis

Interpreting ellipsis lets in powerful cultural ingredients too: local knowledge, point of view, and humor can all play a role. They are so powerful that one might think there is no mechanism here, no skeleton within the mushy flesh, just culture. But now that we've peered into common elliptical holes and exposed the structure within, we can easily see that a strong, well-organized skeleton undergirds even these outlandish cases of ellipsis.

In the movie *Don't Drink the Water*, Jackie Gleason's wife says to him,

"I can still fit into the dress I wore on my wedding day, can you?"

Does this mean he wore a dress? Obviously, as listeners we are supposed to substitute *pants* for *dress* and *you* for *I* throughout: the wife means "Can you [fit into the *pants you* wore on *your* wedding day]?," not "Can you [fit into the *dress I* wore on *my* wedding day]." We have to sense the relevance of extragrammatical knowledge and know just where to stick it into the silent ellipsis. We make crucial substitutions while the grammatical parallelism remains intact.

As a teenager, in my first foray into romance, I said to a young woman, another uncertain soul, "I love you." Wanting to be sympathetic, but not quite as convinced as I was, she said, "Me too." This means either "I love *you* too" or "I love *me* too," and circumstance tells us which is meant. We have to be ready to make this extra systematic shift in point of view.

Jokes, ads, and flippant remarks are full of imperfect ellipses. Consider:

You have to be a good liar, and John just can't.

Here we have to find the verb (*lie*) inside the noun *liar* to get to the speaker's meaning: "John just can't [lie]." Even a current laxative slogan uses ellipsis to catch attention:

For regular people who aren't always.

Here the listener grabs an adjective inside a noun phrase to fill the gap. The machine is so precise that we can humorously tweak it now and then.

Literary Silence

Often we are deliberately even vaguer than all this. We are elliptical in order to not say too clearly what we mean, not be too blunt. Then we may say, "You know what I mean...?" Questions like that are vague and bald at once—they call for us to throw our emotional being, not just grammar, into figuring out what has not quite been said. The province of literary intent is built upon the sharply etched edifice of grammar.

See if you can unpack this elliptical piece of Shakespeare:[33]

True hope is swift,
and flies with swallow's wings;
Kings it makes gods,
and meaner creatures kings.

Here is where it starts:

True hope is swift
and true hope flies with swallow's wings.
It makes gods kings
and it makes kings meaner creatures.

Now we front the objects in the second sentence:

True hope is swift
and true hope flies with swallow's wings.
Kings it makes gods
and meaner creatures it makes kings.

Now we do ellipsis; that is, we delete one of the two identical subjects connected by *and* in the first sentence, and one of the two identical subject + verb sequences connected by *and* in the second sentence.

True hope is swift,
and ____ flies with swallow's wings.
Kings it makes gods,
and meaner creatures ____ kings.

So *it makes* is dropped, and Shakespeare rests. It would be a fascinating venture—not one for this book—to figure out why this is not current English. One notion is clear: as the grammar changes over time, so do the possible ellipses, and so does the challenge for the child.

The literary interpretation of silence can become infinite. Just why does what does not get said, not get said? Here the literary critic may enter the scene. When we say, "Would that I could," is our failing to say something a metaphor for our failing to do something? Silence has become a metaphor itself. When grammar finishes recreating what is deleted, there remains an open world for literary interpretation.

Summary

Ellipsis involves the projection of one sentence into another. What we can call the *principle of ellipsis* lies at the core: dialogue is a continuation of each other's sentences. If children (and adults) are to successfully reconstruct and give meaning to what a speaker has left out, an entire web of abstract principles, concepts of grammar, and interpretive insights has to come together. We have looked at a few of these:

Dialogue trumps visual context in interpreting ellipsis.
Grammar must include a notion of *natural unit*.
Reconstruction can lead to independent objects and independent events.

Besides all this, the child has to keep his cultural wits about him, alive and awake, to see the humor and special knowledge needed to hear the sounds of silence and to know just when the language tells him to include the world around him.

It seems like the acquisition of ellipsis should simply follow in the footsteps of the initial acquisition of grammar—in other words, as the child constructs each new level of grammar, she should construct a parallel level in silence. Yet learning to interpret ellipsis is not so immediate. As her grammar for ellipsis, the child sometimes holds onto a more elementary grammar than she uses in other areas of language; recall the suggestion that for interpreting what's been left out, children beyond toddler age seem to obey the principle "Reconstruct just the noun and not its modifiers," harking back to the early *Want cookie* stage of their development.

8 The Pantheon of Plurals: From Possible Worlds to the Ethics of Our World

Once a child, upon being asked why his parents slept in the same bed, answered,

"Because they are husbands and wives."[1]

What an odd error! Neither person is a plural being. Was the child's answer just an "error," or is Universal Grammar again at work?

Actually, adults propagate a similar (but not identical) dazzling illogic. Take common sentences like these:

Dogs have tails.
Birds have beaks.

Or even:

Unicycles have wheels.

The word *unicycle* means exactly "one wheel," so how do we link it up with the plural *wheels*?[2] The plural seems to be rather undisciplined. Some people point to cases like this as examples of careless thinking, but in fact, as we'll see, they are clues to an interesting property of mind.

As the last three sentences illustrate, the "narrative arc" of this chapter will sweep wide and high. We will begin by looking at what plurals involve. At first, one might wonder what there could be to say about that little *s* in English! Rapidly, though, we will find that we have to encompass whole phrases, higher structure carried by recursive *and*, and some fairly intricate notions of distributivity and the interaction of sets. Studying plurals will inexorably lead us to study quantifiers and questions—three elements that the grammar of each language puts together in its own way like an intricate puzzle. Finally, plurals will indeed draw us upward and outward to study properties of mind: to question how much grammar and cognition interact, and what the grammar-cognition conundrum suggests about teaching and ethics.

One of the great errors of intellectual life and everyday life is to leap too quickly from assumptions about language to assumptions about mind. Educational policies, political attitudes, and our interpersonal relations all suffer because we underestimate each other by overestimating how much what a person says tells us about how the person thinks. This chapter will, I hope, give at least an inkling of the challenge involved.

Why Plurals Are the DNA of Grammar

In this first section, we will explore the intricacies children have to weave through as they encounter the thickets of distributivity, word morphology versus phrasal morphology, and quantifiers like *every*. More broadly, we will look at meaning from the perspective of grammar. Later, we will turn the telescope around and see how grammar looks from the perspective of meaning.

Plural Conclusions: Why Plurals Invite Abstractions

Common sense tells us that *plural* means just "more than one." Its origin lies simply in concretely counting objects. Here, already, common sense misleads us. In order to count objects, we must decide that they belong to a class. If I have a yellow apple, a red apple, and a green apple, then I have three apples. This conclusion requires that I have an abstract idea of an apple that is not necessarily any of those three colors. So *plural* refers automatically to a mental abstraction. It instantly leaps beyond the realm of simple objects—for children as well as adults.

One can, for example, imagine saying this to a two-year-old:

Listen to music, eat your dinner, clean up, and after you do *those things* we can sing.

None of those actions really are "things," and yet we build a plural out of them and expect a young child to understand.

In our most ordinary chats with children, we toss around abstractions, using plurals. Holding a banana, we might say to a child, "Do you like bananas?" Yet there is only one banana present. We expect the child to know that our question is about the "concept of a banana" as a prelude to giving her a single banana.

This argument may have a dizzying kind of familiarity. Once again, reference is obscure, but now it is the reference behind plurals. The grammatical principles we've looked at in earlier chapters keep reappearing.

How Multiple Plurals Link to Each Other

Each thing in a plural (*unicycles*) gets linked to one element in the other plural (*wheels*). We have seen this brand of meaning before: in *You each have a pencil*, for instance, *you* refers to a group of people and *pencil* refers to a group of pencils, distributed one by one to each of "you." The surprise is that two plurals also trigger this property. Such one-by-one distribution is called, once again, *distributivity*.[3] Do children operate with such a "highfalutin'" concept? We need only to ask them.

Ana Pérez-Leroux and I found children's understanding of distributivity earliest with the word *home*, where no plural is involved.[4] Here is roughly how we explored this. We showed each child a picture of a small neighborhood where Johnny, a dog, and a horse were playing together. Also pictured in the neighborhood were a house, a doghouse, and a barn.

We told the children this story:

"A dog and a horse came out of the doghouse and the barn to play with Johnny. Then it started to rain. Johnny said, 'Let's all play at my house.'"

Then we said either,

a. "Then everybody went home."

or

b. "Then everybody went to his home."

In (b), the context pushes the child to interpret *his home* to mean that everyone went to Johnny's home, although the grammar allows both the single interpretation "Johnny's home" and the distributed interpretation "each to his own home." But the single-interpretation option is ruled out for (a), "Then everybody went home." Here grammar allows only distributivity, contrary to the story context, so that everyone goes to his own home:

horse → barn
dog → doghouse
Johnny → Johnny's house

So the word *home* in *Everybody went home* contains a hidden element:

Everybody went home = own home, that is, the home of each person referred to by the subject of the sentence

We found that three-year-old children knew this restriction. We combined this experiment with careful studies of the contexts of the naturalistic data. It became clear that at the two-word stage in acquisition, there are children who say things like "Fraser home," meaning that Fraser is at his own home. They can also use *home* to refer to their own home, showing the word's differential reference: "Tractor home" means the tractor is at the child's own home.

It turns out that the simple word *home*, far from being an egocentric term for which the child has just one referent (her own home), is in fact a word that children use to point both toward and away from themselves: it can refer to the child's own home, someone else's home, or (by three years) a distributive set of homes.

Children are eager to distribute with plurals too—a kind of democratic urge. Being as direct as possible is always best. Yoichi Miyamoto did just that with this simple choice that you can easily reproduce.[5] Put two dolls next to each other and ask a child,

---

Exploration 8.1
Distributivity preferred
(plurals across people)

"Do those dolls have two hands or four hands?"

Or just ask (referring to the child and yourself),

"Do we have two hands or four hands?"

The child may say "Both," but if you then ask why, her explanation will probably include something like "We/The dolls have two hands, but four together," allowing the distributive reading.

Or perhaps one can elicit distributivity. Show a child this picture of three dogs:

Ask,

"How many tails do dogs have?"

It is hard to imagine a child saying "Three" and not "One." But contrast this with a second question, again referring to the picture:

"How many tails do the dogs have?"

Here, *the* allows us to see the dogs as a group, and "Three" is a natural answer.

Now that we have looked at distributivity, we can come back around to our *Unicycles have wheels*–type sentences. To explore with a child, try asking casually, without any special introduction, about something that a creature or an object obviously only has one of.

Exploration 8.2
Singular plurals
(plurals across subjects and objects)

"Do dogs have tails?"
"Do cats have heads?"
"Do cars have roofs?"
"Do cars have steering wheels?"

The method is obvious and the answers are never a problem—almost always the child will say "Yes."

But in fact there's more to it than this. Children take the idea where adults fear to go. Anne Vainikka, in work replicated by Uli Sauerland and his colleagues,[6] found that children up to six or seven years of age readily say "Yes" to questions to which adults say "No":

"Does a dog have tails?"
"Does a child have noses?"
"Does a girl have belly-buttons?"
"Does a boy have tongues?"

What is going on here? Is there a sense in which a plural could include a singular? In fact, if you ask a group of people, "Who has children?," a father who has only one child will raise his hand. If you ask, "Who has friends?," your question will include a person who has just one. Or if someone is describing a room to you and you ask, "Does it have windows?," the answer can be "Yes" even if it has only one window. The use of generics, as in the banana example, does not really exclude a singular instance, so why not? English allows using a plural for a singular only when both are possible, not when only one is; we would not ask, "Does your car have roofs?" Perhaps it is this contrast that children lack.[7]

Merging Meanings: Plurals upon Plurals

Let us follow a line of reasoning that may have some promise. We have seen before that a morphological ending can apply to an entire phrase. Recall the discussion of possessive phrases like this in chapter 6:

the man on the corner's hat

This is really [the man on the corner]'s hat, where the 's is applying to the whole phrase; apparently children are competent at saying and understanding such constructions. The same happens with -er; recall the child who talked about "a bike-rider with no hands," where the -er occurring physically on the inside of the phrase (rider) had the meaning of an -er on the outside of the phrase ([ride bike with no hands]-er).

It seems as if children want their morphology to apply to whole phrases and not just words. Perhaps, then, the child is converting

Does a dog have tails?

into

Do dogs have tails?

by allowing the plural to apply to the entire clause:

[dog have tail]-s

Then the sentence can allow distributivity between the words as if -s were attached to both *dog* and *tail* just as in the adult grammar. If the child's grammar is consistent, then if possessive *'s* applies to whole phrases, plural -s should do so as well. In twenty years, I have not heard of a child who really rejected "distributive" readings. There is something very deep and powerful at work here.

Sauerland sought to find the limits.[8] In a small experiment, he asked children,

"Does Fido have tails?"
"Does Ernie have heads?"

In other words, instead of a plural common noun (for example, *dogs*), his experimental question used a proper name (*Fido*). Suddenly some children stopped saying "Yes" and said "No." So what is the difference? Notice that proper nouns do not normally accept pluralization:

*Do Fidos have tails?
*Do Ernies have heads?

"Does Fido have tails?" and "Does Ernie have heads?" prevent a "Yes" answer because a proper noun is intended to pick out an individual: just one dog Fido and one puppet Ernie. The spread of plural over a phrase requires that each noun can take a plural; but here, one noun—the proper noun—cannot. This blockage lends credibility to the claim that according to the child's grammar, non–proper nouns (so-called common nouns) are really being pluralized in questions like *Does a dog have tails?*

Showing that children impose limits actually reveals that the grammar must be at work: they extend the plural to each noun only if it is a count noun that accepts plurals, and then they "distribute" across two groups. Now we can say that children seek consistency in linking the plural to the whole phrase, just as they seek to link the possessive to the whole phrase. The cases where the child answers differently from an adult speaker are not errors but efforts at abstraction.

We will gradually see that the adult grammar demands that we put plurals on phrases too, not just on words. First, look at this well-known grammarian's bugaboo:

two brother*s*-in-law
two brother-in-law*s*

Which would you say? Many people find the plural on the whole phrase more natural.

Exploration 8.3
Trouble with in-laws?
(plural phrases)

This is easy to explore with children. Ask a child about typical known items and perhaps some novel noun + modifier phrases with a request like this:

"Can you finish this sentence for me? John has one brother-in-law and Bill has two ____."

Most likely, the child will in fact say "Brother-in-laws." Then just keep going with these puzzlers:

"John ordered one pastrami on rye and Bill ordered two ____."
"Bill brought one hamburger with cheese and John brought two ____."

Will the child answer "Pastrami on *ryes*" or "*Pastramis* on rye," "*Hamburgers* with cheese" or "Hamburger with *cheeses*"—or even use a double plural like "*Hamburgers* with *cheeses*" (recall "husbands and wives")? What would we hear from a short-order cook? My bet would be "Two pastrami on *ryes*," but "Two *hamburgers* with cheese." The differences seem delicate and open to individual variation. A child might seek greater consistency and go strongly for a phrasal plural.

If the plural is really on the outside, then it may even affect phonology. How would you finish this sentence?

John has one subscription for life, and Bill has two ____.

Might you finish with "Two subscription for *lifes*"? This example brings a sharp phonological diagnostic to bear. Only if the plural ending -*s* is actually attached to the word *life* will we hear the plural of the word *life* itself, where the *f*-sound in *life* becomes a *v*-sound and the plural ending -*s* is pronounced *z*: *lives*. If the plural -*s* is instead attached to the phrase, these changes cannot happen, and the plural of the word *life* is impossible:

*two subscription for *lives*

Facts like these show that a razor-sharp system controls how plurals attach to phrases.

Exploration 8.4
Cutting corners
(more phrasal plurals)

It is a familiar story: adult and child grammars always look alike when we look closely. So let us keep looking. Consider this array:

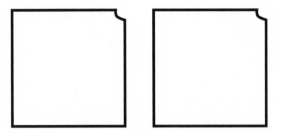

Then ask a child (or yourself),

a. "Is the corner of the boxes cut?"

Conceivably the child will say, "That's silly. Two boxes can't have one corner"—but most likely he will answer "Yes." Most of us take (a) to mean exactly the same as (b):

b. "Are the corners of the boxes cut?"

We easily apply one plural to the words *corner* and *boxes* at the same time. We do this with other expressions as well. For example, look at these figures:

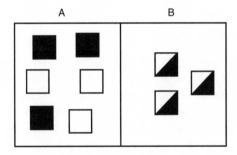

Now, if I were to say,

"Show me where part of the squares are black,"

which squares would you point to? Most people would point to either A or B, with a preference for A.

We have some prior knowledge in hand that suggests the ambiguity is real and more pervasive for children. In an experiment that Ed Matthei and I devised,[9] several hundred four- to seven-year-old children were shown the pictures above and were given instructions like

"Can you show me where some of the squares are black?"

One-third of the children pointed to B, while all adults point to A. The children seem to be taking the phrase as a unit:

[some of the square]-s are black

Here is where most adults seem very surprised. For adults, *some* in *some of the squares* applies only to the whole set, not separate squares. But they should not be surprised: children are doing something very logical, and they are using the sophisticated tools of grammar to do it. In fact, when they get the B interpretation for the request "Show me where part of the squares are black," adults may be doing the same thing with *part* that children do with *some*; that is, they allow it to apply to individual squares:

[part of the square]-s are black

Actually, it is not obvious why *part* and *some*, both of which have some quantificational force, have different wrinkles for adults, so it should not be surprising that children try to make them the same.

Seeking Agreement

What exactly pushes the child toward linking plural to phrases and not to single words? Look again at the combination *husband and wife*. It acts like a plural in that it takes a plural verb:

A husband and wife *are* married.

It is just as if one said, "They are married." The grammar looks at the two words, treats them like a unit—a plural unit—and chooses the verb *are*. The concept of agreement is that "subject and verb 'agree'"; however, the agreement does not happen between the verb and *individual* nouns, but between the verb and the *collection* of nouns that is the subject. The subject [*husband and wife*] simply *is* a plural from the point of view of the verb, for adults as well as children. So the mind creates a plural as soon as we put *and* between two nouns. For adults, then, plural can be present as a property of a phrase.

We are back to the "higher structure" above *and* that we discussed in chapter 4 on Merge. In this case, the agreement (here, *plural*) must be marked on the higher *and* so that it can agree with its (*plural*) verb. In other words, marking the highest *and* with plural ensures that both the noun and the verb at the same level of the grammatical structure carry plural.

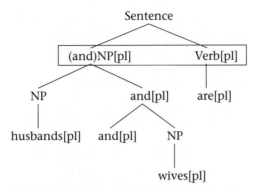

So the child is, in a way, putting the plural where it belongs, on *both* nouns, so they together justify marking the combination as a plural. No wonder "Why do your parents sleep in the same bed?—Because they are husbands and wives" seems possible to a child.

In fact, Susan Carey Block and her colleagues have shown that children do not discriminate singular from plural until the age of twenty-four months, when they recognize the effects of plural in the *verb*:[10]

The cats are here.

It is the presence of plural marking in two places that triggers a sharp discrimination between singular and plural.

Why would verbal agreement signal such a decision to be "semantically strict"? Maybe Universal Grammar carries a connection like this:

Syntactic forms are linked to strictly deductive concepts; don't use plural if singular will work.

Often we can be vague; *I traveled to Mississippi by train* could mean that I took several trains. But when syntactic agreement is present, it requires strict truth: if a plural produces agreement, the meaning has to be nonsingular. This hypothesis is probably too strong, but it may contain some truth—which a child cannot apply until he figures out the mechanics of agreement.

The type of agreement we have looked at, between subject and verb, is the tip of the iceberg of agreement in the world's languages and therefore in Universal Grammar. Many languages require almost every noun, verb, and adjective to show agreement with something. English has hints of overt agreement with plurals: *these hats* is grammatical, not **this hats*. However, English displays much less agreement than other languages. For instance, in *the hats* the article is unchanged. Many grammars add a plural marker to the article so that it agrees with the plural noun (*the* + plural *hats*), giving the child evidence of plural agreement hundreds of times every day.

Enforced Plurality: Blocking Phrasal Plurality

You might now ask, can we ever force a plural to stay put? There seems to be no way to block the spread of plurals to all nouns. Is there any way to make that little morpheme behave and stick with the word it is sitting on? The best way to lock down the plural is by choosing a proper noun as the other noun in the construction (recall *Does Fido have tails?*) or by marking the other noun with a quantifier like *every*. To see what happens with *every*, look at this picture—

> **Exploration 8.5**
> **Three-headed monsters**
> **(scope failure with quantifiers)**

—and ask yourself (or a child),

"Does every boy have three heads?"[11]

Here all adults agree that the answer is "No," even though we are staring at three boys with a total of three heads. There is no distribution among them. Leontine Kremers has done pilot work showing that three-year-olds say "Yes." Other evidence suggests that children do not apprehend *every* perfectly at first (we will return to this point).

Thus far, our discussion circles around two simple claims about plurals and acquisition:

1. Plural can apply to an entire phrase.
2. Plural invites one-to-one distribution between groups.

How does *every* change things? It seems to shift interpretation from a group-to-group (or set–to-set) concept to an individual-to-set concept: what set of heads does *each* person have? One can feel concepts and grammar bumping into each other in these examples. Sentences like these constitute a major topic of philosophical and linguistic discussion: what is the best mode, the best formula, to represent the mind-grammar connection here?

The Meaning of Grammar and the Grammar of Meaning

We have been looking at meaning while leaning on grammar. How does grammar look from the perspective of meaning? What does the word *meaning* mean, anyway? That question is surely too tough; in fact, it may encompass all of human nature! Here we will take just an informal glance at a narrower question: how do we fit words to the world we see?

How the Eye and the Mind Carve Up the World

We humans have a lightning-quick ability to arrange what we see. When a child gazes around a room, things organize: objects, groups, paths are delineated. We can yank many of these patterns up to consciousness easily. If I say, "Point to dark things you see in your living room," you can do it within milliseconds. Suppose I say, "Point to soft things." No problem. Now, how about "Dark, soft things," or even "Dark, soft, old-looking things"? It is easy for us: old brown pillows, worn black sneakers, . . . and whatever else.

We have just carved up a living room to create totally heterogeneous sets, combining different sense systems and provinces of mind—color, age, feel. No logic holds the ingredients together other than my request, born with a bit of mischief in mind: I deliberately concocted a collection of features that have no natural unity at all.

Such mental sets—"mindsets," if you will—may be a human speciality.[12] First, we have a mind that can isolate any kind of individual object. From there we build groups of things (sets) that share defining features. So we go from a kind of conceptual singular to a conceptual plural. The groups—or plurals—are then subject to other kinds of operations—like distribution across yet another group: *Birds have beaks* connects two sets in a one-to-one relation.

Our sentences, our *verbal* edifices, can create sets that confer legitimacy across perception, imagination, and emotion. Often those *mental* edifices are rather questionable collages, as this story reveals:

John thinks Bill is a phony, sneaks drinks, maybe steals, and probably lied to his own brother. Those things, all together, bothered John. They made him move out of the apartment. But none of those things turned out to be true.

Even though *those things* are far from facts, still we can honor them with a plural pronoun: *They made John move out.* It is the very same pronoun we use for undeniably real groups: say, heroes as in *They died for their country.* The genuine fragility of reality—John's illegitimate suppositions—seems to be replaced by the stolid fixtures created by plural pronouns: *they* implies a set of real things. It's no surprise that we get the queasy feeling that language can distort reality, that it confers an indefensible legitimacy upon shadowy impressions. Children, like adults, have to straighten out the often shaky perceptions propped up by the conventions of grammar. Plurals—sets sometimes created by personal perceptions—show how the connection between words and the world can be deceptive or even coercive.

How Questions Carve Up the World

Our grammars invite and enable the "partition" of the world into creative conglomerates.[13] Earlier I illustrated the creation of a "mindset" through the grammar of adjectives: "Point to dark, soft, old-looking things." The grammar of questions also equips us to command and communicate unique mindsets. Suppose I ask,

"What are things that you got from your parents, that you've owned for more than ten years, that are less than a foot long?"

You might answer quickly, "Books, pots, bracelets, Greek coins, vase in the shape of an owl, metal model dinosaur, and probably more." The capacity to survey our knowledge in an original way—letting our neurological impulses somehow dart through thousands of brain strands with a unique formula ("from-parents, ten-years-plus, small") guiding it—is a breathtaking ability, and no theory of neurology can begin to capture it. (The speed of modern computers, though, provides an intriguing analogy and has given birth to an important domain of cognitive science.)

Words like *what, which, when* are, of course, the building blocks of questions. Interestingly, these words have some obvious inner structure:

what = wh + that
which = wh + each
where = wh + here
when = wh + then
whether = wh + either

Because of this, it is unlikely that children learn each word as a single lump; to understand and use these words, a child must be looking for that inner structure. One child I knew asked, "Who person said that?," to make it clear that *who* involves people. A nonnative speaker once asked me whether it is all right to say "our house whose entrance," thinking that since *whose* contains *who*, maybe it applied only to people; but *whose* seems to have lost the "person" feature of *who*.

Although Universal Grammar gives every language-particular grammar the power to ask questions, each grammar seems to lace its question words with little puzzles the child has to solve. For instance, grammars vary in what question words cover. To take just one case: English uses *how* in some questions and *why* in others; in Japanese, just one question word covers the same situations. This tension between what is given innately (the power to ask questions) and what the child has to learn (for instance, how the question words in the language surrounding her carve up the range of possible questions) must be the reason why English-learning children often confuse *how* and *why*. "How do you eat grapefruit?" I once asked a child. "Because I am hungry," he answered—understanding me to ask "Why?"

Does Grammar Follow Cognition?

Are grammar and mind perfect mirrors of each other? Let us begin with a very natural hypothesis:

The growth of grammar follows the same path as perception.

Children move from individual reference (bare nouns), to plural (*-s*), to defined sets (*every*) over which special operations (such as one-to-one linking) are defined. If this trajectory is right, then we might naturally expect that the acquisition of question words like *who* and *what* will take the same path.

Children do hear evidence that a *who* question can have an individual answer:

A: Who is playing outside?
B: (Individual) Mary.

There are cases where the grammar suggests a single person even if more are present. In English, we say,

"Who *is* playing outside?,"

not

"*Who *are* playing outside?,"

whether only one child is playing, or a whole class. (Again, languages differ: some languages like Dutch actually do allow plural verbs in questions. And even within English there are pitfalls and seeming inconsistencies: the child hears both questions like "Who is playing outside?," where *who* takes a singular verb, and relative clauses like "the boys who are here," where the verb is plural.)

Children also hear evidence that *who* can and sometimes must refer to more than one person:

A: Who is playing outside?
B: (Plural) Some girls.

Finally, children hear evidence that *who* can refer to a set (an enumerated list):

A: Who is playing outside?
B: (Full list) Mary, Susan, and Janice.

In fact, in English, *wh*-words (*who*, *which*, and so on) can *require* an *exhaustive* answer.[14] A clear case comes from the courtroom:

Who was in the car the night of the murder?

If John, Mary, and Bill were in the car, then to mention just one individual ("Mary") or to supply a plural ("Mary and Susan") not only would be false, but would actually constitute a form of perjury. To answer "Several people" would be evasive and insufficient. The answer must comprise the full, exhaustive list.

Harvard Law School professor Alan Dershowitz unknowingly alluded to this distinction in discussing the Martha Stewart perjury trial on TV. He said, roughly, that we must read the transcript and see the exact question she was asked to know whether perjury was involved. If the question was

"Tell us the reason you sold stock," then giving just one reason would not be a lie; but if it was "For what reasons did you sell stock?," then mentioning every reason, like inside information, is required. Knowing which question was asked is important precisely because questions with *what* require an exhaustive answer.

There is a small way out—namely, some notion of pragmatic relevance has to be applied. If I say, "What is in the icebox?," you do not answer, "Food, stale air, molecules, metal." My question implicitly asks "what *food*" and therefore it requires only that you mention foods in your answer.

Singletons

Colleagues and I have explored the hypothesis "The growth of grammar follows the same path as perception" as it relates to questions with *who* and *what*—that is, whether children indeed move from individual, to plural, to defined sets in their handling of *wh*-questions.

Early work suggested that children do not see exhaustivity where they should.[15] In this initial research, Zvi Penner, Petra Schulz, and Barbara Pearson worked with over 150 children, some English-speaking and some German-speaking. They showed the children pictures like this: one girl with a sweater and one without; two girls with sweaters and one without; and so on up to five girls with sweaters and one without.

Then they asked the children,

"Who is wearing a sweater?"

(or of course the German equivalent for the German-speaking children). Using pictures of one, two, three, four, and five girls with sweaters made it possible to test whether the predicted acquisition path would appear: individual, plural, set. Would the youngest children point to one picture of a girl with a sweater (the individual or singleton response), would older children point to two or three pictures of girls with sweaters (the plural response), and would still older children point to all the pictures of girls with sweaters (the exhaustive response)?

The results of the experiment were quite startling.[16] When asked "Who is wearing a sweater?," German-speaking children up to the age of about four and a half and English-speaking children up to the age of five regularly pointed to just one girl, the singleton response. It seems that very young children do not show the exhaustivity feature in their grammars. However, fewer than 2 percent of children at any age ever chose a plural answer, a percentage far smaller than even the usual "noise" most experiments have. Children went from the singleton response straight to the exhaustive one: they showed no evidence of a plural stage at all. It was the opposite of what we expected. Children beyond the age of seven who were diagnosed with language disorders answered more haphazardly and inconsistently, but *none* of the children consistently gave a nonexhaustive plural interpretation. In this case our little model, "The grammar follows the mind," was just dead wrong.

So here the grammar and the mind are not perfect reflections—there is no plural possibility in answering a *who* question, for adults or for children, that allows us to mention some of the people who fit the profile of the question, but not all of them. There is a gap here—one could imagine a planet where there really are questions that allow nonexhaustive but plural answers, but this is not the case for English and other languages around the world. To allow a natural plural response, we have to actually *disengage* exhaustivity by adding the notion of *kind*. If I ask,

"What kind of people are wearing sweaters?,"

you can answer,

"Girls like these"

(pointing at two). The fact that children never proceed through a cognitively logical stage tells us, perhaps more clearly than any other kind of evidence, about a deep property of grammar whose acquisition is not a reflection of obvious mental categories.

Let this be a cautionary tale. The assumption that grammar straightforwardly mirrors the mind is almost always wrong: the demands of communication (cognitively, neurologically, and pragmatically) are just different from those of thought or sight. What children do not say or understand properly is not a surefire guide to how they think. In that vein, the children who pointed at only one girl wearing a sweater were certainly perceptually and cognitively aware that many girls fit the description. In fact, one said, "I don't know which one to choose." It was in their understanding of what the grammar demanded, not in what their minds saw, that they differed from adults.

In daily life, it is easy to think otherwise. If someone asks a child, "What do you need for school?," and she answers, "A pencil," it is easy to grow irritated and say, "But you forgot your lunch, your books, and your gloves" and conclude that she "just doesn't listen" or "is a bit slow." It is more likely that the child understood the grammar of the question differently. One wise parent of a twelve-year-old with language problems told me that she has to remember to ask carefully, "What are all the different things you need for school?" She is finding another way of making the exhaustive thrust of the question explicit. Her explicitness might eventually lead the child to see all *wh*-questions as exhaustive.

■ ■ ■

Exploration 8.6
Pictures
(plurals across objects)

Here are some ways to explore the singleton, plural, and exhaustive options discussed above. Do children understand when a variable response is called for, or an exhaustive response? Take seven pictures of people (one person in each picture). Lay the pictures in a row—say, three right-side up and four upside down:

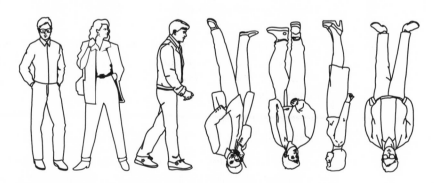

Ask a child,

"Who is upside down?,"

and see how many of the upside-down pictures she points to.

You can probably elicit a plural response, too. Show the child this picture:

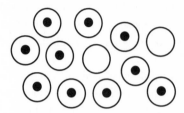

Now ask,

"Do circles have dark spots? Show me."

Pointing to all the circles with dark spots would be laborious and unnecessary; pointing to just a few (the plural response) suffices to answer the question.

Now set the pictures of people in a different right-side-up/upside-down order, or draw a different number and pattern of circles with and without dark spots, and use *every* in your instruction:

"Show me every upside-down picture." / "Show me every circle with a dark spot."

This calls for a lot of work on the child's part, but the instruction is unmistakable: he needs to point to every relevant picture or circle.

Double Questions: Who Bought What?

The exhaustivity requirement becomes compulsory and unmistakable for adults in double questions. (Often, again, more complex structures reveal a sharper version of simple principles.) Double questions make exhaustivity crystal clear:[17]

Who bought what?
[John bought apples, Mary bought bananas, and Susan bought pears.]

Here we have to form two sets, link the members of each by pairs, and be exhaustive. This requirement is not something we are taught in nursery school—or even in high school—yet as we will see, a large number of four-year-olds understand it with no difficulty.

Double questions like this—as short as three words!—provide the most important range of data in this book. They engage the most sophisticated aspect of grammar and lie at the center of much current linguistic research. The double question is a central feature of the Diagnostic Evaluation of Language Variation (DELV), a dialect-neutral test developed by Harry Seymour, Jill de Villiers, Peter de Villiers, Barbara Pearson, the Psychological Corporation (Harcourt Assessments, Inc.), a host of intellectual and methodological advisors, and myself.[18] The DELV is based on features of grammar that have two crucial properties: they are so fundamental that they do not vary with dialect, and they are able to reveal language disorders. The double question is one such feature. Facts about the behavior of double questions come from the most sophisticated work in linguistic theory, and at the same time these questions seem to give the best insight available into a particular language disorder. (It is a token of the maturity of linguistics as a field that the most sophisticated theoretical work has the most direct practical value. The relationship between linguistics and communication disorders begins to resemble the relationship between microbiology and medicine; sophisticated microbiology is often the source of new pills for the most ordinary diseases.)

A typical double question invented for the DELV is this:

"This girl caught different things in different ways. She caught that crab with a net and the fish with her fishing pole. (Pause) How did the girl catch what?"

If you are a competent adult speaker of English, you take the two *wh*-question sets (ways of catching and things that were caught), link the members of each set one to one, and require your answer to be exhaustive. This must be the goal toward which children proceed. The reference to a set is even more stringently required in these double questions (although there are a few exceptions) than in questions with a single *wh*-word.

Children give four types of answers to double questions like "How did the girl catch what?"[19]

1. Paired, exhaustive responses (correct): "She caught the crab with a net and the fish with a pole."
2. Singletons (incorrect): "A crab." "With her pole." "Crab and fish."
3. One pair (incorrect): "The crab with a net."
4. Other answers that are really evasions: "She fished a lot." "She was playing."

Some children always give a double response, some never do, and many do sometimes but inconsistently. Children in the last group probably have the right grammar, but they cannot always bring it to bear and therefore revert to a singleton grammar.

Typically developing children give appropriate answers to questions like these two-thirds of the time at the age of four. However, they rarely produce such questions themselves. I know of no examples in the CHILDES database, and I know of only a couple personally: one of my children, looking at pictures in "Goldilocks and the Three Bears," asked, "Whose bed is who?" The grammar still wasn't quite right, but the pairing intent was evident. No doubt children do produce double questions, but rarely enough that only a pair of attentive ears will catch one.

Children with language disorders answer appropriately less than one-third of the time and remain consistently behind through the age of nine. Children up to the age of twelve who have been shown to have ongoing problems with language continue to prefer singleton answers, even in contexts where adults take pairing to be virtually obligatory.[20]

Exploration 8.7
How to live in a questionable household (double-question games)

Anytime two or more people are together is a good time to launch into this double-question game. The trick is simply to be sure that the context provides two pairable things that can be questioned. Just ask,

"Who is sitting where?"
"Who is eating what?"
"Who is wearing what?"

"How am I eating what?"
"Where did you put what?"
"When did you see what?"
"Why did you buy which food?"
"Which toy goes in which place?"
"Which shoe goes on which foot?"

Playing this game is the stuff of family fun. Once they've played it, children will most likely start forming such questions themselves. This kind of delightful stimulation has a far greater chance of being beneficial than playing Mozart to the unborn. The more casual the atmosphere, the more likely it will prove helpful. Tim Roeper at five years asked spontaneously, "Which foot is which foot?" (meaning "Which foot is which?").

Here is a more complex version—a triple *wh*-question—for older children (say, six to eight) who clamor for more. You can ask for three answers:

"Who told John to do what when?"

If the middle question is an indirect question following a so-called mental verb, the answerer has to link only the first and last *wh*-words:

A: *Who* can you tell *how* to play *what*?
B: I can tell *John* how to play *baseball*, and *Fred* how to play *badminton*.

That is, in this case the answerer does not need to specify "how" (does not need to say, "I can tell John to play baseball carefully, and Fred to play badminton with abandon"). Asking such questions should tell us whether children know that. Apparently this knowledge is not automatic: work by Ana Pérez-Leroux hints that Spanish-speaking children and even adults may answer the indirect question and that English-speaking children do not see right away that an indirect question does not have to be answered.[21]

The Cognitive Question

Now let us turn to the most important question: what critical ingredient is necessary for grasping paired questions? Or, the other way around: what critical ingredient is missing if a child does not use or understand paired questions correctly? We have identified something that could be very deep, so we should look at deep possibilities as well as superficial ones.

The children may lack the notion of a linguistic "variable," like a hidden algebraic *x* that is (1) necessarily a part of *wh*-words, *every*, and nonspecific plurals, and (2) a prerequisite for linking two variables, where two things co-vary as in double questions. This is different from the capacity to handle plurals and their openness to distributivity. Recall that *Children have toys* (plural) allows one-to-one or one-to-many relations (each child has one toy or each child has many toys), but *Every child has one toy* (with quantifier *every*) enforces the one-to-one reading. It is the latter relation I am speaking of. (There remains substantial discussion about how to represent it linguistically—to which an understanding of the acquisition path may contribute.) The hypothesis we will explore is that in the grammar of a child who does not grasp paired questions, one deep linguistic feature could be missing that links *wh*-words and quantifier words.

To say that a child lacks the notion of a variable could mean several things. The idea is genuinely still open both in a technical sense and in a broader cognitive sense. It could, for instance, mean that

1. a cognitive ability is missing,
2. a capacity to *connect* a cognitive ability and grammar is missing, and/or
3. the understanding of a semantically complex lexical item like *what* is missing.

What does *missing* mean in this context? Researchers do not really know at this point. It might mean "truly absent." The inability to handle variables might be a real defect in Universal Grammar. This would be analogous to color blindness, a deviation from natural visual ability. Or it might mean that some factor is interfering with knowledge that a child actually has. This would be analogous to having an immobilized broken arm. A person in a cast is not suddenly missing the idea of an arm; the knowledge of how to use the arm is there, but it cannot be acted upon.

Which meaning of *missing* turns out to be correct has considerable implications. If some factor is interfering with knowledge that a child has—and I would say the likelihood of this is very great—then intervention makes sense. On the other hand, if a cognitive ability is truly missing, then it makes no more sense to try to induce comprehension of variables than trying to force a color-blind person to see colors, or to encourage a five-foot-tall person to "try" to be six feet tall. People with severe retardation, or victims of accidents, might really not have fundamental knowledge. Our challenge is to be aware of this possibility, but not assume it in a way that can damage the dignity and the future of a child. It is a large expectation, which, in my view, has not been well observed in any of the social sciences, where far-reaching and overly simple judgments about human nature are bruited about quite cavalierly.

Invisible *Every*

One avenue of linguistic explanation looks particularly attractive.

In Chinese, question words actually contain an audible quantifier: it is as if English speakers said *wh-somebody* for *who* and *wh-something* for *what*. Taisuke Nishigauchi has made a related proposal for English that fits the acquisition path. If some grammars put a visible (audible) quantifier inside questions, maybe other grammars do the same invisibly (inaudibly). So perhaps *wh*-words in English contain a hidden *every*.[22] In other words, the child must decide that a word like *who* is really [*wh* + person + *every*], therefore that answering a *who* question demands supplying an exhaustive set. This is really not so far-fetched—we have already noted that *which* has a morphologically collapsed *each* inside it, and similarly for the other *wh*-words.

Creating two sets and then *pairing* them exhaustively is a further step, but a natural one. Roughly speaking, pairing is like extending distributivity to *wh*-words, that is, one-to-one matching. (It remains a current intellectual challenge to state precisely what pairing is.)

Nishigauchi's proposal allows this hypothesis about children's acquisition of *who*, *what*, and the other *wh*-words:

Children do not initially know that *wh*-questions contain a hidden *every*.

Children with language impairments have great difficulty seeing the hidden *every*.

We can carry this line of thought further. If *every* is difficult to acquire when it is hidden inside a *wh*-word, maybe it is also difficult to acquire when it is explicit. Uri Strauss, Barbara Pearson, and I have found that children avoid forms with *every* for a long time.[23] Studying the CHILDES transcripts of six children up to four and five years of age, Strauss found only twenty-five uses of *every*. Of those, seventeen occurred in adverbial compounds like *every time* and *every day*, which are different from the *every* + *noun* type where the noun set is exhaustive. So only eight were *every* + *noun* combinations: *every boys and girls*, *every farmer people*, *every glasses*, *every people*, and so on. It looks suspiciously as though these children's grammars allow plural agreement with *every*, as with *all* (*all boys*). Children in fact use *all* long before *every*—but note that *all* carries exactly that plural feature. (A recent study of utterances by eighteen children under the age of five revealed only ten instances of *every* + *noun*, while children use *all* perhaps thousands of times.)[24] There is no doubt that children do not grasp all of the many peculiar properties of *every* immediately. In fact, it is still not clear why the adult grammar allows *each of the boys* but not *every of the boys*, for instance.

Following work by William Philip, the DELV team searched the DELV database and found children who did not seem to register *every* (that is, who disregarded it in answers) or regarded it as a plural.[25] To study this more formally, we showed children pictures like this:

We then asked,

"Is every boy on a bike?"

Some of the children consistently said "Yes" to this question and others like it. They seemed to be answering the question "Are boys on bikes?" The plural option echoes the few naturalistic cases found in the transcripts, like *every glasses*.

The plural option seems to be what children fall back on as they acquire *every*. This is different from acquisition of *who*, which children first understand as asking for a singleton answer and then as requiring an exhaustive answer, without passing through a middle, plural stage.

If *wh*-words and *every* really are connected, their acquisition should somehow be connected. Exploring the DELV database, Uri Strauss showed that this odd but consistent response to questions with *every* correlates with how children understand paired *wh*-questions.[26] Those children who made errors answering "Who bought what?" were for the most part the ones who did not correctly analyze "Did every boy ride a bike?" And their errors were in the same direction: they tended toward the interpretation that arises if we assume that *every* is just not present. They gave erroneous singleton responses to "Who bought what?," and they answered "Did every boy ride a bike?" as though they understood it to be a plural question ("Did boys ride bikes?"). They seemed not to understand the hidden *every* at all in *wh*-words, and they seemed to misconstrue *every* as a plural marker when it occurred explicitly.

Imperfect *Every*: A Glimpse of Sophisticated Theory

In some respects, this section goes beyond the intended thrust of the rest of the book. It outlines a more specific theory of exactly how *every* is acquired. Some arguments may seem a little opaque, but they will give you a taste of how linguistic ideas come together abstractly.

William Philip has shown (for six languages with various collaborators) that children consistently misconstrue *every* quite systematically in response to the following situation and question:[27]

"Did every boy ride a bike?"

They often point to the extra bike and say, "Not this bike." The DELV has revealed the pattern robustly with over a thousand children.[28] In other words, the children actually treat *every* as if it applies to both nouns in the same sentence, just as they do with plurals—in other words, as if the question means "Did every boy ride and was every bike ridden?" Here the children recognize the presence of *every*. However, they do not treat it as a modifier of a noun; rather, they treat it as a modifier of the whole sentence, as if one were to say, "Everyly, a boy rode a bike." Note that English has the bare adverb *most* in addition to the overtly adverbial *mostly*: *I play baseball most* means the same as *I play mostly baseball*. If English has *most* and *mostly*, why not *every* and *everyly*? Most grammars in the world have a sentential adverb like *always*, but many lack a noun phrase modifier like *every*. Therefore, the idea that *every* equals *always* may be a natural first assumption dictated by Universal Grammar. Parallelism in grammar should lead the child to expect that *every* could also be an adverb. That is, could a child actually assume that a bare *every* means "every time" or "always"? That would explain why adverbials like *everytime* show up first in the naturalistic database. And parallelism should lead children to adverbial interpretations for other quantifiers like *most* (see exploration 8.8).

Apparently, then, there is an intermediate stage between "no *every*" and "adult *every*." Can we make all these things fit together? What follows is a sketch of an idea.[29] As noted in chapter 4, the fundamental operation of grammar is simply to merge new information into the old structure. Support comes from the claim that both *-er* and plural *-s* can attach to an entire phrase. We should therefore expect that a child's first move, when confronted with a mysterious *every*, is to merge *every* to the whole phrase or sentence, instead of to just one noun. When children hear *every*, they must either ignore it or attach it somewhere. Let us say that a child hears the sentence *Every boy rides a bike*. If she just attaches *every* to the sentence, then she has given the sentence a structure like this:

every [boy ride bike]

In this case, *every* would apply to both *boy* and *bike*; it would distribute, just as the plural does.

So we have proposed that *every* can appear in a range of structural positions, from outside the sentence to inside a word. Here is a vision of the structural path, which needs to be validated by a full account of how the whole panoply of quantifiers emerges:

1. applies nowhere (child ignores *every*),
2. applies to the whole sentence (*every [boy ride bike]*),
3. applies to a phrase (*every boy*),
4. applies inside a word (*every* inside *everytime*),
5. applies invisibly (*who* = *who-every*).

Does this range of possibilities define an actual sequence that children pass through in mastering *every* and *wh*-words? Answering this question poses a real research challenge, since so many steps may happen silently before a child decides to use any particular quantifier. We have some evidence that the sequence is not exactly right, for we have noted that *everytime* appears very early in children's speech, along with other forms like *everyday* and *everywhere*—but *every + noun* (as in *every boy*) is virtually absent. (It is possible, though, that children perceive words like *everywhere* holistically as a single word without parts, in which case it is misleading to consider the *every* in such words as a real instance of *every*.) Also, it is possible that the structural path outlined above may not be manifested in what a child says, yet still be a part of mental growth; that is, it may represent silent stages through which a child passes. Why would a child have silent stages? It is natural if the child knows (unconsciously) that he has only partially grasped a construction. Many second language learners—who in part reproduce the acquisition process—silently refrain from using phrases that they partly understand but do not control.

So here is the *interpretation* path:

1. There is no *every* in noun phrases and no *every* in questions; therefore, singleton answers are given to *wh*-questions.
2. *Every* is outside the sentence, merged at the top ⇒
a. *Every* applies as a plural—a plural prefix instead of a suffix. So *Every boy is on a bike* is the same as *Boys are on bikes*, which is not exhaustive.
b. *Every* is *overexhaustive*: it applies to both nouns. Children answer "Is every boy on a bike?" as if it meant "every boy" and "every bike."
3. *Every* applies only to the noun it is next to, as in the adult grammar.
4. The child realizes that questions with *wh*-words have a hidden *every*.

Is this sequence right? It is difficult to be sure, but it does reveal the kind of step-by-step building of a mechanism that many in the acquisition community believe the growth of grammar to be.

Is this idea outlandish? Some people are startled by imagining a word like *everyly*—or incredulous at the thought that their four-year-old may not control the adult form of *every*. It is very possible that the situation is more complex. Maybe children really do have, at least by age four or five, a representation of *every* inside a noun phrase like adults'—but the representation is not secure. Under situational duress, children reach back to earlier grammars, closer to the Universal Grammar starting point, and this may lead to their making mistakes longer than their best knowledge would lead one to expect—much the same way anyone, in a tough situation, might mumble a bit, be unable to make phonology flow, or the way second language learners revert to more primitive representations of their native language after a long day. Until the grammar is secure, Universal Grammar-based misinterpretations are quite possible, and may affect a child's school life and ability to do, for instance, math problems that involve *every*, if math is stressful.

How can one tell where children are? Two good guidelines are these: until children use a form regularly, it is likely that it remains insecure (which is why they do not use it); and it is unlikely that children younger than five will use *every* in anything other than adverbial constructions. We get good evidence that they have mastered *every* when they can reject context (for example, when they can look at the boys/bikes picture and say, "No, not every boy rode a bike").

A full account would bring all quantifiers into play (and, I should add, a number of sophisticated questions about logic and the full semantics of quantifiers that we are not considering here).[30] If children were totally unable to grasp a variable, then we would predict problems with other quantifiers as well—problems with interpreting, for example, *Each boy has one hat, Some boys have one hat, Most boys have one hat*. In fact, we saw in chapter 5 that children may not control *some* perfectly, and experimental evidence shows that the same types of problems arise with *most* as with *every*.[31] While there is no *everly*, there is a *mostly*. It was not surprising to discover that children might take sentence (a) to mean the same as sentence (b):

a. Did most boys paint houses?
b. Did boys paint mostly houses?

Exploration 8.8
When *most* is *mostly*
(anchoring quantifiers)

You can explore children's understanding of quantifiers yourself with hats and some lamps. Take a pile of hats and put a hat on all but two of the lamps in a room, leaving some hats left over (so, if you have ten hats and six lamps, there will be hats on four lamps and six hats left over):

Then ask a child,

"Are most hats on lamps in this room?"

Will the child say "Yes," as if you had asked this question instead?

"Are hats on most lamps in this room?"

How much is invisible in the grammar of children? This is one of the deepest questions we can ask.

More Invisible Reference

If *every* can be hidden, we predict that other quantifiers and reflexives can be, too. A quick look reveals that this is so.

Two people went to a hotel, where the desk clerk asked them, "Are you married?"—to which they answered "Yes" because each was married to someone else. The deception works because we understand *Are you married?* to mean "Are you married [to each other]?" without having to say "to each other." Many plurals contain hidden *each other*s too.

To explore this with a child, you could construct questions like this, making stories to fit *friends, enemies, classmates,* and so on.

Exploration 8.9
Hidden quantifiers
(silent *each other*)

John is Mary's friend and Bill is Fred's friend, but John and Bill do not like each other. Are John and Bill friends?

As adults, we would instantly answer "No"—but in fact, each man is a friend *to another person*, so when we consider the two men together, the plural *friends* should be acceptable. Why do we overlook this possibility? Because there is really another hidden quantifier here: we take *friends* to mean "friends [to each other]" where *each other* isn't mentioned. The same holds for *enemies, rivals, acquaintances, lovers, classmates,* and so on.[32] Yet of course not every plural contains a hidden *each other*. If we say, "They are haters" (or liars or swindlers), we do not necessarily mean that they hate each other. Do children know that a hidden *each other* can exist and where it does not exist? One could tell stories like the one above and find out.

Intervention: Bringing the Missing Knowledge Out

If a child has trouble with a linguistic construction—say, always gives singleton answers to questions that call for an exhaustive list—the usual approach is to bombard the child with examples. I would certainly say that general exposure to language is always a good idea. But bombarding a child with repetition of what he has not mastered just puts him down. It is a constant accusation of ignorance or stupidity, however "kindly" or good-heartedly we engage in repetition. Instead, we can recognize that situations are inherently specific, so we should look for a precise gimmick that helps the child see the central point—here, that *who* can require the listener to answer with more than one person or thing. So let us try to imagine contexts that will help the variable characteristic emerge. It is not easy. Every situation that allows *multiple* reference seems to allow just single reference as well. However, it turns out that some adverbs and verbs are incomprehensible without a multiple answer.[33] For questions like

Who played together?

and

Who shared the ice cream?

a singleton answer is really not an option. So we can ask the child questions of this kind in an effort to promote the realization that *wh-* is exhaustive. We can bolster the implication with questions like this:

Who is looking at each other?

Since we are dealing with a primarily unconscious realm, simple explanation will always feel more difficult than illustration. "Explanation" is as wrongheaded here as a football coach hiring a physiologist to explain a pass play.

Conclusion

Just as the tiniest elements give direct insight into the principles of physics, so the smallest ingredients in language can give us direct insight into the principles of mind that the child brings to bear. We have seen this at work again with plurals and quantifiers. The reference for plurals can be complex, and phrasal structure is involved. Quantifiers may be misapplied—too broadly—or be invisible.

These notions are not just "technical." They implicate both cognition and ethics.

Ethics and Education: The Social Role of a Modular View of Grammar and Cognition

How Cognition Can Trigger Grammar

A fundamental ingredient in advancing a child's developing grammar is how the child sees that a sentence fits—or fails to fit—a situation. We understand situations without words; that is, we have a nonverbal mental version of situations. What type of situation could bring the meaning and syntax of *every* alive for a child?

Let's say that in an art class, three children are making American flags (which of course have three colors). The teacher shows them a flag, says they should copy it, and gives the group one red, one white, and one blue crayon. The situation itself is clear enough so the children already know what is needed.

Now imagine that each child has so far used only one color (one has used red (black in the picture here), one has used blue (here, gray), and one has used white (here, light gray)):

It would be true to say,

"Every child has a color and every color is being used by a child."

However, it's a misunderstanding to interpret this sentence as meaning

"Every child has used every color."

In fact, Mari Takahashi has shown that younger children readily answer "Yes" to the question "Is every child using every color?" in situations like this.[34] Let's imagine that our flag-making children's grammars are at this stage.

Nevertheless, the flag-making children do know that they are supposed to use all the colors to finish their flags. Let's say the teacher asserts,

"Every child hasn't used every color yet, so keep on working."

How should the children understand this sentence? They understand the situation (each is supposed to use all three colors to finish the flag) and they want the sentence to fit the situation. After all, it is what the teacher said, so it should be true. So they undertake a *grammar change* to bring the logic of the situation and the truth of the sentence together: let each *every* apply separately to each noun, and link them. Each child has to use all three colors. Then it comes out right.

This scenario of grammar change means that the child is using an independent cognitive representation in the process of fixing how the grammar of her native language works. It suggests again that we must be wary of assuming that a failure to understand what looks like the simplest of sentences must surely reflect a cognitive problem, not grammar. It seems almost impossible to most people that understanding "Who ate what?"—where the child already knows each word—could be anything but a cognitive problem. But this illustration of how *every* could be acquired suggests that seeing *how grammar reflects thought* is what challenges the child, not the thought itself.

Here is another case in point. Piaget and Inhelder assumed that problems with quantifiers must be cognitive problems.[35] The evidence shows inconsistency: sometimes children give answers showing that they grasp quantifiers and double *wh*-questions, and sometimes they do not. When they do not, they seem to revert to an earlier grammar where *every* is absent. But sometimes they do it right. That must mean that they really do have the grammar, or an inkling of the grammar, but they cannot exercise those abilities all the time. Why? It could be another neurological factor that we do not even know how to think about.

However, from the cognitive point of view—while some deficit could also be present—inconsistent responses suggest that children can form an implicit idea of an exhaustive, paired set at some fundamental level. If they could not, then they would *never* give paired answers—just as someone who is five feet tall is never six feet tall, not even occasionally. So Piaget and Inhelder's assumption that problems with quantifiers must be cognitive problems is clearly in doubt. Extending grammatical results to cognitive claims requires great caution.

This leap from grammatical deficit to mental deficit is so automatic, so deep in the history of education, that overcoming it is no easy task and calls for personal vigilance and the reconsideration of educational policy. At the moment, failure on language-oriented tests can contribute to children's being placed in Special Education classes, where the assumption is that they have cognitive difficulties. It is hard to overestimate the importance of the need for caution. To underscore it with an anecdote: a child, born in the United States to a professor, was first tested and because of grammar misunderstanding (due perhaps to a Caribbean dialect) was placed in Special Education, which assumes cognitive impairment. When the professor complained and more rigorous examination took place, the child was moved within one month from Special Education to Gifted Education.

Ethical Modularity: Cognitive Caution

So this is where we are: we have identified a difficulty with the notion "variable" that appears to be connected to core properties of grammar. Therefore, the problem could appear in the grammar of any language. The problem's exact nature and its connection to cognition and other realms of how we process sentences remain unresolved. Meanwhile, it is something we can be aware of in intervention, in children's readers, and in how we converse with children. One nugget of a negative conclusion should stay with us: every direct connection between grammar and cognition should be treated with suspicion. Like doctors trying out unproved techniques, we should suspect all of our approaches to cognition. Suspicion is warranted on both scientific and ethical grounds. In the scientific realm, we have already seen a case where assuming a simple connection between grammar and cognition made precisely the wrong prediction (the hypothesis that comprehension of *who* goes through a plural stage). In the ethical realm, we should keep a child's dignity in mind even as we consider possibilities that may endanger that dignity. A college student told me of the scars left on him because he was designated as retarded, though it later emerged that he had a hearing deficit and was unusually capable. A parent told me that his fifteen-year-old, who does not seem to grasp the variable nature of *wh*-words, just has no concept of what a "list" or a "group" is. Surely he does have such concepts if he can put several things on his plate at once at dinner. He just does not know that the *wh-* in questions calls for that list. If a child does not correctly represent a variable in grammar, we cannot make any claims about how the rest of his mind works. Any claim that a person is inherently incapable of a certain concept puts a label of inferiority on him that can permeate our actions and social relations so profoundly that we are not fully aware of it.

So let us articulate the opposite, heavily modular view regarding grammar and cognition. Suppose we argue that one-to-one mapping (distributivity) is like stereoscopy in vision and sound. The same principle governs two quite different mental capacities. We expect them to be separately represented. There is no one stereoscopy center that could be knocked out by a blow to the brain, so that one simultaneously lost the ability in both vision and hearing.

Suppose we argue that one-to-one mapping is separately represented in language, vision, sports, conscious reflection (what we are doing now), mathematical reasoning, and perhaps even social relations. Could we have isomorphic emotions? Who knows? Shakespearean plays (following classical notions of dramatic orderliness) often end with everyone getting married, as if there is something emotionally satisfying and inevitable about such pairings.

We definitely have the visual capacity to see one-to-one connections. A teacher can spot the fact that every child in his class has a T-shirt, or that some do not, or that some T-shirts are in a pile on a chair. If he had to deal with the sets of T-shirts and children independently, instead of T-shirt + child pairs, life would be harder. On the other hand, people vary in their ability to "see" colors mentally. We may think four objects in four different places are the same shade of green, but when we put them next to each other, they turn out to be different in a way that our eyes were incapable of computing without immediate adjacency. It can be hard to shop for a new shirt to match a pair of pants if you do not bring the pants along.

Visual pairing, tactile pairing, sound pairing for music, and athletic pairing of motion in sports or ballet most likely require a pairing mechanism that is independently represented in the mind and not quite identical from one mode to another. Pattern recognition for sight, touch, and words and the conglomerate that comes together in thoughts about things like style may share properties, but it is far from clear that one conceptual scheme underlies them. Visual patterns might involve sets of connected and embedded pairs, a kind of visual recursion that from a mathematical point of view is vastly more complex than verbal recursion. Yet mental visual recursion does not allow extraction (though zooming in and rotation are possible).[36] Imagine seeing a house and then doing "across-the-board window-extraction," where all windows appear in your imagination systematically lined up on the left outside the house:

Making this type of conversion in our "mind's eye" is simply not a built-in human mechanism. If it were, then vision would be like English grammar, where we ask a question by moving the object of the verb all the way to the left:

What does every room in a house have ____?

So we can actually say something about a visual object that we cannot easily carry out visually in our imagination: extract the windows as a separate set that we see as a unity. Most likely, such an extraction operation would be useful for planning intricate architectural symmetry, but it does not describe how humans see visual patterns.

We are tiptoeing here around one of the deepest questions in psychology and biology: how the architecture or the intrinsic logic of one module might get used by another. Pairing in one module might facilitate pairing in another. Patterns of pairing in vision might help grasp pairing in grammar. It could be that visual pairing of T-shirts and children engenders a supramodular notion of pairing that the child can extend to *every* in the sentence *Every child has a T-shirt.* Yet we must always remain clearly aware that a *trigger* connection is not an *identity* connection. The pairing would be separately represented in the mind and would be slightly different from module to module. Cognitive scientists do not yet quite know how to formulate this question because it goes to the deepest philosophical issue of the extent to which the different parts of mind are actually connected. One consequence should be clear: the parent of the teenager who cannot understand *Who bought what?* moves too quickly in assuming that the same factor underlies an inability or unwillingness to make a grocery list.

Modularity and Dignity

The modularity of mind is not just a tantalizing abstraction, but a proposition about humanity that delineates our capacity to honor each other's dignity. The ethical weight of this issue is immense. If we ever say that another person "cannot think something"—even if it is a natural personal response to an impasse in conversation or a necessary human judgment by a teacher—it is a challenge to that person's humanity and therefore to his or her dignity. Still, those judgments have far less weight than claiming the authority of science in leaping to an estimate of "human intelligence." Our ethical posture should be this, I believe:

Do not to extend a judgment about the character of one mental module to another module.

In a way this is common sense, but it is common sense that is not very common. It is very hard to prevent ourselves from extending a judgment about language to a judgment about mind. Every extension of an observation to "general intelligence" probably runs afoul of this dictum.

Professional Ethics

A kindergarten teacher once said to me, "I see—learning language is more mechanical, like learning how to tie your shoes, than learning new concepts like 'subtraction.'" Indeed, such a metaphor is what language specialists need to keep in mind, not the Piagetian cognitive one. Broad cognitive claims almost inevitably overstate a child's deficit and undermine adults' ability to treat children respectfully. Even if cognitive scientists do not have the mechanism and its modular connections perfectly worked out, it seems wise for all "language practitioners" to champion the metaphor that most carefully safeguards a child's dignity. Parents and teachers need help—need protection—from the inevitably exaggerated implications of educational technology, such as the infamous IQ tests, which after seventy years or more cannot point to a single reliable concept we can call "intelligence." The natural conclusion is this: we should assume that any person's problem in "understanding" is local to language until really proven otherwise. The community of scholars studying people with "learning disabilities" struggles to establish this notion as well: a deficit in one area, like reading or math, represents no fundamental deficit in human sensibility.

How do we match our obligation to inform the public of our knowledge—partial and imperfect though it may be—with the obligation to work against its misuse? There is no alternative to simply being as careful and scrupulous in the presentation of that knowledge as we know how to be. We should not—as doctors once did with patients—decide that people cannot handle important knowledge. In the past, it was customary not to inform patients that they were dying so they would not be upset. Now we see having this knowledge as the right of any person to determine the circumstances in which the end of life comes. It is necessary to warn people of heart attack symptoms, even if those symptoms are sometimes indistinguishable from harmless forms of indigestion. If an operation has only a 75 percent chance of success, it must be the patient, not the doctor, who decides whether the risk is worth it. Language acquisition presents a similar obligation—both to alert parents to potential grammar problems and to enable them not to be misled by the natural path of grammar development. Parents have a right to be involved in the assessment of their children's language abilities and therefore a right to knowledge about the current state of research. If we are uncertain about our health, we both inform ourselves and go to a doctor for further evaluation, and the advice is analogous in case of uncertainty about a child's linguistic growth: both inform yourself and consult a speech therapist.

We will return to questions about dignity and professional ethics when we return to the image of human nature that the perspective on language taken here implicitly advocates.

Microdialects and Language Diversity

9 Language Variation: Emotion Overtakes Structure

Some would say we have looked only at the body of grammar, not the soul.[1] Indeed, so far we have looked at only the common skeleton of grammar: the universal and invariant concepts like word, sentence, and recursion. That is the easy part. The soul of grammar is how it contributes to our sense of identity. If we speak a dialect, it seems to holler out who we are. When we consider grammatical variation and dialects, all dimensions of humanity seem to come flooding into view. Our social attitudes completely dominate our concept of grammar when dialect is the topic of discussion, as if everything about grammar were emotionally motivated. Language leads us to make both gross and finely calibrated judgments about each other, often misguided.

Since our judgments "come from the gut," they are very hard to dislodge. Linguistic attitudes are maintained at both a conscious and an unconscious level, which makes them devilishly insidious. Those—even linguists—who claim that they are untainted by language prejudice have not grasped how deep its unconscious roots are. It may be that linguistic judgments are part of a biologically driven mode of personal interaction—much like aspects of sexuality that are not within elementary mental control. If we could just "decide" not to be affected, then pornography would not be offensive, but our reactions are partly automatic. As with race prejudice, people have a strong intuition of inevitable truth in making linguistic judgments, both positive and negative. Just hearing someone's accent or dialect may cause us to think "So and so doesn't seem so bright" or "So and so must be smart" (think of many Americans' reaction to hearing a British accent, which "feels" more intelligent to them). Where exactly does such an opinion come from? Often it is a judgment about grammar, not content.

Unfortunately, language prejudice remains intellectually acceptable in modern society. People do not feel embarrassed about making fun of other people's language, much as a generation ago no one felt inhibited about racially oriented humor. A caricature almost always involves an exaggerated imitation of language style.

It has sometimes been suggested that language prejudice increases when race prejudice declines. If we must have a way to accept or dismiss someone in a few seconds, race is convenient, but if not race, then "improper English" serves as a device for instant social analysis. Is language prejudice increasing as some progress is made in fighting race prejudice in the United States? It is hard to say.

Linguists are fond of saying that "a language is just a dialect with an army."[2] It is in fact true that where dialects are linked to armies, they are often called distinct languages, which provides a kind of political barricade against prejudice. Scandinavian languages are often mutually understood—and yet we have separate labels for Norwegian, Swedish, and Danish and separate textbooks dictating correctness in each language. What is the educational fallout from all of this? Our culture is full of concern over big issues stemming from language variation: body language, African-American English (Ebonics), bilingualism, and code-switching (moving between dialects). Related issues—outrage at misspelled words, parents' hyperconcern about slight differences in pronunciation, the changing status of profanity—are related but petty fellow-travelers of language prejudice.

While our educational apparatus mounts a large campaign against race prejudice, little is done to combat language prejudice, partly because such an education requires some knowledge of linguistic structure. Instruction in grammar never explains why dialect variation is just another version of Universal Grammar. And no one explains that we can no more violate Universal Grammar occasionally than grow a third foot when we feel like it. Without this perspective, grammar instruction inevitably teaches to a norm that amounts to suppression of dialects.

As the chapter unfolds, we will look at the emotions and sense of identity that are bound up with language variation, note that even young children are sensitive to it, and start to explore where our strong, human response to linguistic differences may come from.

Uncontrollable Attitudes and How We Process Them

A large part of the reason we have dialects, different speech registers, and rafts of new words brought into the language by teenagers eager to forge their own language space is that language conveys much about our attitudes in indirect ways. We will see that broad concerns are mapped onto linguistically precise differences. Pronunciation, vocabulary, and intonation can deliver a speaker's *attitude* about what he says, at the same time his words convey his meaning. It is quite astonishing that we can also process attitude and meaning in parallel—indeed, our sense of a person's attitude often crystallizes before the content of a sentence does. Meaning and attitude seem woven together like braided hair—how do we pull them apart?

The features that convey attitude can be extremely subtle. Even just a slight shift toward an ironic tone can make a sentence imply its opposite. Or the opposite of irony: an over-earnest denial can lead the hearer to quite a different view. Different listeners may well have drawn different conclusions when Richard Nixon said, "I am not a crook," or George W. Bush said, "We do not torture."

To return to the machine metaphor that motivates science: some formula, which crosses all the domains of mind and sensation, allows us to form instant opinions about people, their motives, their danger or appeal, within a few milliseconds of hearing them speak. It does not take half an hour to decide that someone made a menacing remark. It happens simultaneously with decoding the grammar. Do we unpack the personality woven into sentences the same way we unpack a compound noun? That is a question for the future; but the comparable speed of the two operations tells us they may share something—that both our emotion generator and our sentence analyzer may have a similar machine behind them. (This is not the last word on emotion. We will discuss a different order of thinking—slow thought—when we consider human nature in chapter 15.)

Impressions of Identity

The way we speak is in some sense part of our *identity*, but not always under our conscious control. Though people can often code-switch and use different dialects, command is sometimes imperfect. For example, a friend from Scotland traveled back there on his honeymoon, and his wife said that she suddenly couldn't understand him because his brogue reappeared dramatically, though he wasn't really aware of it. At the 2000 Democratic National Convention, Jesse Jackson sought to start a chant, as he often does—but this one failed. He called, "Stay out the Bushes," and the audience started to repeat but then faltered. Why? Because he was using an African-American English locution, *out* + noun phrase, where Mainstream American English (for mysterious reasons) uses *out of* + noun phrase (*stay out of the bushes*). The Mainstream American English speakers in the audience apparently found the phrase somehow odd or hard to grasp without its preposition. Jackson's language contains African-American English features—even when he is addressing Mainstream American English–speaking audiences—of which he is unaware. Those features are also, quite possibly, a real part of his attraction to other constituencies.

From the way a person says what she says, we also make immediate *judgments* about identity. We let ourselves generate an impression of *who* a person is before we hear *what* she says. A Southern drawl (or just a *y'all*), a Brooklyn *dese* or *dose*, a Boston *pahk the cah* lead to instant geographic, intellectual, class, and political assumptions. These can be amazingly sharp and subtle. In Boston, there are two forms of *r*-lessness, heard in two ways of saying *Harvard*: *Hahvid* and *Haavid*. The first is upper class and the second is decidedly lower class. A person from elsewhere in the country may not hear or notice the difference, but those who live in Boston will immediately detect it.

Stories about dialect can be amusing and make for lively anecdotes. For example, during a U.S. Senate debate over a bill on sexual harassment, it was noticeable that those for it said *ha-RASS-ment* and those against said *HAR-assment*. A friend asked his fiancée from the West to start saying *awnt* rather than *ant* for *aunt* before they got married because the *ant* pronunciation bothered him, and his bride was sure to be greeting his aunt frequently at the wedding. And so on.

Yet the fact is that our reactions to people's different ways of speaking —the view we construct of their identity—can deeply affect and even threaten their lives. The implications of some anecdotes can be quite profound.

Consider social class. One linguist friend from the South told me this story. When he was a child, he came home one day and said something about "CEment." His father responded, "We're moving North, I can't have my children talking that way: it's 'ceMENT.'" Likewise, merely whether we hear a person say *UMbrella* or *umBRELla* can cause us to instantly pigeonhole her one place or another along a social continuum. Grammar can instantly enforce or deny social stratification: among the many customs thrown into disarray during the social revolution of the 1960s, the distinction surrounding formal and informal pronouns gave way to universal informality on European campuses (in France, everyone was *tu* instead of *vous*); but now customs have changed again, in part, leaving students and professors uncertain about how to address one another.

In World War II, the U.S. Army used linguistic devices to determine the political involvement of chemists. The chemists were asked to read the word *unionized*. If they said "Un-ionized," they were politically acceptable. If they said "Unionized" (belonging to a union), the Army gave them a second look.

A relative of mine said his life was saved by his northern German dialect. He was in a concentration camp called Theresienstadt in Czechoslovakia. He and a colleague from southern Germany—both chemists with advanced degrees—were assigned to make disinfectants. On a visit to the camp, Adolf Eichmann spoke to them about sanitary conditions. My relative's southern partner was quickly sent to his death, but Eichmann addressed my relative as "Herr Doktor" and kept him alive simply, he believes, because of his more acceptable northern dialect.

Child Attitudes

Children are busy acquiring attitudes as well as words, and they seem to grasp aspects of language variation early on. For instance, they quickly sense that we talk differently to strangers than to our families. If they are bilingual, they know to use one language at home—but once they are out the door, the other language comes out. Children rapidly become aware of dialect differences too. Those who tape children have found that African-American English is instantly more prevalent when adults who don't speak African-American English—or even just authority figures—leave the room. Even three-year-olds can code-switch.[3]

And children learn that there are different styles appropriate to different ages. I once overheard two five-year-old girls talking about playing house. One said, "Do you want to be the one-year-old or the two-year-old?" The other asked, "What's the difference?" The first answered, "If you are one, you just say 'ga, ga, ga,' but if you are two, you say 'me want.'"

Children are sensitive to minute variations in the weight of words (though they may be off target now and then). For instance, even fairly young children can recognize ironic intonation. An undergraduate did an informal experiment in which she asked children to choose which of two characters really didn't like oatmeal. One character said, "I like oatmeal," and the other said, with heavy irony, "Oh, I just LOVE oatmeal." She found that five-year-olds easily identified the ironic intonation as implying the opposite of the meaning of the actual words in the sentence.[4] One could try the experiment informally with younger children and see how they respond. Knowing how early children are sensitive to ironic intonation would be useful information for parents because we often speak to each other and to children with a tone that reverses the meaning of our words. Children may, or may not, understand.

Do children make real social distinctions on the basis of language? A parent from the South, living in the North, is alarmed because her four-year-old won't say "y'all" though it is dear to her Southern culture. Why? *Y'all* actually fills a gap in Mainstream American English, which fails to distinguish, as other languages do, between generic (*you* = one) and specific (*y'all* = you specifically). "Can you go to the moon?"—a generic question—might easily be answered "Yes," but "Can y'all go to the moon?" is quite a different question, asking about you personally. Since *y'all* has a unique and useful role in grammatical terms, the child must be resisting using it for social reasons.

In sum, as soon as children begin to make social distinctions, those distinctions will find reflections in their use of language and their response to the language of others.

Signals of Informality

There is a whole community of scholars who study when people use formal or informal modes of address.[5] The variation can be very subtle. Mountain climbers will use only informal modes of address above a certain altitude, but will return to formal modes when they descend again. Prostitutes use informal language just before and during their activities, but return to formal modes of address afterward. The use of informality itself has changed over time. In the nineteenth century, informal language was used primarily by people at superior social levels to address people at inferior social levels: a landowner addressed his peasants with informal language but might address his wife with formal language as a mark of respect. In modern times, the situation is reversed: informality represents equality and intimacy.

In general, informal speech often becomes "acceptable" over time. Were we all to speak to our families the way Jane Austen's characters speak to each other, we would feel pretty phony. Surprisingly strong distinctions can arise from one generation to the next. All three of the following expressions are acceptable in written English today:

Who did you talk to?
Whom did you talk to?
To whom did you talk?

Fifty years ago, *whom* was preferred and *who* was informal. Today, *who* is normal, *whom* feels slightly pompous, and *to whom* borders on the archaic.

How do children enter this ever-changing pool of attitudes? They may not grasp irony at the age of three, but they will be sensitive to differences in informal and formal speech. Expressions like *aw c'mon, gimme, just 'cuz* all convey strong feelings via their informal phonology. The ways overtones and undertones in our pronunciation carry all sorts of ineffable feelings and the way they are bound to phonological rules must have large innate components as well. Some of it works across species: we know when an animal is threatening or in pain. The emotion carried by language is very real for children, though difficult for us to describe because we have little skill in formulating the curves of feeling carried by sounds.

One generalization seems plausible: informality is linked to phonological contraction. That is, dropping vowels or consonants implies a commonality of feeling and experience. Phonological ellipsis is much like the syntactic ellipsis we discussed in chapter 7. Sounds can be dropped because we know how to resurrect them. In a sense, the shared, silent resurrection creates moments of community.

Nevertheless, languages vary along these dimensions as well. Dropping subjects is a sign of informality in English: *Wanna go to the movies?* lacks *do you*, and *Seems OK to me* lacks *it*. These are informal expressions in English. In Spanish, however, one can drop subjects without the same sense of informality. Dropped subjects are a part of the grammar in a more formal way (to which we return in chapter 10). A child must then discriminate what is a normal part of the grammar and what is not. As we will see, the informal grammar may, in a sense, derive from an entirely different language family.

If informality is marked by deletions, and informal speech gradually becomes normal, how does language ever become richly structured? Every generation for centuries has claimed that language is declining. But it can't decline forever; it must be enriched somehow. The reason we cannot see how language is enriched is that the sources of enrichment are often subject to prejudice. For instance, teenagers not only introduce new words but also often lead the way in allowing grammatical changes to enter the language, though it is a slow process. A case in point is the preposition *like*, which is on its way to becoming a conjunction as well (*Like I really want to go to the movies*). Although it may clang in the ears of elders, it is really a form of innovation that future generations will be quite unbothered by.[6]

African-American English (Ebonics)

It is safe to say that every grammar or dialect contains elegant subtleties of its own that anthropologists and linguists delight to discover. All languages spawn dialects—they are often the most vital part of language—and dialects sometimes resemble a child's language. The resemblance is deceptive. A classic and at times tragic case is African-American English, which is frequently labeled "broken" or "immature" English. Children are made to feel ashamed of it, teachers refuse to tolerate it in class, school administrators use it as a basis for sending (sometimes) bright children into Special Education classrooms from which they never emerge.

In the fall of 1996, African-American English captured national attention more dramatically than any other linguistic topic in recent memory, when the school board in Oakland, California, sought to classify African-American English as a distinct language and African-American English–speaking students as bilingual (a classification that would have brought funding for special programs in its wake). (This was the so-called Ebonics controversy.) The public response was largely to challenge the legitimacy of the African-American dialect altogether. The Linguistic Society of America then issued a special statement defending the legitimacy of *all* grammars in the strongest terms.[7] As the prominent sociolinguist Walt Wolfram put it, doubts that African-American English is a normal grammar should have no more legitimacy than the Flat Earth Society's doubts that the earth is round.[8]

The incident recounted earlier about the 2000 Democratic National Convention briefly illustrates the parity of dialects and standard languages. In the chant "Stay out the Bushes," Jesse Jackson used an African-American English locution, *out* + noun phrase, where Mainstream American English uses *out of* + noun phrase (*stay out of the bushes*). The Mainstream American English speakers in the audience apparently found the phrase somehow odd or hard to grasp without its preposition. But notice that Mainstream American English itself drops prepositions in compounds (*broom-swept*, not **with-broom-swept*) and in dialogue (*Where did you go? New York*—but not **I went New York*). The dialect uses the same principle as the standard language, but in a different place—a theme we will explore at greater length in chapter 11.

In chapter 10, we will examine the idea that all speakers are bilingual. That is, when we look closely, we see that all of us have multiple grammars. This should provide direct intellectual underpinning for the position taken by the Oakland School Board.

Still, gut-level responses to language, born of social prejudice, remain turbulent. Arguments over Ebonics seem analogous to the demonstrations held outside art museums early in the twentieth century when Picasso-like modern art was exhibited in Chicago. Work in sociolinguistics does not really explain the sheer magnitude of emotion that language elicits. Some people feel that civilization itself is threatened if standard grammar is not upheld. The presence of "Black English" in schools, on TV, and in pop songs feels to some people as though the legitimacy of African-American English grammar is being forced down the nation's throat and strangling "proper" English. They feel that something culturally vital is lost if their language changes and indeed, as we have seen, evolution in language does involve loss as well as gain. As with modern art, a change in attitudes will probably come slowly.

Conclusion

In this chapter, I have sought to cast the net wide before pulling it tight again. We have looked briefly through the lens of social distinctions. These general mental factors loom large in our motivation and understanding of language, but a grammatical engine underlies them; broad concerns are mapped onto linguistically precise differences (such as vowel reduction, dropping subjects, word choice).

In chapter 10, we will explore the idea that all speakers have multiple grammars, which may come from different language families. Our strong response to dialect comes from our subconscious awareness that quite different, even alien, principles underlie the special properties of dialect. To understand this claim, we need first to look more closely at how grammars vary. In chapter 11, we will see, for instance, that a subpart of the African-American English verbal system builds upon the concept of events whereas Mainstream American English builds upon the concept of time. Differences like this can explain why dialects can feel both strange and exotically interesting at once.

10 Are We All Bilingual?

We have acknowledged the social side of grammar, but we remain far from explaining why grammar exerts such emotional force in our response to other people. We need a deeper understanding of how grammars vary before we can see that our response to dialects has something to do with how grammars choose between opposing principles.

So far, our discussion has been strewn with the subtle challenges of English (where can English speakers do Merge? what rules are recursive?). Those challenges are each just a half step away from Universal Grammar and innate knowledge. We have asked how this universal or that (compounds, questions, ellipses) is reflected in English. We have left to the side all the real differences among languages and dialects. What does the child do when he has to make choices: is it English or Swahili or French or German that I am learning? A critical decision the child has to (of course, unconsciously) make in figuring out whether a particular construction is part of English is whether it obeys an automatic rule (is open to recursion) or whether it is an exception linked to specific words.

My answer goes against the grain again: I will argue that it involves two phenomena that have a contradictory flavor. First, I will claim that somewhere inside English we can find the seeds of most other grammars. Second, I will claim that those hints of other grammars are not minor deviations, but may reflect different *organizing principles*, all available in Universal Grammar.

Here's a taste of the two arguments. When John F. Kennedy said,

"Ask not what your country can do for you,"

it had quite a different force than if he had said,

"Don't ask what your country can do for you."

He returned to the Germanic roots of English, now left far behind—the time when English could put the verb in front of a negative (*ask not*) or even first in a question, as in Shakespeare:

Say you so?

JFK's locution, reaching back to Shakespeare, may have unconsciously symbolized the fact that our language, like our culture, carries its history with it. Grammars gain and lose new organizing principles and we feel the gain and loss, though unconscious of their origin. Traditional grammarians err when they think that the loss of the subjunctive in English (*If I was you* instead of *If I were you*) means the loss of a whole frame of mind. The distinction returns elsewhere in the language. But they are right in thinking that the grammar could be shifting at a deep level. We will work our way toward a rudimentary explanation of how the deeper shifts work and how dialect is often the leading edge of change.

When we see that one language, English, contains hints of other grammars, we must add another layer to the acquisition conundrum: how do children decide that English is essentially English and not, for instance, Spanish, if pieces of Spanish pop up here and there? The answer is that rules from another language apply to just a few words (usually verbs). The core language has rules that apply to all words in a category (nouns, verbs, and so on).

Is Grammatical Consistency Possible?

Although we imagine that Mainstream American English is consistent and dialects are inconsistent, it is just as often the reverse (and this is true of other languages and their dialects as well). The grammar we take to be "standard" is chock-full of odd vagaries and inconsistencies. They become the basis of severe prejudice, cocktail party conversation, and spelling bees. Although individuals may bounce between delight, exasperation, and ridicule when confronted with such exceptionality, a sober look once again reveals the presence of intricate abstract principles.

An important question is, why do inconsistent "exceptions" survive? It is easy to be blind to what keeps those "exceptions" stable. One might think the rules of grammar would uniformly and rapidly drown out the exceptions. Take the rule for past tense in English: add *-d/-ed*. Early in language learning, most English-speaking children apply the rule to all verbs. If children say *standed*, for instance, what keeps *stood* alive in the language, even inside a word like *understood* whose meaning has drifted from its origins?

One answer (currently being investigated by a number of scholars) is that grammars are inherently inconsistent because they contain a variety of subgrammars; so, for example, English has subgrammars that resemble German, Spanish, or Chinese. Seeming "exceptions" involve rules borrowed from other grammars.

Ironically, the most powerful abstractions in language (transformation, movement, quantification) invite the creation of subgrammars—for instance, the German form of verb movement embedded in a corner of English grammar—that are limited in domain but just as natural a part of Universal Grammar as the dominant form. In physics, the notion of a common deep abstraction about motion—the presence of gravity—at once shows that all movement belongs to a common theory and that subtle factors produce 1,000-fold variation in examples of movement. Grammar is a less extreme case. All the variation, the odd wrinkles we find, reflect the same universals.

Multiple Grammars inside Vocabulary

We all have an intuition about our internal multiple grammars from vocabulary. English, for instance, has Anglo-Saxon, Latinate, and Greek words and derivational rules to accompany them (such as rules that specify which suffixes can attach to which adjectives to form nouns). Confusion arises because the divisions among vocabularies are not clean. Janet Randall did a splendid study of English speakers' intuitions about the Latinate and Anglo-Saxon portions of their vocabulary.[1] For a Latinate adjective like

civil

adults and children accepted two nouns:

civility, civilness

The same was true for other Latinate adjectives:

trivial, triviality, trivialness
fertile, fertility, fertileness

However, for Anglo-Saxon adjectives, the adults and children accepted only the noun ending in -*ness*:

evil, *evility, evilness

The same pattern holds with the suffixes -*er* and -*ian/-ion/-al*. The (primarily) Old English suffix -*er* can apply to Latinate words, but the Latinate suffixes -*ian/-ion/-al* cannot apply to Anglo-Saxon words:

Latinate stems + *-er* or *-ian/-al/-ion*
beauty, beautifier, beautician
propose, proposer, proposal
pretend, pretender, pretension

Anglo-Saxon stems + *-er* or *-ian/-al/-ion*
hit, hitter, *hittian
win, winner, *winnal
lend, lender, *lension

Why the asymmetry? English speakers really have two grammatical systems. One has "generalized"; the other has not, and remains restricted to its (Latin) origins. Amazingly, without instruction, five-year-old children have internalized two vocabulary systems, identified their affixes, and labeled one "general" (*-ness*) and the other "restricted" (*-ity*). The children who took part in Randall's study knew that *evility is impossible, but that both *evilness* and *civilness* are acceptable, though it is unlikely that they had heard either. So English contains rules that apply to Latinate words and rules that apply to Anglo-Saxon words (that is, rules that honor multiple grammars), plus other rules that cross over and see no difference between Latin and Anglo-Saxon. A kind of deep inconsistency is present—unless, of course, we see ourselves as fundamentally bilingual, in the sense of having a major grammar and several minor grammars (or subgrammars). An Anglo-Saxon affix from the major system (like *-er* or *-ness*) can be adopted into the minor Latinate system. But there is an asymmetry: no Latinate affix is adopted into the major system. The largely unconscious task for the child then is to find evidence that determines which is major and which is minor—is there a minor form of English inside German or a minor form of German inside English?

Multiple Grammars inside Syntax

Such claims move beyond common sense when we start looking at syntax. The idea of multiple grammars or universal bilingualism—a view that Charles Yang, Anthony Kroch, and I have been exploring recently in acquisition and historical studies—is a theoretical claim whose consequences overturn linguists' usual perspectives.[2] The arguments below are quite compressed. My goal is to give you a taste of the data and arguments, not to thoroughly explain them—that is, to enable you to appreciate the ideas, even if the refined distinctions involved make some of the data hard to swallow.

A Case Study: German inside English

Are there really pieces of German, Italian, Chinese, and so on, lodged in corners of English? Consider these odd but perfectly English constructions:

"Nothing," said Bill.
Into the hall scampered the children.
It matters not what you do.

The last form involves a rule of German:

Move the main verb to second position in all main clauses.

In real German, a wider array of cases are possible, all disallowed in English. Translated, examples of some of these might read like this:

Meat ate Bill.
There sings John.
At home cooks Fred.

These sentences seem somewhat off-base in English because the verb-second rule is only marginally a part of English grammar.

Expressions like *Matters not* (the German-like form where the main verb falls before *not*) vary with more typical English expressions like *It doesn't matter* (where English speakers put an auxiliary verb before *not* or *n't*). In both languages, some verb must appear before the negative in these sentences. German moves the main verb to that position, while English sticks in a *do*. When someone says, "Matters not," he just chose German—that is, he reached into the German subgrammar inside English.

Every language utilizes the array of Universal Grammar options in a unique way. That is why linguistics professors like the late Ken Hale of MIT have appealed to the U.S. Congress to help save dying languages. Just as biodiversity is important among plants and animals, because crucial biological discoveries may rest on having each remaining genetic combination available for study, so the existence of all the world's remaining languages is crucial because we learn about Universal Grammar from the way each language realigns the constellation of grammatical operations. Could a language link click sounds or umlaut (the phonological fronting that changes *u* to *ü* in German, for instance) to quantification? If African click languages or languages using umlaut were to disappear, we might not be able to ask.

Our social ears have to be open, too. Ask anyone and they will say *matters not* sounds more serious than *it doesn't matter*. Maybe that is why it shows up in headlines ("Why Audiogalaxy Case Matters Not") and ads ("Size

Matters Not: Star Wars Miniatures").[3] This feeling is not inherent to the construction itself; rather, it attaches to the construction's marginal status within our larger grammar, marginal and older constructions often being linked to stronger emotions. If you say both "It just isn't so" and "It just ain't so" to speakers of Mainstream American English and ask which form is more sincere and deeply felt, most likely they will take the momentary use of dialect (*ain't*) as a sign of seriousness. An Arizona politician shifted dialects to achieve just this effect: "We must not permit the State of California to deplete the water supply of the State of Arizona. Ain't no way we're gonna give 'em that water."[4] Within the African-American English dialect itself, where *ain't* is used more regularly, this pragmatic difference may not be present.

Why Informality Is Grammatically Changeable

Missing Subjects   The fact that some languages omit subjects more readily may make them feel "more informal" to outsiders. In those languages, however, speakers may choose different avenues into informality because subject deletion is just normal. There are lots of ways to be informal, from a lighter tone to swearing. For some people, swearing is a sign of informality, trust and intimacy, while others perceive it as gross and repulsive. These social responses to grammatical choices are deep within us, and we cannot turn them off with a small dose of anthropological awareness.

Speakers of Spanish and Italian (and Chinese, German, and other languages) drop subjects where English requires them. To use Spanish as our example:

Que pasó a Juan?—Se fue.
[What happened to John?—Went.]

Inflection in Spanish provides information about person, gender, and number, so it has been suggested that the subject is really built into the inflection on the verb. It seems that the subject is just unnecessary. Though this explanation has some hope within grammatical theory, it does not explain the pattern of exceptions in English, where a certain set of verbs does allow the subject position to be empty:

Seemed pretty as a picture.[5]
Looks nice out, doesn't it?
Rained today.
Doesn't matter who wins.
Never happens that John is late.

The particular verbs that allow missing subjects are just the ones that have what we can call an "empty subject," *it*: *It rained today, It looks nice out today, doesn't it?, It doesn't matter who wins.* There is nothing that the *it* really refers to. It just fills up the subject position when we mean something very general.

Sometimes *I* subjects disappear under what can be called "diary drop":

June 21: went to the store, bought bread, fell asleep early

But this is limited to special circumstances (which the child must correctly perceive as special).

The depth of the grammatical difference between English and Spanish emerges sharply in subordinate clauses:

A: Where's John?
B: Went home.

A: Where's John?
B: *Everyone thinks ____ went home.

English absolutely requires the speaker to use *he* in the subordinate clause. The subject cannot be dropped. However, this is not the case in Spanish. The following sentence is perfectly good, though the subordinate clause has no overt subject:

Todo el mundo piensa que ____ es amable.
[Everyone thinks ____ is nice.]

Its counterpart with overt subject in the subordinate clause is fine as well:

Todo el mundo piensa que *el* es amable.
[Everyone thinks *he* is nice.]

We can see, then, that the grammars of English and Spanish overlap. For a specified set of verbs, English allows missing subjects as if it were Spanish. But the grammatical overlap does not extend to subordinate clauses. Languages of the world consistently allow more variation in the main (top) clause than in subordinate (lower) clauses, but linguists have not yet grasped the abstract principle that explains this fact naturally.

English differs from Spanish in its semantics as well. The meaning of

Everyone thinks he is smart.

is ambiguous in English. It can mean either "Everyone thinks that he himself is smart" or "Everyone thinks that some other 'he' is smart." In Spanish, the missing subject is linked to the quantifier, and only the "he himself" reading is available. Schematically (and using English words):

Everyone thinks ____ is smart =
Everyone$_x$ thinks [empty]$_x$ is smart

The identical subscripts mean the same person is involved. In other words, in Spanish a missing subject in the subordinate clause is always understood to be the same as the subject of the main clause; an overt subject is always understood to refer to a different person or people. Thus, Spanish has an explicit syntactic difference for something that is ambiguous in English because the empty subject in the subordinate clause gives a unique reading unavailable in English. One consequence is that a common intuition is correct: grammars vary in their precision of expression (which is far different from the common but mistaken view that "concept Y cannot be expressed in language X").

Missing Objects: Presupposed Participants One might think that we use context—our environment—in interpreting sentences whenever it is handy, as the discussion of ellipsis in chapter 7 strongly implies. Actually, though, languages vary on this dimension as well. Asian languages allow context sensitivity of a sort that English does not. One linguist has dubbed the difference "hot versus cool languages," where the "hot" ones presuppose context, as though speaker and hearer both have their fingers and eyes on exactly the same set of objects, while the cool ones require extra explicit reference.[6]

There are constructions where English ignores context as a potential communication crutch, but Asian languages use it. I became aware of this when a visiting Asian student handed me a gift, saying,

"Let me give you."

An English speaker has to say,

"Let me give you this,"

even though, since the speaker has the gift in hand, the pragmatics make the meaning totally clear.

Why do we have to include *this*? In other situations, it is superfluous. For instance, imagine a stalled car. People are lined up behind it, and someone says,

"OK, everybody push!"

We find that we have no sense of ungrammaticality here—no need for an extra *this*. So why is the object obligatory after *give* but not after *push*?

This is a deep grammatical question that cannot be answered just by looking at context. A clue comes from the idea that it is in true double object constructions that the object is required. We say, "I handed Bill this," and not "*I handed Bill." The single object/double object grammatical contrast is extremely intricate in English, and pursuing it would lead us away from the central point. Nonetheless, there is evidence suggesting that some English dialects can leave out the indirect object as if they were Chinese.[7]

If context is just overwhelmingly obvious, then in even narrower corners of English we might find a true Chinese grammar. Suppose one person said,

"I'm looking for my shoes,"

and another replied,

"I'll look too."

Ellipsis rules would tell us what is missing. However, it is interesting that this version is impossible:

*I'll look for too.

The transitive preposition does not allow its object to be missing. That is a grammatical fact of English. All these expressions are impossible with a missing verbal object no matter how clear the corresponding physical object is in context:

*John stood next to.
*Bill looked at.
*Mary stepped on.
*Michael took the bike from.
*John rolled the ball under.

Nonetheless, one day I caught myself saying to a child under a blanket,

"Can I put my feet under, too?,"

and the situation was so well defined that no object was required, despite the transitive preposition. The question did not feel ungrammatical, like *Can I look for too? Here we see the language momentarily departing from its grammar—or, as I suggest, we see an entirely different grammatical gestalt emerge: a tiny piece of "Chinese." It is the syntactic version of suddenly saying the French words *Bon voyage* inside an English sentence. And it fits the core sense of a "hot context," where speakers presuppose more context than speakers of "cool" languages do. (The title of the TV show *Six Feet Under* chooses an implied object too. Maybe the producers enhance the show's appeal by tapping into another grammar type.)

We have looked at two corners of English where pieces of other languages may be hidden: missing subjects and missing objects. English, Spanish, and Chinese each have different requirements about expressing subjects and objects, yet we find elements of the Spanish and Chinese systems within English. Now let us apply the same sort of analysis to verbs.

Deep Ideas: Do Grammars Carry Worldviews?

Event and Environment   We will now look at some grand metaphors, and I will give them a stronger twist than my colleagues might:

Grammars choose either *environment* or *event* as a descriptive axis.

A Chinese-style grammar focuses on environment, while Native American–style languages focus on events. Event reference, in turn, can focus on *time* (past, present) or the *nature* of the event (progressive, result), often capturing the same situation with slightly different semantics.[8]

We will see that African-American English can project a gestalt for events with a larger range of distinctions than Mainstream American English because it engages a further grammar type. Again, it is the surface of language I am speaking of; I am not making any claim about some deeper mental reality. I am not saying that, instant by instant, different cultures represent events or attitudes with fundamentally different ingredients. They just use different hooks to hang their speakers' perceptions on, to use for communication, which can in turn create a different coloration in each situation.

The same view holds for the riches of vocabulary. The word *charming* came into English from French. The fact that English did not previously have the word *charming* does not mean that there were no charming English-speaking people or that one English-speaking person could not think that another was charming. English speakers just did not have a label for the thought. (And, who knows, maybe the marvelous *I/thou* poetry was created to find a way to say that someone is charming. It might be that English love poetry was partly motivated by the loss of *wit*, the intimate form for *we* (while both formal and informal *you* remained): people wrote whole poems to capture what a single word used to capture. Thus, the absence of certain grammatical elements may promote poetry.)

A critic might rightfully retort, "But vocabulary differentiation must reflect cultural preferences." It is quite true that wherever we differentiate kinds, we have to differentiate words (the steel industry, for instance, has many words for types of steel). Nevertheless, the cultural power of vocabulary does not tell us how culture connects to grammar itself.

Time Lines and Event Types   As noted above, languages using the "event" descriptive axis can focus on *time* or the *structure of the event*. Time systems articulate these concepts:

Time
- past (*ate*)
- imperfect (*was running*)
- future (*will do*)
- past perfect (*had done*)
- future perfect (*will have done*)
- hypothetical, or subjunctive (*might*)

Event systems capture these properties:[9]

Nature of events
- inceptive (beginning)
- goal-oriented
- resultative
- progressive
- iterative (repeated)
- habitual
- stative (in a state)

Languages often choose one system or the other, but usually they have a subsystem that allows a combination of them or has explicit lexical pointers. English has all three: the time system, the event system, and pointers. For instance, it has a lexical particle *up*, a pointer that captures result or "completiveness":

John ate the cake.
John ate the cake up.

The *up* does the work. Children grasp this quickly, though one can hardly see any actual "upness" in the meaning that gets conveyed.[10]

We will discuss progressive, resultative, and habitual modes when we come to African-American English. First, let us look at Mainstream American English—which, as we will see, is actually an odd language.

A phrase like

the painted house

describes an object and entails a completed event. The sentence

The house was painted.

describes an action and locates it in the past. Often the two locutions are close enough that an editor might substitute one for the other:

He thought about the house that was painted.
He thought about the painted house.

If we embed them into the right context, two styles of perception emerge:

I saw the painted house.
I saw the house painted.

In one case, the hearer imagines a timeless object; in the other case, an action over time.

Michiko Terada investigated at what age children know the difference between result (*painted house*) and event (*house painted*).[11] She showed children two pictures, one of a gray house being painted white and one of a white house being painted gray:

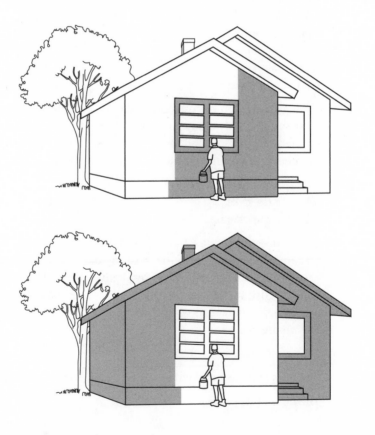

She asked the children to say which picture fit each of these statements:

Someone is painting a house gray.
Someone is painting a gray house.

She found that three-year-old children already grasped that *painting a house gray* refers to an action, while *a gray house* refers to an an object.

Exploration 10.1
Action or result?
(adjectives before
and after the noun)

You can easily explore this difference informally with a child. You will need three boxes: one turned-over box and two boxes full of, let's say, toys. First, show the child the three boxes and then turn over one of the full ones.

a. Point at the box that was turned over to begin with, and ask,
   "Did you see this box turned over?"

b. Point at the box that you turned over in front of the child, and ask,
   "Did you see this box turned over?"

c. Point at each turned-over box, saying for each one,
   "Can you see this turned-over box?"

If the child understands the difference, she will answer "No" to the first question, "Yes" to the second, and "Yes" in both cases to the third. (You can continue the game with any type of container—bottles, cans, buckets, and so on.)

Languages have an astonishing variety of ways of representing time perspectives and event perspectives. We will just touch the edge of this variety in capturing English dialects in the next chapter.

Disappearing Present Tense   In English, time structure and what I have dubbed event structure (which is traditionally called "aspectual structure") have to work together. It seems that Mainstream American English is losing its tense system. There is no semantic present tense in the syntactic present tense—a fact that is very difficult to convey to adults learning English as a second language. Grammatical "present tense" actually fails to anchor the verb in time. A sentence like

Mary eats hotdogs.

refers to the fact that she generally eats hotdogs; it does not say that she is eating a hotdog right now. The English "present tense" is a form that refers to a person's characteristic activities across times or outside of time (in which case it is called a *generic*) or as a property of that person. (Each of these options actually invokes a different semantic theory.) It cannot be used to point at *now*. If I come into a house looking for John and ask,

"What's up with John right this minute?,"

and you answer,

"He sings songs,"

your answer is inadequate as a source of information about what John is doing right now. If *now* is what you want to communicate, you have to say,

"He is singing songs."

This is not true for many languages, like German, where the counterpart of *He works* can mean "He is working."

The complex English structure consisting of a form of *be* + a main verb + *-ing* (*is running*) really draws together the tense (time) and aspectual (event) systems to capture indirectly what other languages capture directly. Its mongrel quality makes it perplexingly difficult for second language learners to grasp, though first language learners have no trouble (a fact linguists cannot yet explain). As far as I know, English-speaking children never mistakenly use forms like *John sings songs* to answer questions like *What's up with John right this minute?* It would be part of parental lore if they did.

Exploration 10.2
Inside and outside of time
(progressive versus generic)

There are several ways to explore generic tense with children. The simplest way is to casually ask a question like

"What is Mom up to?"

Does the child answer with "She is reading" or "She reads"?

Toys offer many opportunities here. Holding a (silent) doll that has the ability to talk, ask,

"Does it talk?"
"Is it talking?"

Or point to a bike in the garage and ask,

"Does it go fast?"
"Is it going fast?"

A gathering of vegetarians and nonvegetarians at a vegetarian dinner would give the opportunity to ask,

"Who eats meat?"
"Who is eating meat?"

Time for a digression on the confusing surface of grammar. You may have noticed cases here where the surface of language provides a puzzle. If I refer to *a talking bear*, it may not be talking right this minute. That might seem to tell the child that *-ing* does not mean "ongoing." The seeming contradiction—that *-ing* conveys "ongoingness" in some situations but not others—should be confusing to the child until he sees that another concept has applied from Universal Grammar: unmodified adjectives describe a timeless property. In English, *verb + ing* is an adjective when inside a noun phrase; therefore, "ongoingness" is canceled in cases like *a talking bear*. The distinction is clear in these two sentences:[12]

Can you see the talking bear?
Can you see the bear talking?

After the noun, *talking* is still a verb linked to time. Inside the noun phrase, it is outside of time.

If a child understands this distinction, she has a foothold on both the time system and the event system. She can also see how a semantic property (ongoingness) can be blocked, or rendered optional, when one form (verb: *talk*) is turned into another (adjective: *talking*) and stuck inside a third (noun phrase: *the talking bear*).

But why is English being so indirect? Why does it require a tense marker and a progressive just to refer to the present (*John is running*)? That is a deep question to which linguists do not yet have a genuine answer. However, some clues are piling up. Suppose Universal Grammar has a dynamic principle (not yet understood) that makes event structure emerge in a language when time structure becomes obscure. Then the progressive (*is + -ing*, illustrating with third person) can be seen as a kind of transitional expression: it combines the *generic* with the *progressive aspect* to achieve the equivalent of present tense. It is a combination of time structure (present *-s*) and event structure (progressive *-ing*). But now we have taken a truly counterintuitive step: proposing that two kinds of grammar combine in one sentence!

Again, I expect this to be a startling conclusion, one that may engender immediate resistance. It is surely unorthodox, but most surprising claims—like the idea that gravity affects big and small objects equally—have a flimsy and contradictory quality. The way to evaluate ideas is to use them and see what work they can do for us.

Actually, we have already found the multiple grammars concept a helpful route to explanation. Recall that we found it useful in chapter 7 to think that children may use English grammar to interpret the first half of a sentence like

The girl pushed her car and the boy did too.

= The girl pushed her car and the boy did too [push car]   (*not* [push his car])

and a Spanish- or Chinese-style grammar to interpret the second, elliptical half. Future research may reveal many more cases like this.

Microscopic Semantics

When I was a child, someone told me that pork could have worms in it that could get into people's insides and live there. The news threatened my view of biological integrity to the point that I had nightmares. But the view is one we need to accept. A professor of biology told me that more of the human body is composed of parasites and bacteria than is composed of our own organs. Likewise, "English" grammar has pieces of other grammar-types inside it. For those among us who view English with classical senti-mentality, all dialects feel like alien organisms. This is partly why there is a visceral antagonism among some Mainstream American English speakers toward the use of English dialects like African-American English, though the same forms used in the dialects are quite natural in other languages.

Yet for those who see grammars from a formal perspective, the same principles are always at work, no matter how many grammars cluster under the umbrella of a single language. The grammar amalgam creates a kind of beauty of heterogeneity in language.

But are these incredibly subtle differences real at all? How can something inside one language be attributed to two different grammars? In English, the time/event meaning differences in sentences like *He thought about the painted house/He thought about the house that was painted* are evanescent—they seem to disappear when we concentrate. One feels, "Well, but the two sentences could have the same meaning," or "If I try, I can get both meanings for both sentences." Still, in other grammars the same distinc-tions are thunderingly loud.

These hints and thoughts in hand, let us now ask what a "dialect" is, and train our microscope on African-American English.

11 The Riches of African-American English

There is an essential logic to African-American English. I can at most provide an overview, but my goal, as usual, will be to articulate connections to Universal Grammar and to other languages, explore the challenges for the child, and discover the reasons for common prejudices. The topics range from familiar questions of negation (*I don't got none*) to less familiar issues regarding aspect (habitual *be*) and little-discussed interpretations of verbs.

I have warned that ideas have an instant impact upon us, with an obvious upside and often a hidden downside. The idea of African-American English itself contains a negative bias, which leads to my first caution: To talk of "African-American" English (or any other dialect) immediately creates a contrast and forces us to name the form of English that is viewed as the "main," nondialectal language. Often the name is *Standard American English* or *Mainstream American English*. But by using a term like *Mainstream American English*, we etch a fake image of a uniform grammar shared by Americans, which does not really exist. In fact, Mainstream American English and African-American English are both abstractions. In his book *The Word on the Street: Debunking the Myth of "Pure" Standard English*, John McWhorter sets straight the view that there is a single respected "standard" mode of English, plus some helter-skelter dialects.[1] Everyone speaks a helter-skelter dialect full of lexical and grammatical oddities with a local flavor. In order to proceed, we need these artificial abstractions, which give the impression of two separate entities. By warning that they *are only abstractions*, I can only hope that the harm done is limited.

How Is African-American English Not Different?

To speakers of both Mainstream American English (MAE) and African-American English (AAE), the difference between *John tall* and *John is tall* and the difference between *when a man help himself* and *when a man helps himself* may sound major. But with respect to these constructions, MAE and AAE are in fact evolving along the same path—they are just at different stages of the journey. This is what I will call the *progressive dimension* of the relation between MAE and AAE.

Deletion Is the End-State of Contraction

MAE has a rule of contraction that operates *within* a sentence:

John is tall. → John's tall.

It never occurs at the *end* of a sentence:

I know how tall John is. → *I know how tall John's.

AAE has exactly the same rule of contraction, but it effects *complete* contraction—that is, deletion. Thus, AAE speakers can say,

"John tall,"

where MAE speakers say,

"John's tall."

But note that the contexts where MAE contracts and AAE deletes are exactly the same. Deletion is possible within a sentence in AAE (*John tall*) but not at the end of a sentence:

I know how tall John is. → *I know how tall John.

Where MAE contracts, AAE deletes, and where MAE cannot contract, AAE cannot delete. The same rule applies in both cases—it is just that AAE extends the rule a little further than MAE.[2] This example—full deletion as opposed to partial deletion—captures what a typical dialect variation consists of: the same rule with slightly different conditions on its application.

Note that MAE-learning children sometimes delete *is*:

It big.
Toy here.

These forms look just like AAE forms and would be acceptable in AAE. But is the MAE-learning child's form truly identical to the AAE form? Linguists are not sure. It seems that MAE-speaking children delete the copula even when they are referring to times other than the present. In AAE, however, only the present tense form can delete. *Is* is deleted, but never *was*. So a sentence like

Johnny here.

can only mean "Johnny is here" in AAE, not "Johnny was here." This is a crucial restriction on possible meanings.

He Run: The End-State of Inflection Loss

A second prominent feature of AAE—lack of third person -*s*—again points toward a common evolution in MAE and AAE. Inflection is a major indicator of "correctness," and failing to inflect verbs according to the MAE system elicits shame, outrage, and indignation. If a person says, as Jesse Jackson did at the 1992 Democratic National Convention,

"when a man help himself"

instead of

"when a man helps himself,"

a major social gulf emerges (although as a "speech error," dropping of -*s* is common in all dialects).[3] In fact, John Baugh has demonstrated this prejudice by making telephone inquiries about apartments.[4] He found that if the person answering the call heard a dialect, the inquiry was often refused. So dialect details can have consequences: if you fail to add the -*s*, no apartment.

Why? It is not entirely clear why features like -*s* are seen as bellwether markers of education. If we look back at Old English, we see that verbs used to be highly inflected. To use the present tense of *dēman* "to judge" as an example:

Singular	1st person	dēm-e
	2nd person	dēm-est
	3rd person	dēm-eþ
Plural	1st, 2nd,	dēm-aþ
	3rd person	

Gradually, these person-number inflections have disappeared, until only one is left in MAE:

I deem	we deem
you deem	you deem
he, she, it deems	they deem

If we step back in history, then, the overwhelming fact is that MAE is impoverished with respect to its Germanic origins. Shakespeare could write,

Thou singest.

We would feel foolish adding an -*st* to a verb when talking to friends or family. There must have been a time when deleting -*st* was perceived as a mark of educational impoverishment, just as dropping third person -*s* is perceived today. Imagine refusing someone an apartment because he failed to add -*st* to a verb! ("Hast thou (you) an apartment available?")

In a sense, the third person singular -*s* is the lone remaining representative of an entire tense- and agreement-marking system. AAE is slightly ahead in the same process that MAE is undergoing. Likewise, we are losing touch with a complex system of tense differentiation, which allows the mind to dance around an event in a way that has special literary qualities. Consider:

John *must have been being revived* at just the moment Anne died.

Expressions like this, with five verbs in a row, suggest an elegance of temporal expression that could be lost if the time system is simplified, though it will still be possible to get the essence of the thought, since every language has other ways to get at any meaning. Perhaps we unconsciously see that final -*s* as representing an entire, but now dwindling, system of grammatical expression. It is as if the language were abandoning a whole network of connections. Maybe this is what lies in part behind the outsized and intellectually indefensible social response to dropping this little affix in AAE.

In reality, the network is already gone: where some languages mark number, gender, and person on their verbs, MAE barely marks person. Most verb forms carry no marking at all in present tense (*I run, you run, we run, they run*), with, I might add, no major loss of communication. And quite apart from the presence or absence of -*s*, even the present tense meaning of -*s* is disappearing. The restriction of its meaning to generic is the unmistakable clue that a deeper change beyond superficial morphology is involved. The loss of inflection *and* meaning is irretrievable and is part of the evolution of MAE itself; no AAE influence is needed. MAE speakers cannot by will alone rekindle the older grammar and make the expression *He sings* mean "He is singing." AAE represents the inevitable future.

Another Grammar inside African-American English with Event Structure

As noted in chapter 10, Universal Grammar seems to make several verbal systems available: systems oriented toward environment or events—and within events, toward time (tense) or the nature of event structures (so-called aspect). Another key to accepting the legitimacy of AAE lies in grasping that its verbal system is aspect-oriented, whereas the verbal system of MAE is tense-oriented—equal though different options within the universe of human language possibilities. I have argued that all grammars have subgrammars like dialects, and so the relation of AAE to MAE is perfectly normal.

What replaces the system of tense that is receding in AAE and now starting to recede in MAE? It appears that AAE is becoming one of the event structure grammars we looked at in chapter 10. Lisa Green and Michael Terry have begun to piece together the abstract system from a tradition of careful sociolinguistic work by William Labov, Walt Wolfram, Donald Winfred, and many others.[5] Linguists have a descriptive foothold, the outlines of a system, but much more remains to be uncovered.

One of the aspects that an event structure grammar articulates is *habitual*. And indeed, a classic fact about AAE is its use of habitual *be*:

He be playing baseball.

This use of *be* is often thought of as generic, but in fact, it refers to habituality over a set of real times and not possible times. Thus, an AAE speaker can say,

"He fights, but he don't be fighting,"

which means that he has the ability to fight, but does not do so often. The construction does have some tense properties, as shown by the fact that

*He be fighting yesterday.

is impossible in AAE. Nor can one use habitual *be* with verbs denoting states:

*He be knowing the answer.

Habituality requires agency and is to be distinguished from iterativity. AAE does not allow constructions like this one, which simply denotes an action that repeats frequently:

*The clock be ticking all day long.

Nonetheless, a second property of events that AAE expresses is *stativity*. Consider these sentences:

I did play baseball yesterday.
I done played baseball yesterday.

To speakers of MAE, they probably seem to be just variants expressing the same idea. But to speakers of AAE, there is a difference. A clue to their meaning lies in the tag questions that they allow:

I did play baseball yesterday, didn't I?
I done played baseball yesterday, ain't I?

The tag questions suggest that the event is being presented in a different manner in each case. The event system marks the situation as a state, not an action, Michael Terry argues,[6] which makes the contrast between these sentences like the difference we saw in chapter 10 between *The house was painted* and *the painted house*. MAE does not have a straightforward way to attribute a state to a person. Being in a state of having played baseball is a possible state, and one to which someone might want to refer, but MAE forces its speakers into cumbersome circumlocutions like

I was in a state of having played baseball.

since English, perhaps curiously, does not allow us to convert stative verbs into adjectives. While *the painted house* is possible, **the ran man* is not.

So the verbal system of AAE itself can convey habituality and stativity. A system seems to be present, and if so, we should find more aspectual distinctions. We do: AAE has a *remote past* referencer, *bin*.

He bin ate. (MAE "He is in a state of having eaten some time ago.")
I coulda bin went back to work.
I bin had it.[7]

The meaning "remote past" seems to be involved, but it is not completely clear how to characterize this meaning. Should it be represented in tense terms? We can put *bin* together with stative *done*. For example,

He bin done ate.

means that he was in a state of having eaten some time ago.

Any generative system automatically invites one operation of Merge after another. When several items like *bin* and *done* are merged into an AAE sentence, the MAE speaker's understanding is quickly outstripped. Most MAE speakers have some notion of *done* or *bin*. But just like recursive possessives, when aspectual markers are *combined*, they have their own logic—which seems like illogic to those who do not have a native grasp of the system. It is the fact of composing new meanings inside the aspect system that tells us that a system, not occasional lexical items, is present.

Here are some further combinations and distinctions from Lisa Green's wonderful book *African American English*.[8] These distinctions are immediately expressed in AAE and much more circuitously achieved in MAE with, for instance, adverbs (see glosses below):

Habitual resultant state

She gotta be there for nine, so they *be done gone* to school. ("...so they have usually already gone to school.")

Anybody who don' have no money and jus *be done got paid* must be on drugs. ("It is usually the case that anyone who doesn't have money who just got paid must be on drugs.")

Future resultant state

I *be done forgot* next week. ("...will have forgotten...")

Modal resultant state

Once you put your hand on the plow, you can't look back, cause you *be done dug up* something else. ("...because you will dig up something else.")

I make any kind of move, he *be done shot* me.

Remote past resultant state

You shoulda *bin done called* me down there.

He *bin done put* that in there. ("He put that in there a long time ago.")

Parallel to *bin* denoting "remote past," AAE may have a construction denoting "remote future." It may be that although both

ima

and

imana

in sentences like *Ima go* and *Imana go* seem to be reduced forms of *I'm going to*, the *imana* form denotes remote future. This is just a hunch—it needs more careful study, but it would fit in. It is what the viewpoint "A language's verbal constructions form a coherent system" tells us to look for.

We have looked at only a few concepts expressed in the AAE verbal system. However, together they exhibit just the sort of variation from MAE that suggests that a different overarching grammar generates the distinctions and attaches them to features of the auxiliary verb system. Once an MAE speaker gets the hang of it, a kind of linguistic envy may set in. Why does MAE not have such an elegant way to combine event perspectives? Teenage speakers are sometimes accused of "affecting" AAE as a form of protest. Perhaps, though, not being blinded by prejudice, they just become aware of new linguistic resources unavailable in MAE.

The distinctions we have been exploring and the generative system behind them are what an AAE-speaking child must acquire. It doesn't look easy, especially from an MAE point of view. When do children master these distinctions? Here is how Janice Jackson has pursued children's knowledge.[9]

Imagine that Cookie Monster is sick in bed and cannot eat. Meanwhile, Grover is eating cookies. Now we ask,

a. "Who be eating cookies?"

and

b. "Who is eating cookies?"

Five-year-old AAE-speaking children will answer (a) with "Cookie Monster," correctly identifying him as the one who habitually eats cookies even if he is not eating them now, and will answer (b) with "Grover." A child who does not answer (a) correctly is probably not a speaker of AAE—that is, the child may be an MAE speaker or an AAE speaker who has a delay or deficit in learning AAE. For comparison, note that in one of my college classes, 25 out of 26 students (none of them African-American) wrongly interpreted (a) as if it were (b).

Now we have a vision of AAE showing that it is almost identical to MAE in its system of contraction/deletion of copulas and at the same time has begun to build a quite different grammar within the auxiliary, based on a different language family, the same way that several vocabularies flow into English as a whole. This heterogeneity is just what we expect, because we find it in all languages when we peer through our linguistic microscope carefully enough to really focus on the details. From this point of view, AAE is at one leading edge in theoretical work aimed at uncovering the various possibilities that Universal Grammar makes available for differentiating aspectual relations. It should in turn feed into a larger theory of events.

Much has been made of connections to Africa in the vocabulary of AAE.[10] That is not the perspective I take here, although again, the two possibilities constitute another example of the inherent eclecticism of grammars: these aspectual features may have historical connections to African languages, or they may have arisen spontaneously from the dynamics of language change. Their origins are not as important here as our vision of what living grammars are like: they are full of grammatical microcosms that carry generative power.[11]

Why Grammatical Negation Elicits Social Negativity

Ask a non-AAE speaker what AAE sounds like and chances are the answer will be something like "I ain't got nothing." Negation has a grip on the prejudiced imagination of MAE speakers. It may well be that more than raw emotion is involved. Negation is another domain where MAE speakers may feel that AAE is "sloppy" or "unsystematic"—but where in fact, AAE simply uses a different grammar than MAE, a wholly systematic grammar that is found in other languages as well.

MAE speakers can correctly grasp the *thrust* of negation in AAE, in attested examples like these:[12]

I sure hope it don't be no leak after they finish.
Sometimes it didn't have no chalk, no books, no teacher.
I ain't never seen nobody preach under announcements.
Don't nobody want to go to the movies.
No game don't last all night.
Nothing can't tell you it wasn't meant for you.

But MAE speakers can easily misanalyze them through the filter of their own grammar. Let me explain.

Worldwide, the variation in how two negatives fit together is extremely intricate. Two general modes are possible. In the first type, *cancellation negation*, each negative cancels the previous one (*I don't want to wear no shirt* = "I want to wear a shirt"; *You cannot not go* = "You have to go"). In the second type, *negative concord*, all the negatives together equal one negative—a kind of extensive agreement. Cancellation negation is found in MAE, and negative concord in AAE.

Here, perhaps, is where the hostility is born. To MAE speakers, it seems like a violation of the logic of cancellation to allow agreement among negatives. Because humans process language automatically, MAE speakers cannot stop using their MAE "grammar analyzers" on AAE sentences, so they feel that *I don't got no coat* simply fails to honor the meaning of *no*. So the negation system epitomizes where AAE is deeply at odds with MAE. It is no wonder that double negation causes agitation.

Conflict is not the only shadow cast by dialect. It may also have the seeds of the future in it.

Dialect as Future: Engines of Language Change

The engine of change in grammars is hard to see. The factors are very difficult to analyze and tease apart. They create a linguistic soup rather than a body easily carved at the joints with a scientific knife. Still, the types of factors involved in language change are clear:

1. Geographical factors. Languages that exist side by side geographically inevitably influence one another.

2. Generational factors. Each generation brings in a platterful of new words and small grammatical shifts. Larger social shifts may promote larger grammatical ones.

3. Internal factors. Another engine of change—not well understood—lies in the grammars themselves. As we have seen, they contain the seeds of other grammars, which shift in both domain and strength.

Dialects are often harbingers of what will happen in the dominant grammar. The dialect may take a next step that the dominant grammar resists because of social conservatism or events. For instance, following the Norman Conquest, the form of English that was dominant at the time resisted incorporating Latinate words from the conquerors' French, but upper-class English speakers took them in, creating two parallel forms of the language. (Shakespeare often says things twice, once with Anglo-Saxon words (*belly*) and once with Latinate words (*stomach*).) One profound harbinger of the future, as discussed earlier, is the loss of inflections like third person -*s* that has gradually begun to happen in AAE. Another is word order.

As noted above, English word order reflects a Germanic system that has been evolving for 500 years. English as a whole no longer inverts main verbs like *sing* in forming questions:

*Sings she folk music or opera?

MAE also no longer inverts *have* (although British English does: *Have you any money?*); it inserts *do* instead:

Do you have any money?

MAE does continue to invert *be* (as does British English):

John is here → Is John here?

But if it were consistent, it would not.

AAE takes the next logical step in the grammatical evolution. We find questions where *do* is inserted with *be* and the move away from verb movement is complete; the logical direction of change is fulfilled:[13]

Do it be dark?
Do he be sleeping in that car?

(Sentences like these often strike the MAE speaker's funnybone. The reason isn't exactly clear. Our responses to language remain deep and mysterious, dangerous in their impact upon others, and probably not something in which we can take much pride.)

Fleeting evidence from MAE-speaking children shows that some may see the deeper consistent generalization before they restrict their grammar by inverting forms of *be*:[14]

Do it be colored?
You don't be quiet.
Allison didn't be mad.
This didn't be colored.
Did there be some?

In using this construction, children and AAE speakers are reaching for the future, but our MAE culture holds them back.

Orthogonal Systems or Allied Systems?

We have argued that the diversity inherent in Universal Grammar is on display in AAE. A dialect does not display random, minor deviations from the mainstream language; instead, its differences form a system. The system itself may not be a variant of the mainstream system. Instead, it may represent a different grammatical family and may point to the future direction of grammatical change. The AAE dialect offers at least three different perspectives on MAE, partly allied and partly orthogonal. Our prejudices—our emotions—are reflections of these differences.

1. Alien dimension. A new kind of verbal system based on aspect rather than time is emerging in AAE, making use of another axis around which Universal Grammar allows languages to organize actions.
2. Progressive dimension. AAE is taking a logical step in the long arc of language history, where word order changes slowly: eliminating inversion for *be* as well as *have* (*Do he be here?*).
3. Contradictory dimension. In the realm of negation, AAE is applying a system of concord found in many languages, though not in MAE: one sentence can have several negative words, which all agree in expressing a single negation. This system seems to be at cross-purposes with the MAE system—seems "illogical," perhaps even aggressively so.

AAE and MAE speakers are all bilingual, because they sense the presence of multiple grammars within one language. Americans abroad who are proud of understanding AAE rap music where foreigners do not, can understand it partly because they have AAE latent in their knowledge. That latent knowledge, which frightens language conservatives, gradually is having an impact on MAE.

Educational Implications: Can Schools Be Savvy about African-American English?

Learning Mainstream American English Is Not Easier Than Learning African-American English

Let us deal with a frequent objection. It is often said that people should just learn MAE anyway; if they did, it would take care of all the problems. If you are an MAE speaker and you think that suggestion is easy, then try this. Most languages prefer the consonant sequence *ks* as in *lacks* to the sequence *sk* as in *ask*. This means that, phonologically, it is easier to use the dialect form *aks* than the standard form *ask*. Try, for the next four hours, to say "aks" whenever you mean to say "ask" and punish yourself if you fail: you may not say anything for 30 minutes if you use "ask" once—just what a child put down by a teacher might experience in school. It is very hard work to monitor your speech constantly. It feels like remembering to say "sir" after every sentence, which Marine recruits learn only with great effort.

The serious point here is that not all people can easily control their dialects; for many, it is extremely difficult. One of the remarkable observations and ironies about the Ebonics controversy was that many of those who said children should not use Ebonics (AAE) had clear traces of AAE in their own speech. They were no more able to drop AAE at will than most Americans with a Southern accent can adopt a Northern accent at will. There is tremendous variety in people's ability and willingness to code-switch. It is not reasonable or realistic to demand it of everyone.

I do not mean to say that all language commentary in the classroom is out of place. Education should enrich students' vocabularies, literary sensibility, sense of logic and style in writing, and facility with language. Controlling the use of dialect is quite a different matter: it amounts to an effort to stamp out the use of structures that the grammar of AAE requires. Of course, some students (mindful of prejudice) want to be alerted when their expression seems "dialectal." It has often seemed to me that writing teachers should have two pens: one color for style, another for dialect, if the student (or parent) requests it, but only if. As with choosing clothes or appearance, we have a right to choose how we speak, even though others may disapprove (as many parents' reaction to nose rings clearly shows).

The Impact of Grammar Correction

Children naturally pass through other grammars on the path to MAE. They may touch upon German, Italian, or Chinese, traces of which are still found in the corners of adult English grammar. Beyond that evolution, there are characteristic child utterances that frequently elicit a hot reprimand—perhaps hotter than most parents and teachers realize: "Don't say 'me and Johnny'" or "Don't say 'I don't got none.'"

There is plenty of evidence that grammar is hard to correct and that children do not learn from being taught rules. In some cases, one can tell that the child generates a phony rule.[15] A child who says "Him go" can consciously substitute *he* for *him* ("He goes"), but she is using an extra rule of memory, not a rule of grammar, perhaps like adding *ma'am* at the end of a sentence. Generally, teaching rules does not help a child speak differently, so the reprimands tend to multiply.

What, then, is the impact of parents' and teachers' corrections? The child may well feel condemned for something she cannot correct. Or he may acquire the idea that judging people by their grammar is appropriate and legitimate. Everyone judges speech ("Gee, he talks too loud"), but this is really quite different from judging grammar.

One might say, "Surely parents have the right to prefer one dialect in their own household," just as some parents decide to raise their children bilingually. However, if a child who says, "I don't got none," is corrected at home, what will he think of a playmate who says the same thing? Language prejudice is no stranger to the nursery school.

The challenge of raising children without language prejudice seems formidable. However, it is the obligation of linguistics to make it perfectly plain that dialects are legitimate forms of grammar and that promoting prejudice against them is therefore intellectually ill founded and regrettable, even if socially understandable.

Grammar correction is really an education away from appreciating the nature of language and toward creating prejudice. Because our responses to language are so deep, language prejudice is one of the most insidious ways in which we mentally downgrade each other. Every parent should be aware of what it means to teach prejudice. Ultimately, people decide for themselves how they wish to talk. It may never be too early to respect a child's linguistic rights. Most parents have a tremendous effect on their children's values, including their linguistic values, without using reprimands that are very difficult to follow.

To my mind, genuine education about dialects—not about lexical items or about entertaining peculiarities, but about their systematic nature—should be a part of every high school curriculum. It takes some time—more than these few chapters require—to really feel the equality of dialects. It is an aspect of civic understanding that seems well worth a month of the high school English curriculum. If Canadian children must learn both French and English, though some English-speaking children are in far-flung provinces with no French speakers, why not have American high school students spend a single month in four years learning how AAE works? In my experience, the study of dialects brings an English class alive, and high school students love the opportunity to study something full of vitality in their own social and musical culture.

Societies with recognized bilingualism have long seen knowing both languages as an important part of citizenship. In Switzerland, for example, some primary school classes are taught in the Swiss dialect of German and others in (note the name) High German.[16] Language policy is ultimately a social question, not just a linguistic one, that needs to be decided by an informed public.

IV Finding Philosophy and Morality in Every Sentence

12 Philosophical Consequences: The Path from Mathematics to Human Dignity

Is the Whole Mind a Generative Grammar?

We have been looking at how the molecules of language get built, using the strongest magnification we can muster. While we have been awash in linguistic detail, larger implications and deeper issues about human nature have hovered in the background. At this point, we can address these issues only with uncertainty—but we must at least try to address them, if we are to honor the commitment to appreciate the implications of our views, and to encourage this approach to the larger mind, however uncertain we may be.

We will start by looking at where philosophers and linguists connect. In fact, much of modern philosophy has arrived at an image of human nature similar to the one sketched here.

Do Common Principles Operate across the Mind?

Is grammar actually a model for how a good part of the mind works? That is the position I advocate, but still quite speculatively. It is not only a question of advocacy. It would be derelict of me not to acknowledge that if we have a model of one module of mind, it will dominate our sense of the others until those are rigorously spelled out. If we do not discuss how far other mental abilities resemble grammar and how far they do not, the default understanding that people will come to is that grammar *is* the essence of mind, that the principles of grammatical structure are the principles that underlie all mental abilities.

Do other parts of the mind operate like a machine that is both fast and creative, with hierarchies, rules, and recursive properties, and with no fixed mapping to the world? Do they have domains of rigidity, creativity, and openness to personality? From the outset, vision seems different from language in two ways: it is three-dimensional, and personality does not feel like it is at work there—we do not discern color "angrily" or compute geometrical angles "optimistically" when we look at a flower. Nonetheless, vision shares properties with language: it involves hierarchy, transformations, and links to physical coordination, and there is a microprogram of creative individuality in how our eyes dart around a room.

Do we generate emotions the way we generate sentences? And do the modules for emotion and language, with their internal rules, guide each other the way hand-eye connections allow the two highly structured motor and visual modules of the brain to communicate? Can we achieve the same distinctive individuality in the way our face responds at each moment as in the way we summon and modulate words to fit each moment? Is there something at the heart of it all that resembles, say, how gravity lies behind all motion? I would like to suggest that the systematic "generative power of grammar" is found throughout the mind/brain. That is, I am suggesting once again that we are creative via automatic formulas. We will find structured connections between modules, "interfaces" among our abilities. The fact that we can talk about what we see is much like the fact that we can experience emotions of joy (beauty) or sorrow (ugliness) connected to what we see. Moreover, what cannot happen will define the "interfaces" of what can. While we can describe in detail what we see, we cannot describe in any detail how our internal organs are connected, so there is no interface between our language and our internal organs like the one between our hands and our eyes. In what follows, I will make much the same argument again, from different vantage points.

Let us speculate more on how generativity could be represented elsewhere. As suggested in chapter 2, our human capacity to generate unique emotions may be no different from our capacity to generate unique sentences. Physical coordination requires the same kind of creativity. Each time someone throws you a baseball, it arrives at a slightly different spot, so a hundred of your muscles must be organized in a slightly different way to catch it. And each of us might catch it with our own slightly different style (organization of muscle instructions), so microcreativity is ever-present.

Let us imagine how syntactic trees can be an interface, like cogs in connected wheels, to other parts of mind. First, recall the syntactic trees used to represent grammatical structures, like this one:

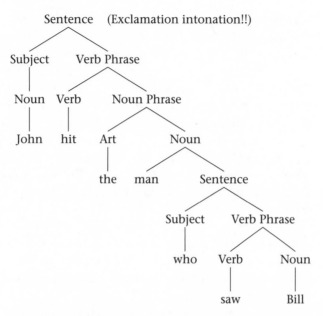

The tree's various elements, configurations, and labels represent a host of linguistic concepts: categories (noun, verb, action), functions (subject (here, *John*) is agent of action), reference (pronouns (such as *who*) refer to nouns), recursion (one sentence can have another sentence inside it). The nodes in a tree bear systematic connections to nodes below them—and to much more that linguists have not investigated or do not yet understand. Much of that structure must be fixed or innate, though it may not be inevitable or obvious.

At the bottom of syntactic trees come words, which carry amalgams of meaning drawn from every part of mental life. On top of the trees, via intonation, we project our personalities onto what we say. In a rough sense, we can think of the *tops* and *bottoms* of linguistic trees as connecting to other dimensions of mind that are not shown here. A mechanical interface—of much greater intricacy—must exist to enable rapid thought across a smorgasbord of mental capacities.

While the broad notion of a *hierarchy* (the tree) is common to many cognitive domains, it must be specifically anchored in each module. For instance, stereoscopy is found in both the eyes and the ears, but it is represented separately in each module, vision and hearing. A cognitive map of the arms and hands—a kind of software program that must exist—might have a hierarchy in which the arm muscles are "higher" than the finger muscles when some motion requires them both.

In the hierarchy specific to language, verbs always control object nouns—that is, are always higher than object nouns—a fact we represent by writing the marker for a verb phrase higher in the tree than the marker for the noun that names its object (*hit the man, see Bill*). Suppose one argued that "hierarchy" is not specific to language and that nouns and verbs are derived from "things" and "actions"—a rather unlikely hypothesis. Still, the innate grammar says that some verbs control nouns—dominate them in a hierarchy—the way an arm, roughly, controls fingers (for example, in a phrase like *hit Bill*). This specific connection between hierarchy and verbal categories is what is attributed to Universal Grammar. It is much like the specific innate structure that provides foot-eye coordination. The connection is just as innate as the foot and the eye. This is an important feature of innateness, often misperceived by professionals. The fact that part of Universal Grammar is used for other purposes does not mean that "grammar is not innate," any more than the fact that eyes are used for many purposes means that hand-eye or foot-eye coordination is not essentially innate.

Such things are the "motors" of thought, and they look just as strange as motors always do. If you lift the hood of a car, it seems amazing that such an odd collection of wires, screws, and pipes should make any kind of sense, much less organize sufficient energy to move a ton of metal. Looking at neurological pictures of the brain taken with an MRI machine, it seems equally hard to imagine the brain as a source of cognition.[1] So it should be no surprise that our cognitive maps—like the syntactic trees that represent sentences—look odd or even like a total hodgepodge. It all fits the speculation: the fact that we can coordinate arms, legs, words, music, and a host of emotions when we dance means that we have cross-modular powers organized by the formulas in our brains. Rapid thought requires formulas that connect different modules, just as a carburetor connects gas and wheels. The carburetor is built into the car—though it looks strange—just as hierarchical structure for nouns and verbs is built into grammar.

The Representational Mind

These are not isolated views. In his 2003 presidential address to the American Philosophical Association, Paul Churchland articulated a similar domain for cognitive representations, quite common now among philosophers:

Suppose also the internal character of each of the representational spaces is not fixed by some prior decree, either divine or genetic, but is slowly shaped or sculpted by...extended experience.... So we begin by expanding the number of representational spaces, into the hundreds and thousands.... And we reach out to include motor cognition and practical skills, along with perceptual apprehensions and theoretical judgment, as equal partners in our account of human knowledge.[2]

Physical actions require a cognitive map. While experience fills in many flexible spots in our cognitive map of the body, the motor systems (arms and legs) are genetic and not acquired by experience. Grammar, though abstract and remote, is just like our arms and legs—an apparatus that we have from birth, whose uses we refine by experience.

In a similar vein, the physicist Steven Weinberg has expressed the view that mentally guided behavior will ultimately submit to mathematical representations:

I do think that we will have an understanding of behavior...in the path laid out by Galileo and Newton: the discovery of increasingly comprehensive mathematical laws.[3]

The heterogeneity of information involved in the construction of action—the fact that we draw from different facets (modules) of mind—is both noteworthy and normal. Physical formulas like "Force equals mass times acceleration" also mix different types of concepts.

Identity and Instant Thought

Social scientists have developed the same concept. Claude Steele has shown that stereotype anxiety affects people's problem-solving abilities at a subconscious level when taking tests.[4] In his experiment, Asian women did better on a math test when they identified themselves as Asian before taking the test than they did when they identified themselves as women before taking a similar test. The stereotype of Asians is that they are good at math and the stereotype of women is that they are poor at math. Whichever stereotype is dominant (as primed by a question) affects how one performs at an instantaneous microscopic level, necessarily below the level of consciousness. Steele's claim is that subtle shifts in the women's unconscious identity affected just how they made rapid, unconscious choices in solving mathematical problems. This conclusion fits the general view that somehow we humans integrate every aspect of ourselves into every act. Among the things we integrate are ideas—new and old, good and bad, half-baked and wise—all marinating together.

The Instant, Unconscious Impact of Ideas

As Malcolm Gladwell shows in his recent book *Blink*, we both receive ideas and exercise judgment unconsciously and almost instantaneously, even when the ideas are quite abstract.[5] I would add that others are instantly affected by every idea that we give voice to. When Einstein proposed the theory of relativity, its impact on realms beyond science was inevitable. If physical interaction itself was in some sense "relative," then obviously everything else could be as well. The effect of relativistic thinking began instantly and is still rippling through the academic world. Einstein himself took the instant effect of ideas into account when he said that he rejected the big bang theory because it would support religion. From the teenager who ritually says, "You never know," to "situation ethics," to the claims of deconstructionists, our ideas all mingle. The notion that fundamental ideas can be unconscious motivates historians to argue, generations later, that an idea could dominate everyone in a particular era, though people at the time could not see it. The reaction to the Enlightenment idea that revolutions are inevitable was a largely literary notion of "gradualism" that developed in the nineteenth century. It certainly influenced Darwin's thought about how evolution occurred, although he may not have clearly realized it if he was sure that all his notions were rooted in pure observation.

These views strike some people as implausible and others as obvious. But even those who accept the impact of ideas often assert that they are able to disregard ideas they dislike by an act of will. It seems far more likely that although we can diminish the impact of questionable and false ideas, we cannot eliminate it. For instance, I believe grades are an inappropriate way to measure academic performance. Yet if someone tells me that a person is "a B student," my image of that person is affected whether I want it to be or not. (And note that the idea need not even be expressed in words; it can have its effect even if it is merely built into the *style* of speech. The white parent who says to a visiting black child, "My, *you* are very good at math," can convey a whiff of prejudice merely by contrastive intonation. Why should it be surprising that the child is good at math?)

Once we accept the notion that ideas can be unconscious—as Freud brought home to us—then we must accept the possibility that wrong ideas can affect us. From there it is a short step to the realization that we are all affected by all ideas at some level.

If this is true, an immediate question arises about certain ideas in this book. How can I guarantee that ideas I cannot define perfectly do not have unintended consequences? I have argued that children may not grasp the hidden variable inside a question word like *who*. But I do not want to say that children who fail to grasp this cannot form lists or possess the notion elsewhere in their minds. It is difficult to protect against such an unwarranted extension. I know of no other way to forestall its impact beyond being as explicit as I can about the view that the modularity of mind means precisely that humans are capable of applying a principle in one sphere, but not in another, unless an interface guarantees a translation between them.

Infinite Dignity

Throughout the book I have emphasized these claims:

1. All rapid action or thought must be mechanical.
2. Any mechanism works by principles that can be captured in a mathematical formula (far from understood in any real detail where the mind is concerned).
3. Each individual has unique formulas.
4. Inner formulas that generate unique actions cannot be fully comprehended by another person (as we began to discuss in chapter 3).

A great deal of humanist philosophy and religion could be summed up this way: our deepest intuition about human nature is that we should respect each other's dignity. Our sense of personal dignity reflects our awareness that we each have such personal formulas and hence are unique as individuals.

No two people are identical. This is not just because any two people's faces, sentences, and meanings are not identical; rather, it is because some aspect of each person's essence is unique. Such a conclusion is a humanistic truism, but is it reflected in theories of the mind derived from mechanistic models and cognitive science? Can we see ourselves as software programs and still maintain self-respect? The reasoning in this book seeks to connect humanistic insights to modern cognitive psychology.

If we each have an unfathomable inner formula, then it should confer a dignity upon each of us that, somehow, we all give credence to. We can condemn a murder while respecting the idea that the murderer's motives remain partly mysterious. We see other people's current actions, but because we are unable to see the formula behind them, we cannot infallibly predict their future actions (this is of course true for ourselves as well).

Our view of children is daily affected by whether we accept or deny this mystery. It has always amazed me that parents speak with such confidence about what their children's unconscious motives are. Such confidence can only come from a belief that a child's unconscious realm is transparent. Is it really?

The Mystery of Slow Thought

One virtue of clear ideas—the beauty of lucidity—is that they give birth to their opposite. The clarity of the computer metaphor throws into stark relief what is special and unknown about the human mind.

I have argued that all of our personal complexity is projected onto the tiny mental acts that compose and govern our actions. Yet there is a stunning discontinuity between ourselves and computers. It is the mystery of what I call "slow thought." A computer can race through any computation involving a domain of information with logical relations. Our minds also work very fast most of the time. Yet we are aware that other thoughts smolder and need us to "sleep on" them. If we have all the necessary information in a particular domain, then why should any thought take a long time? Computers have no operations that suddenly take 10,000 times longer to process than others. Even computer games like "Civilization Two," built to evaluate heterogeneous information, do it by putting all the information into a common computer language and then crunching the output with the usual computer speed. Nothing takes weeks, months, or years.

There is no obvious reason why any thoughts that work like the computer model should take a long time. It is true that in order to solve a problem or come to a decision, we sometimes need to dredge up obscure memories that can take days or weeks to surface. Yet often when we ruminate on something, we know we have all the necessary information—we just need a new way to see it. If all new thinking is just another computation, then it should happen just as quickly as shifting programs on a computer.

We can speculate that the human process of "building formulas" uses a different kind of formula than executing actions. Note that computers undertake "automatic programming" whereby they program themselves following a higher-order program. But again, in the case of the computer everything is fixed; there is no need for extended runtime.

The fact that some rumination is slow suggests that a different kind of thought is involved. Intuitively, slow thought involves *changing assumptions*, looking at things from another angle. We are somehow rebuilding the machine itself. The fact that the process is slow suggests that the mechanisms are different. We do not know how to conceive of them; they are true human mysteries. And, though some people value spontaneous responses above others, most of us feel that slow, deliberate thinking reflects who we are most distinctly. (This book, for instance, took a lot of very slow thought.) Although I have argued that rapid thought contains the ingredients of creativity and individuality, surely slow thought is really where our essence resides, mysterious though it is. In *Blink*, Malcolm Gladwell presents fast thought as strange and unusual, but really we may be closer to understanding that type of thought than to understanding what we do when we "think about things." Although we may have the illusion that thinking is conscious, most of it is not.

Very peculiar human notions, like maturity, signal a mental openness that time produces in the growth of children. And it is whatever King Lear spoke of when he said, "Ripeness is all." If we understood it, a real kind of mental quality is reflected in maturity, but we do not have the terms to think about it with precision. How does a mature person process information differently from an immature one? It is a bit like a banana ripening slowly, where we see a few dark colors but not the real microscopic process that is occurring.

If I knew how to make these sparse observations into a counterweight to the thrust of this whole book, I would. I will simply note that there is a counterweight in the ruminative style of humanistic study that deserves to be respected on its own terms, even though the computer model of the human mind is commonly assumed in the sciences.

Free Will and Determinism

Now we will leave the empirical domain behind and leap into the humanistic realm. What are the human implications that "objectivity" excludes, which most scientific intellectuals strenuously avoid? We must ask about them if we are truly committed to seeing where implications for life and our intuitions about the nature of personal experience can be found in our extrapolations from grammar.

Free Will: Necessary Assumption or Genuine Reality?

If personal dignity arises from our sense that we have an unknowable infinite potential that is our own responsibility, then we should accept the notion of human dignity as referring to something real, not sentimental. If that view is real, then a decent science of the mind should incorporate it. And, if we should honor the proposition that our sense of our own unique dignity is real, then we should match it by our respect for every other person's dignity.

Our mechanical system for generating language has several features that we as human beings link to personal freedom: creativity, uniqueness, endless possibilities. If our grammatical machine has them, do we as human beings fail to have them? The question goes to the heart of modern science: does determinism rule or is free will a possibility? The intuition that we have free will, although routinely denied, can be seen as a pillar of our sense of dignity. We are the authors of our actions and bear responsibility for them.

Is all the systematic creativity inside our grammar really ruled by the iron will of determinism? Are we really contemplating alternatives and weighing evidence when we think we are doing so, or are we marionettes manipulated by unseen physical forces? Many doubters seem satisfied with the "as if" approach: we act as if we had free will, though we do not. Does "as if" really work? Can we still have a sense of integrity if we believe that free will is an illusion?

The Legitimacy of Free Will

Two ideas are emerging here. On the one hand, though free will is an unpopular claim among scientists, it seems to me that we cannot fully accept responsibility for our actions if we do not believe we have free will. On the other hand, a great deal of science depends upon determinism, which says that if physics follows fixed rules, and we are physical objects, then what we do is ultimately determined not by some vague "self" but by inevitable physical laws. There is an assumption here: that properties of mind will resolve into familiar physical interactions. Yet physics has not really addressed properties of mind.

Indeed, these ideas form a paradox: current physical laws are deterministic, yet the mind seems to have free will as a potential. Science derives energy and focus from paradoxes. It is recognizing the legitimacy of both sides that leads to insight. The dominance of the physical sciences has relegated claims derived from rigorous work on mental products to second-class status. If we take the accomplishments of linguistics seriously, then the best move is to assert both that free will is necessarily true and that it is impossible. A resolution of that paradox will leave the essence of each view intact.

Another way to put the matter is to say that the "bridge laws" between mental truth and physical truth remain underconceptualized.[6] In any case, these thorny philosophical issues will not be resolved soon. What do we do with our imperfect knowledge in the meantime? The question is important for two reasons: first, because we are affected by all ideas, and second, because our commitment to our children is to ask, what are the moral consequences of assuming either determinism or free will?

Recognizing (or denying) a notion of free will is central to how we see and treat each other, and—perhaps most important—to how we see and treat children. If we see ideas as having an instant effect, then our choice of free will or determinism must affect how we treat children. If we cannot decide, then our indecision itself will affect them. Our obligation, I believe, is to formulate an idea that safeguards children's dignity. In that light, I would advocate the following humanistic proposition, much like the presumption "Innocent until proven guilty": we should assume that free will really exists, that it is not an illusion, until proven otherwise.

Determinism and How We Talk to Children

Let us look at where deterministic assumptions connect with daily life. Determinism likens human behavior to the seemingly unpredictable but actually fixed path of a rock rolling down a hill. As the rock is rolling, it appears to come to many "choice" points where an observer feels it just bounces one way or another. In fact, though, the rock's trajectory and ultimate resting spot are completely predetermined; we are simply unaware of the deterministic nature of the rock's descent because we cannot project how the shape of the hill, the shape of the rock, and the rock's momentum will interact. Do we, when we think, choose our own destiny, or is the thought process an illusion that follows a biological determinism we cannot witness?

It might seem that we are engaging in more philosophy than we need to here. Yet how we talk to children always reflects our image of the child and the human being within. If we say to a child, "Everything you do is predictable," we deny free will; equally so when we say, "If you tell a teenager to do one thing, she will just go and do the opposite"—as if apparent free will is just governed by a hidden determinism (that some parents think they can control by "reverse psychology"). It is hard to say what a child or a teenager unconsciously concludes about such remarks. They seem like denigrating remarks to me, but they are the common coin of modern life. In any case, it can hardly be doubted that philosophy and views of free will are intricately woven into daily style.

I think a desire to recognize and uphold children's dignity demands that we take the philosophical implications of our own and a child's style of thinking seriously. No one, of course, denies children choices. But we may, in other statements, deny respect for how they make decisions, assuming we can see the forces driving another human being and see where, deterministically, they lead. Claiming "Whatever I say, he does the opposite" implies no thoughtfulness on the child's part. Statements like "You always get upset just because you are hungry" deny the reality of the child's feelings and diminish our view of him (and probably his view of himself) and how he chooses his own destiny.

13 False False Belief Belief and True False Belief Belief

Building an Interface

Although philosophy and linguistics overlap in many ways, the philosophical issues that I address here go beyond what linguists usually address, and I do not do so from an entirely scholarly perspective. However, they are issues that affect us as human beings and therefore it is important that everyone feel entitled to address them, that the perspective from each discipline—and a variety of human orientations—receive articulation.

In the last chapter, I projected a minimal image, dim at best, of what an interface between language and mind looks like: a syntactic tree connected to word-meanings at the bottom and intonation at the top. Intonation projects onto the whole structure at once and carries both attitudes and personality.

The next step in fashioning an interface is not so clear. One option is to look longer at what's been done on the other end, the cognitive end. One pertinent question is this: how do we think about each other's thinking? Much attention has fallen on the thorny question of how we attribute a concept of false belief to someone else.

Right away, let me say that the concept "concept" is not such a great concept. The effort to build an interface architecture is not well served by a notion that floats unanchored in the multimodular space of the mind. The discussion here and in the next chapter is partly aimed at showing how the concept "concept" may cloud more than it reveals—and lead to overstatements of children's immaturity. If we can reduce the notion of concept, get more microscopic again, we may be able to discern a sharper and sturdier connection between language and one form of propositional knowledge.

In a nutshell, the argument will be that we need a fully specified, languagelike symbolic system to represent propositional knowledge that allows deductive reasoning: deducing propositions from propositions. Noam Chomsky has recently suggested that in fact we minimize the unique features that Universal Grammar contains and allow the symbolic system of cognition to form an important, integrated aspect of the interface between language and mind.[1]

Nonpropositional knowledge—equally complex and equally definitive of humanity—races all over the mind on its own, creating paths of intuitive connections that are very difficult to represent in a rigorous way beyond the weak term *association*. It is the kind of knowledge that can cause a red-flushed face when we see an embarrassing picture even if we cannot coherently "say" what is embarrassing.

What Is a Child's Theory of Mind?

The strong view is that children younger than about four "have no theory of another person's mind" and therefore cannot attribute a false belief to anyone else. The question has many dimensions. We will investigate (1) how a child's point of view is relevant, (2) how explicit propositional knowledge is distinct from implicit intuitive knowledge, and (3) how the activity of asking a question calls for special kinds of mental computation.

The following scenario, often replicated with different variants, reveals the basic phenomenon of children's failure on false belief tasks:

Experimenter shows child a box labeled *Crayola*.
Experimenter: What is in the box?
Child: Crayons?
Experimenter: Well, why don't you have a look?
  Child finds toy frog.
Experimenter: What is that?
Child: A frog.
Experimenter: Can you put it back in the box?
  Child puts it back and closes the box.
Experimenter: Who is your best friend?
Child: Tom.
Experimenter: What will he think is in the box?
Child: A frog. *or* Crayons.

Children younger than about four years typically say "A frog" and those who are older say "Crayons." The conclusion is that the younger child, unable to avoid his own knowledge (that there is a frog, not crayons, in the box), has difficulty in attributing a "false belief" to his friend, who could not know what is in the closed box. Exactly what does such an assertion mean? We need to be very careful about saying that the child "has no concept of false belief." *Failure to compute a concept in conversation is not the same as failure to have a concept in a less than fully conscious way.*

Could this be simultaneously a cognitive problem with "other minds" and a linguistic problem with subordinate clauses (*think that...*)? It could be just that, if some cognitive representation for other minds is identical to the linguistic one for a sentence inside a sentence. To represent another person's mind inside our own mind, maybe we need precisely the same structure.[2]

To address the issue clearly, we need to see where false belief could be innately entailed in what the mind does essentially "instinctively" (as Steven Pinker puts it in *The Language Instinct*), and we need to look closely at the question the child is answering in these experiments. Our modular hypothesis will be this:

False belief might be represented differently in different mental domains, and therefore translation among domains is far from automatic.

For example, the same principle—stereoscopy—works for both hearing and vision, but it obviously has a separate neurological representation in each. Could it be that implicit false belief is unconsciously imputed to someone else in a different form and in a different module?

Here are various types of false belief:

Biologically entailed false belief

Most animals dart away when another animal is near. A chameleon will not move because, since its color shifts to match its environment, it is programmed to assume that another animal will not see it. That is equal to saying that the other animal has the false belief that the chameleon does not exist.

Visual false belief

a. A thief wearing bright clothes might duck quickly when he saw a person who might see him. But a soldier wearing camouflage might not duck when an enemy appeared or might not duck quickly because he has absorbed into his physical action the idea that he is not really visible (or as visible) and therefore the idea that the enemy could maintain the false belief that he is not there.

b. An athlete who feints in one direction, but moves in another, does so to mislead—in effect, to build a false belief in her opponent about where she is going.

c. Parents report that children under three years will do things they are not supposed to do when the parent is not looking. In effect, they act under the assumption that the parent has the false belief that they are not doing what they are doing.

Verbal false belief

a. (Imaginary: False assumption) If a child says to her playmate, "I'll be the Mommy and you be the Daddy," she is proposing that the playmate act as if a false belief, of which both children are aware, is true. They pretend they are something that they are not. Proposals like this are often expressed with modals and subjunctives: "Could you be the boy?"

b. (Subordination) A statement like *John thinks that the world is flat* is a true statement that contains a false statement. Such statements underlie many false belief experiments.

c. (Compounding) The jesting title of this chapter, "False False Belief Belief," entails a representation of false belief that is different from the subordination case, namely, a representation in terms of compounds. In essence, it subordinates one false belief to another without attributing the belief to any particular person.

Situational false belief

Using the props of several modules, we are able to understand situations ("contexts") in ways that feel "easier" than understanding sentences. Somehow verbal, visual, and emotional representations help each other.

a. If a person sees someone walk away from a dog, she might infer the proposition *He is afraid of the dog*. She might then say, "Don't worry, the dog's friendly"—an assertion that corrects an inferred false belief.

b. If a child stops a baby about to eat something with dirt on it that the baby does not seem to notice, the child implicitly assumes that the baby does not realize that the food has unhealthy dirt on it. In effect, the child has attributed a false belief to the baby, namely, that the food is all right.

c. Humor often entails playfulness with false belief. Consider: At a party, Jane announces she is going home. Twenty minutes later, she is still there and Al says, to common laughter, "Oh, is this your home?" What is entailed here? Al knows that Jane knows that he does not really think it is her home. Al's question is funny because Jane knows that Al knows that she knows that he is not serious about suggesting that the party is her home. So we have a fairly complex cognitive situation, which takes a five-verb sentence to paraphrase: *It is funny . . . knows . . . knows . . . knows . . . is not serious*. The situation itself—whatever cognitive map it entails—is easier to understand than the sentence with three instances of *know* in it.

Those four kinds of attribution of false belief—plus variants within—make a legitimate academic abstraction about false belief, but they refer to no single biological reality. The child and the adult have notions of false belief, but they are not separable from the visual, social, and verbal modules in which they are represented.

The upshot of all this is that there is no "false belief concept" that, like a floodlight, turns on and lights up all corners of the brain. The same is true for other academic abstractions that go under the title "concept." Are there subtle links between these kinds of representation so that one initiates the other? This is possible, but not necessary. The question will be difficult to answer until it becomes clearer how each notion of false belief is tethered to each module.

How do we humans represent situations so that they hold extra information more easily than sentences do? Presumably we have ways of representing "context" that include language as well as ways of representing language so that it includes context. We can understand visual, verbal, and tactile information bound up in a situation quite differently from the way we understand sentences by themselves. A different matrix for representation of context must be present—but it is far beyond current knowledge.

Those who study false belief distinguish, for instance, *pretend* from *believe*, but no one really gives a rigorous definition of the difference. Some notion of false belief, call it "provisional false belief," is entailed in *pretend*. Though logically more complex, pretense is more available for children's minds when no visual information contradicts the pretense. Adults do something similar. Champion chess players look away from the board when they think ahead because the current position interferes with their projection of future moves.

Even "conscious false belief" comes in various degrees, as when you see a hint of doubt in a child's eyes—a vague sense that what some adult says is not quite right. It is not clear that consciousness itself is a sharp concept, since there are so many forms of partial consciousness. We easily refer to such states of mind when we say, "I gradually became aware that..." What exactly does *aware* mean?

Building False Beliefs: Constructivist Concepts

Our focus here will be the pivotal notion of what we can call *propositional false belief*—false belief in a form that allows further reasoning to be built upon it. It is this notion that I believe underlies children's conversational behavior. It has important educational consequences, but it also has moral implications. We need to capture propositional false belief as narrowly and precisely as possible in order to avoid inviting unfair judgments on children who have not yet mastered it—judgments that extrapolate from the child's handling of false belief to the child as a whole.

Looking at how false belief is represented in language, we see that the grammatical context can enable or disable the projection of false belief. First of all, note that we can construct similar concepts with either subordinate clauses or compounds. A *true* statement can contain a *false* one subordinated within it:

John thinks that the world is flat.

The statement about John is true, but it contains a belief of his that is false. The entire statement can in turn be embedded:

Bill thought that John's professed belief that the world is flat was insincere.

Interestingly, the point of this sentence can be captured with compositional (not subordinative) syntax, using compound nouns:

(It was a) false false belief.

Now consider this:

We thought that Bill's expressed view that John's belief was phony was a way to tease him a little.

This gets hard to comprehend, but we can do it. In any event, the sentence is clearly formed from the rules of English; were we to ask speakers of English whether it is "grammatical" or not, they would say "Yes." We can represent it in some sense like this:

false false belief belief (= a false belief about a false belief)

Note that there is no single word for this complex concept. We have had to represent it by a compound, which we understand by putting together its parts. Thus, even verbal constructs refer to false beliefs with different kinds of abstractions. And of course we (as children or adults) don't readily use the term *false false belief belief,* though it is a legitimate referential construct. Instead, we construct complex (subordinative) sentences like the ones above, which delineate more precisely where the false belief lies. Those complex sentences seem to have an important property:

The structure of the sentence carries the structure of the thought it expresses.

In other words, a sentence inside a sentence is like a concept inside a concept.

Sentences like the ones we have just looked at are not too far afield from real life. More topical cases are easy to come by:

Gore stated that the Bush campaign's assertion that manual recounts are illegitimate was just a political ploy.

That statement, however, was seen as equally insincere and unprincipled by most commentators.

While the evanescent quality of such a discourse might lead one to say that it is just another example of claims about "false beliefs" (recounts are illegitimate), it is really what recursion has done that is impressive: we keep combining concepts to create new concepts that begin with an assertion of "false belief" and build from there. This is not just a false belief, but a false belief twice embedded, a different concept. A proposition can undergo further operations of embedding and evaluation: so next to "false proposition" in our example, we have "insincere proposition" and "political ploy proposition," and these are systematically entangled via recursion. It is easier to construct such embeddings than to move up a level of abstraction and understand the words *false belief, contradiction, denial.*

Now, turning this reasoning around, we can conclude that children do not "use or have a concept of false belief" either. They construct sentences that attribute an untrue concept to another person. Teaching young children the expression *false belief* would be difficult; yet they easily understand or create sentences like

Mom thinks you ate the dessert.

Likewise, it seems easier for a child to say, "That's wrong," or "That's not true," than to learn the word *contradiction.* No one doubts that children can master false belief via embedding before the term *false belief* itself. Why does this seem self-evident? These sentences involve a representation that we can label *false belief,* but no bell goes off saying, "That's a false belief."

Grasping Propositions

For adults, all declarative sentences are propositions, that is, statements susceptible of being true or false. It's not yet clear when children understand that a sentence is a proposition—whether they understand it already when they first say something like "He big" or whether this understanding comes later. For very young children, perhaps a declarative is just an *observation* without any implied parallel possibility that it is a statement that could be true or false. (Exploration 5.17 begins to probe this question.) If an adult makes a false statement ("The door should be closed"), a listening child might think she had not understood or heard right (since the door is open). This is a logical possibility that could be correct, but it is actually very hard to evaluate, if the child thinks that the proposition is an observation. It is time to look where we always look first: at what children actually say. What do they say when they first seem sensitive to propositions?

False Belief and Conversation

Where do we first get hints that children can handle false belief—long before they can really ruminate upon it or perform mental operations based on the presupposition that false belief is present in someone else?

Ordinary conversation engages the most subtle relations among minds.[3] Conversations are full of hints and shadows, but few of us doubt the reality of the minds of people we talk to, though that reality is difficult to "prove." Let us imagine that children respond just to *sentences* as if they were disembodied—hanging out there like laundry on a line. Is that really possible? It is immediately obvious that if you say something to a two-year-old that she doesn't like, she will be mad at *you*, not just at the sentence you said. She must therefore associate the sentence with you in some representation. And if the sentence is in some measure questionable, then the seeds of attributing false belief to someone are present. Consider this conversation between Adam (the child whose early speech transcripts have been studied the most) and his mother, when Adam was two years and four months old:[4]

Mother: That's your brush.
              That's not a hammer.
Adam: Hammer?
Mother: That's not a hammer.
              What makes you think that's a hammer?
Adam: Look like hammer.
Mother: Oh # it looks like a hammer?

Doubt comes first in the single word "Hammer?" Then Adam responds to "What makes you think that's a hammer?" by clearly thrusting doubt on the proposition contained in the question (*That's a hammer*) by saying, "Look like hammer." "It looks like a hammer" is not a natural response to the statement "That's a hammer" (a natural response would be "No, it isn't; it's a brush"); instead, it is a response exactly to the question "What makes you think that's a hammer?" Some kind of falsehood is involved here—a false supposition, a false guess, a false hope—and it is the stuff of daily life. Adam was most probably not using subordinate clauses yet in his own speech, but he seems to display comprehension of something very close to a subordinate clause by grasping that the truth of the proposition *That's a hammer* is placed in doubt by "What makes you think...," which in turn is linked to the person asking the question. If Adam is not using subordination himself, then he may not be able to understand subordination when he hears it in a comprehension experiment. Nonetheless, he can still form (making an inference on a situation) a single sentence like "Why is this hammerlike to you?," where the intonation entails that the speaker (the other mind) thinks something else.

In addition, we easily generate intonation patterns full of incredulity and disbelief:[5]

John: Tomatoes carry nuclear waste.
Mary: Tomatoes carry nuclear waste?!

Here Mary expresses an attitude that departs from certainty. We have an image of her mind, and we attribute her attitude to that mind. One might wager that an ingredient of uncertainty is a part of most conversations. Here's Adam again, under three years of age:[6]

Mother: Go ask Cromer if he would like a cup of coffee.
Adam: Le(t) me # have # cup of coffee?
Mother: Cromer.

Adam's "Let me have cup of coffee?" is pretty clearly an incredulity question that attributes an implausible assumption (a child drinks coffee) to his mother, but modifies it by adding a question. When a child angrily corrects a parent who says, "You forgot your spoon," by saying "Un-uh" and showing the spoon, he is with one word both attributing a false belief to the parent and correcting it.

The hint of false belief could be first represented in the intonation of incredulity, though I suspect (being no expert in it) that intonation does not have a recursive mechanism that allows one intonation to be embedded inside an identical intonation so that one alters the truth value of the other. Intuitively, it is much harder to make an inference that brings tones of voice to consciousness than to make one with explicit words. We do it, but it feels like work. You might hear an adult say, "Something in your tone makes me think you really want to go to a different restaurant."[7] I have never heard of a child commenting on an adult's tone of voice, yet variations in tones of voice are constantly directed at—and surely understood by—children. Once again, we have arrived at a situation where knowledge is present, but the knowledge is in a form that hinders a further operation of raising it to consciousness and thereby being able to comment on it.

Syntactic False Belief

Jill de Villiers has championed the role of syntax in false belief tasks and in fact has experimentally found a specific role for syntactic *complexity*. First, two-year-old children are known to say things like

"She thinks it is mine."

Jill and Peter de Villiers have developed experimental devices that seek to elicit related constructions from children a year or two older.[8] They and I would argue that these children clearly understand that a statement is propositional when it is embedded, and as a proposition it can be true or false.

Also at the two-year-old stage, children will misunderstand questions like the false belief experimenter's

"What does he think is in the box?,"

the parallel question

"Where does she think it is?,"

or a question corresponding to the attested child utterance "She thinks it is mine":

"Whose does she think it is?"

Is the assertion *She thinks it is mine* really different from the question *Whose does she think it is?* Yes; sometimes things that look close together are really far apart, as we will see before long.

Although we are entering territory where highly technical representations of grammar are involved, a few simple distinctions will give the flavor of what is going on.[9] The argument turns on the difference between an *inference*, a kind of situational guess, and grammatical *subordination*, where one sentence is logically a part of another.

Suppose I say,

"John told a lie. The Statue of Liberty was turned upside down."

Now if I were to ask you, "Did the Statue of Liberty get turned upside down?," you would probably say, "No, that was a lie that John told." However, note that I actually said two independent sentences. You inferred (guessed, in a way) that one was "subordinate" to the other.

Guess: the lie = the Statue of Liberty was turned upside down

We make this kind of mental, nongrammatical connection all the time. If I were to say,

"A guy is nailing wood on our house. Carpenters are nice people."

you would infer that *Carpenters are nice people* somehow referred to the guy nailing the wood, although I said two separate sentences that did not need to be connected. Or suppose I said,[10]

"Can he cook? Well, he's French, isn't he?"

The inference (or more strongly, implication) is that being French means that you can cook.

Now look at these sentences:

Mary told a lie. John told a lie. The Statue of Liberty was turned upside down.

What do these sentences assert? I have asked this question of many people, and all of them answered with confusion and uncertainty. Mostly they concluded that both people told the same lie. However, if I said, "Mary lied that John lied that the Statue of Liberty was turned upside down," you would understand because I expressed the idea with repeated subordination—another instance of recursion.

Why is *Mary told a lie. John told a lie* hard? While it is easy to make a guess, it is very hard to put a guess inside a guess without the overt device of subordination. In other words, the unknown mental equivalent of subordination—used for nonverbal false belief—cannot be repeated on itself unless we use a system of representation, namely, language or a mental reflection of it. If you think you can put a guess within a guess without subordination, then try a guess within a guess within a guess (*John told the truth. Mary told a lie. Fred told a lie . . .*). It gets tough as a sequence of inferences, but every day *New York Times* readers handle sentences with five or six embeddings relating to each other.

To put it differently, with no mode of representation we cannot easily, if at all, create an inferential structure like [*guess* [*guess* [*guess*]]], where we are guessing about guessing about guessing. As you read it, you might have a glimmer of what such a thought would be, but it is hard to hold it in mind without seeing it written down. It is just like the old observation that it is hard to count the stripes on an imaginary zebra. The image is not stable enough to allow another module (math) to work on it. As soon as you draw a zebra on paper—an external mode of representation—it is easy to put another module to work.

Grammar can help thought the way that zeroes help numerical representation. A numerical analogy would be this: we perceive a large mass of individuals, we determine that the mass is therefore countable, and we would like that precision. So then we count and arrive at a specific number. Before we began, we had a large mass, the recognition of individuals, countability, and the desire for precision. We do not have the number until we do the count, but counting does not add a concept. This is exactly like realizing that we can understand 1, 10, maybe 100 (say, number of fingers times number of fingers), but very soon we need real, written zeroes to represent the process any further. We cannot manipulate 100 trillion in our minds and state what half of it plus one would be. We can do it easily if we write down the zeroes.

The same information can be represented with Roman numerals or an abacus, but then it is not as available for further manipulation. Multiplication is hard with Roman numerals. An abacus may perhaps allow addition easily (swift-fingered owners of Chinese restaurants who preferred the abacus to a nearby cash register were once common), but not other operations. Slide rules have other advantages and disadvantages. The older mathematicians had coded operations into a set of rapid jerks that sometimes were faster than calculators. We code knowledge in many, many ways—for instance, I have the whole alphabet coded into the motion of my fingers as I type now, though I have no overt mental image of the keyboard alphabet so it would be difficult for me to count the number of letters from my typing knowledge. Language, then, is like a mental blackboard. It enables us to do operations inside operations, just as a blackboard allows us to add as many zeroes as we like to a number.

With these ideas in mind, let us return to our investigation of why young children answer the standard false-belief-experiment question in such a way that they apparently do not attribute propositional false belief to another person. We will see that the problem is not that children are cognitively unable to attribute false belief in any way, but that failure to represent complex sentences may mean that the deductive reasoning required in conversations is much more difficult or impossible.

The Growth of Recursive Subordination

Considerable research suggests that children first attach clauses as if they were new sentences. In fact, a string of relative clauses can easily be paraphrased as a series of sentences joined by *and*.[11] The first of these sentences is just like the second:

This is the toy that I got for my birthday that my dad bought that my sister wants too.

This is the toy that I got for my birthday *and* that my dad bought *and* that my sister wants too.

Suppose that children at first represent a complex declarative sentence like *She thinks it is mine* in the same way:

She has a thought. It is mine.

If so, the two parts of the sentence are connected by mental inference, but not by syntactic subordination.

However, a question *requires* us to make a connection to something subordinate. A question like

*What is it? John wants.

would be ungrammatical, but if we put this sequence into a subordinate clause, then it is all right:

What is it that John wants?

Children must have these recursive forms; as argued in chapter 6, they are needed to allow long-distance questions:

What did John say that Bill believes that Fred wants ____?

So for the child there may be a difference between the statement with a false belief (*She thinks it is mine*), where an inference can connect *she thinks* and *it is mine*, and the question with a false belief (*Whose does she think it is?*), where more than an inference between clauses is needed: a real subordinate clause that allows the mechanics of question formation to work (as is true for the false-belief-experiment question *What will he think is in the box?*).

Propositions and Entailments

If the sentential structure mirrors the cognitive structure that the sentence expresses, it is possible that children who answer the false-belief-experiment question incorrectly have not developed the cognitive embedded structure that is parallel to the question and that will deliver a notion of propositional false belief to conscious reflection. To answer a false belief question, one must have the propositional structure that allows one to derive a further proposition. The classic example of derived propositions is a syllogism: Socrates is a man; all men are mortal; therefore, Socrates is mortal. It is this capacity to derive further propositions—to see logical entailments—that both linguistic and cognitive representations must be rich enough to allow. What reasoning must the child follow? It is roughly this propositional deduction:

The cover of the box indicates the contents of the box (crayons).
My friend will see only the cover of the box.
Therefore, she will think the box contains crayons.

The child must derive the third proposition by a deduction from the first two, which then leads to a subordinate clause representation, from which she can derive an answer to the question.

   A summary may be helpful at this point:

1. A child may have implicit concepts that are not fully conscious.
2. A concept that is fully conscious requires a mode of representation that allows further representations.
3. Sentential recursion allows us to keep embedding propositions to create complex meanings.
4. Propositions allow further propositions to be formulated in terms of them.
5. Answering a question requires us to perform a further operation, to deduce a new entailment, a proposition, as an answer to the question.
6. We can attribute a propositional false belief to someone else via an embedding structure. Such a structure allows a new operation, question formation, which in turn allows us to deduce a further proposition that answers the question.
7. In sum, it is the fact that false belief is embedded in language in a very particular way that makes attributing false belief in questions more difficult.

   Are young children incapable of recursive subordination? This is an important question that is still being studied. However, one can imagine a five-year-old saying something like this—four clauses, two of them embedded, plus one instance of ellipsis, all packed into thirteen words:

"Mom said you said that I ate the ice cream, but I didn't."

If young children can indeed say things like this, then they are not far from meeting the recursion requirement.

Unconscious Entailments

Is it possible to compute entailments unconsciously? I consider this question to be a real mystery, yet one that reflects most deeply on our view of humanity. Does the action "walk to the fridge to get milk" entail a proposition: *there is milk in the fridge*? If so, then many creatures unconsciously make propositional deductions. Freud's approach to the unconscious treats it as a domain as rich as consciousness. Yet to many people it feels like consciousness is special. I have no answer, but in the absence of an answer, what should we think? A conservative assumption is that, to remain as respectful as possible, we should assume that our unconscious—and therefore a child's—has all the mental intricacy of consciousness.[12]

Point of View

Is recursion sufficient to allow a child to project propositional false belief onto another mind, or are other abilities presupposed?

Lurking in this discussion is the question of how a child computes another point of view, which has been a focal point of work by Bart Hollebrandse.[13] The suggestion that children actually have no "theory of another person's mind"—taken rigorously at face value—would lead us to expect that a child cannot compute another point of view anywhere because a point of view also requires a mind. However, even the simplest of requests like "Come here" requires a child to see the word *here* from another person's point of view. If children couldn't do this, a child might respond to his mother's "Come here" by saying, "I *am* here" (from his own point of view).

Pointer words (deictics) engage point of view in a way that children can handle, even if the situation is complex. Chris Tanz found that nursery school children can switch several pronouns at once.[14] In Tanz's study, children were able to respond to the request

"Ask *her* what color *she* thinks *my* eyes are"

by turning to another child and asking,

"What color do *you* think *his* eyes are?"

So, as with false belief, it is not simply the concept "point of view" that we must tangle with, but how it is represented in particular mental systems.

Now let us return to the mystery of why children do not grasp questions. Again, this will be an oversimplified conjecture. If I say,

"John thinks that the world is flat,"

I am linking the clause *the world is flat* to *John*. But if someone asks me a question, then pragmatically it is the questioner whose point of view I am pulled toward. We can feel this effect emotionally when we consider a question like this:

Who is your best friend, me or Johnny?

It is clear that the questioner has a point-of-view attitude that is very pertinent to how the listener answers. So when a question about *the hearer's point of view* arises, it is potentially in conflict with *the questioner's point of view*, which must also be coordinated with *the sentence subject's point of view*. It is as if we filled in the question *Whose toy does she think it is?* with the speaker's and hearer's points of view:

(*I* ask) whose toy (*you* think) *she* thinks it is.

This is an oversimplification, but it captures the rough idea that the child is computing point of view on top of recursive subordination. In other words, the computational challenge does not end with the derivation of new propositions. The child must compute those propositions with an awareness of the complex points of view entailed in simple dialogues.

This is an additional challenge to thinking on one's own. Many teachers will ask a child a question that they think the child knows the answer to but then find the child somehow intimidated. One might jump to the conclusion that the questioning teacher is "unfriendly"—but in fact the problem may be that computing the whole situation is more complex than one thinks.

■ ■ ■

| **Exploration 13.1**
Shifty pronouns
(maintaining point of view) | Point-of-view questions can easily be constructed around the dinner table. For example, a father might nod toward his daughter and say to his son, |

"Ask her if *she* thinks *you* would like to eat *my* vegetables."
("Do *you* think *I* would like to eat *his* vegetables?")

Some children treat *ask* as if it were *tell* and may just say "No," so you will need to be sure the children you are conversing with understand the difference. See if they give different answers to these requests:

"Ask me something."
"Tell me something."

Then start with simple questions:

"Ask me what color my eyes are."
("What color are your eyes?")

Then:

"Ask me what color I think your eyes are."
("What color do you think my eyes are?")

And so on.

The Art of Abstraction

We have seen that the standard false belief experiment poses both grammatical and cognitive challenges for the young child, involving questions and point of view. Other mental operations—other modules—are involved as well and make children's eventual computation of correct answers to the false-belief-experiment questions even more remarkable.

Hidden further within the false belief controversy is a point about the nature of thinking itself—namely, that most of good thinking involves a kind of systematic forgetting.[15] The concept of "abstraction" means the loss of particulars.

A 2004 *Newsweek* report on memory cited a study of rats whose "intelligence" was inversely proportional to their memory.[16] The better they were at remembering things, the worse they were at "figuring things out." Famous mnemonists also reportedly have tremendous ability to retain detail and little ability to rise above it.[17] What is the connection?

The *Newsweek* article pointed out that when we think, we subtract as rapidly as we can all of the particular anchors in a situation, leaving ourselves to the greatest extent possible with "general" or "generic" observations. That is why remembering meaning and forgetting actual sentences is crucial to comprehension. The field of parsing is largely about building a model of how, moment by moment, we delete knowledge. Our minds automatically separate people, locations, and events from each other and put them in different sets. The fact that Sam and Mary went to the movies last week ends up in Sam's "evening date" set and the fact that they saw

Crouching Tiger, Hidden Dragon ends up in his "movie" set, making questions like "You and I went to the movies last week, but what did we see?" and "I know I saw *Crouching Tiger*—but was it with you?" commonplace. Students legitimately are annoyed if their teacher remembers insightful remarks made during class, but forgets who made them and thus fails to give students the individual recognition they may deserve. In a meeting one can hear, "Someone suggested, I forget who, that we open the store an hour earlier." It is what we often want: to consider a proposition independent of its author. This "loss" of particulars is part of the process of forming abstractions like "I go to movies about five times a month." The general idea knocks out the particular facts.[18]

Kinds of Propositions   I have argued that deducing propositions from propositions is hard work. But there are different kinds of propositions whose truth and falsity have vastly different criteria. The false belief task requires the child to evaluate a specific situation, not a general proposition. It might be, as we have seen before, that children can compute abstract propositions more easily. Remember how tricky definite articles—reference to particulars—turned out to be. Let's investigate a little.

The attraction of abstraction is evident in a well-known human foible: we generalize too quickly. We hear statements like "John misses meetings" when in fact he missed only one. Children do it too. "I don't like Johnny because he takes my toys," says a child, and the parent points out, "He did that just once, but every other time you had fun playing together."

The presence of particulars is usually linked to definite articles. Consider this statement:[19]

John thinks that bananas are blue.

We know instantly, simply by invoking what we know about bananas, that it is false. But watch what happens when we add a definite article:

John thinks that the bananas are blue.

This statement invokes a totally different mental search. It *presupposes* that a particular set of bananas exists, and we have to figure out what bananas they are before we can decide whether John's thought is true or false.[20] In other words, John's thought could be true in many ways: a play could involve blue bananas, a child could paint bananas blue, or a story could be about animate bananas that are unhappy. When beliefs have to be evaluated by first locating a range of particulars and then grasping a proposition about them, two quite different tasks are entangled.

All of the false belief situations involve remembering not only the proposition, but also the point of view (who) and the specifics (the place, the person, the toy). It is this three-way computation, not any of the individual ingredients, that may well challenge a young child. It could be that the child who drops the point of view or drops particular places from memory is just too quickly invoking abstraction.

So what does this add up to? The typical view is that children move from the specific to the abstract, but we have seen evidence that abstraction comes easy and that learning to be specific is the hard work. It is not going up the ladder of abstraction, it is coming down the ladder of abstraction that is hard, demands attention, and easily goes awry, so that the child (or the adult) falls off. That is why politicians aim at sound bites, easily "understood" by everyone, because "the facts" are so hard to keep straight.

■ ■ ■

Exploration 13.2
Are bananas blue?
(false belief and generics)

We can try to shine light more directly on children's grasp of falsehood and presupposition. (Related explorations on reference are found in chapter 5.) First ask,

"Are bananas blue?"

This tests whether the child can recognize that a proposition can be false. A different situation arises when we violate the conversational custom that both partners in a conversation should have common ground (for example, by introducing an object into the conversation before referring to it with *the*). If you ask,

"Are the bananas blue?,"

it will be natural for the child to respond, "What bananas?"—accepting the presupposition that the bananas exist but pointing out that the conversational common ground (which bananas you are talking about) does not exist. In an experimental setting, children gave this response (though not always) when they were asked,

"Do you like the elephant on my head?"

Many five- and six-year-old children said, "What elephant?," although some just said "No."[21]

Now let us complicate matters a little. Show the child a row of black bananas:

Then ask,

"Are bananas black?"

In this case, you are asking a question about generic bananas (which are yellow) in the face of incompatible particulars (the row of black bananas). If the child understands the generic force of the question, she will answer "No." But if you ask,

"Are the bananas black?,"

presumably she will allow *the* to seek the particular and immediately answer "Yes."[22]

The Abstraction of Particularity: An Individual Art   What justifies the word *art* in the title of this section? Once again, I will make my familiar claim: each of us develops an individual art of abstraction; each of us sees personal, emotional, social, or mechanical generalizations somewhat differently from other people. For example, even in a fairly technical field like computer science, some people seem to have an intuitive grasp of how to tackle problems that is very different from others' grasp, and far from pure "logical deduction."

We relate to each other differently not only because of our own personalities but also because of how we put together abstractions about others. Whether we deal with juvenile delinquents or faculty members, we put together an implicit vision of positive and negative traits that allows each of us to relate to others differently. How do you bring out what you sense as the latent good will of a juvenile delinquent while being wary of his temper, or the latent generosity of a faculty member who is shy? So our individual formulas, our individual "art," is at work again even where we think that a systematic sort of "common ground" is present.

I would conclude, then, that knowing just when to drop particulars is an art with many social aspects. In every discussion, we seek acceptable abstractions by remaining aware of individual points of view, or by trying to abstract away from them. Even nursery school situations show the difference. One child likes shallow water, another likes deep water. A third might suggest, "Oh, here's a spot where there's a little of each," and a fourth might say, "Let's play in the sand instead"—forgetting which person likes what, but simply seeking a more abstract way out of a contradiction. How the young child develops this art is far from transparent. Whether a deep maturational event or a single psychological principle is involved remains open. Still, it is always important to see the full intricacy of the endpoint in psychological growth in our effort to envision the early stages.

Multiple Methods for Thinking

Karen Searcy, a biologist, suggests a nice metaphor, entirely relevant to the notion that our mind/body can represent a single concept in different ways: the body has dozens of clocks in it.[23] Clocks regulate all sorts of biological processes—sleep, hunger, remembering to water plants. Interestingly, diverse notions of time often make their slow way to consciousness as a single "concept," though much remains unconscious. If I suddenly say, "Gee, I haven't had couscous for a long time," or "Yes, I know that face, but I haven't seen that guy for twenty years," what is the mechanism that enables me to make that temporal judgment—how was the memory stored so that I know? Why can we use *faster* both to describe one race car flashing ahead of another by a few milliseconds and to claim that the Austro-Hungarian Empire declined more quickly than the Roman Empire? The same term covers quite different mental mechanisms.

Those innate unconscious notions are no less sophisticated—nor any less defining of humanity—than conscious ones. A child may be perplexed about ambiguous *words* relating to time: does *soon* mean "a few minutes" ("We'll eat soon") or "a few months" ("Coming soon to a theater near you")? Still, very human awareness of time is present when the same child rushes to grab his grandma with an intensity that reflects his awareness of the fact that he has not seen her in six months. Even an infant must already have multiple representations of time.

Nonverbal False Belief Tasks

False belief experiments have been carried out entirely without language. In the nonverbal version of the false belief experiment, the participating child sees a picture of a boy putting an object in one place, then a picture of a girl (out of sight of the boy) putting it in another place. The experimenter asks the child, "Where will the boy look?" Some children assume the boy knows the object's new location even though he never saw the object moved.

It is primarily (though not exclusively) children who do not demonstrate full knowledge of recursive subordination who make this mistake. To turn this around: why, when children have set the recursive mechanism for subordination in their language (in English, the fact that *that* comes at the beginning of a subordinate clause, not at the end as in some grammars: *John thinks that Bill is here/*John thinks Bill is here that*), can they handle nonlinguistic false belief contexts better? *Better* is perhaps the crucial word, since some children who do not show knowledge of syntactic complementation still succeed in the false belief task. It is like the mathematics analogy: Arabic numerals represent numbers and, with the help of zeroes, are ideal for doing mathematical operations. Roman numerals can represent the same numbers as Arabic numerals, and it is possible to do mathematical operations with them—but it is much harder. With a generative form of complementation, the subordination structure is readily available as a mental structure and is easily invoked; for children who have mastered linguistic complementation, the false belief task is easier. But children have many forms of thinking available. It seems natural to expect that other methods of inference—usable but less ideal, like Roman numerals—can still capture false belief. Which mental metaphor does the child unconsciously reach for? It is like reaching for the Arabic numeral system with zeroes, Roman numerals, an abacus, or a slide rule to do a math problem. The child may not always grab the right one or have developed the full set. If the child has not developed one of the grammatical options that help in the false belief task (say, subordination or compounding), then those options are not available at all. Other methods may take more work, like an inference between two independent sentences. If so, the child may more easily move to an abstraction not bound to an individual perspective. But if situational support is strong, other methods of arriving at various kinds of false belief *are* possible—false belief is simply not a single mental entity. (What is "situational support" for a child? Have you ever met a child who cannot reason his way around a math problem very well but who is wonderfully adept at discussing intricate sports situations? The logic of baseball is so familiar that the child can make logical extensions without difficulty.)

Nevertheless, failure on nonverbal false belief tasks and its putative link to an allied form of grammatical representation—though no loss of humanity is involved—could reflect a significant handicap. It might lead to difficulty with the kinds of computationally intricate tasks that school demands or with other activities—like solving children's whodunits or other mysteries.

In sum, the grammarlike model, which may be derived from grammar itself, is that recursive subordination (or recursive compounds) could be essential to recursive false belief in a cognitive representation:

Bill denied that Alice believed that John thought that the world was flat.

Therefore, grammar really can help represent thought—it is like a blackboard that helps us keep track of a lot of zeroes. The blackboard is essential to the thought, but the blackboard is not the thought itself.

Language That Helps Thought

I have argued that language is a blackboard for thought, nothing more. Could concepts inside words help organize another module, like vision? Elizabeth Spelke has explored circumstances where there is an arguable connection.[24]

Certainly a child would know that these arrays are different without help from language:

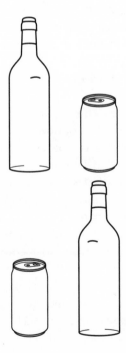

We do not need the verbal expression *The can is on the right on top and on the left on the bottom* to be able to see the difference. However, again, if we construct a complex concept, then notions like "right" and "left" might be important. Try making a mental map using these instructions:

Go this way (pointing) to the corner, then go the other way; go two blocks and go the other way; then go a mile and go the other way.

Now try it using these directions:

Go left to the corner and turn right; go two blocks and turn left; go one mile and turn right.

The contrastive term *the other way* in the first version could in fact carry the same information as *left* and *right* in this version, but it would be much harder to build a mental image with the *this way...the other way* instructions than with the *left...right* instructions. In effect, the words *left* and *right* allow an independent reorientation at any point, which in turn makes it easier to construct a mental map with a kind of meta-instruction: at each turn, go the opposite way from the way you went last time.

What to conclude from all of this? Again, it is not the ideas but the organization of ideas that is at issue. Is the notion a thousand or a million a new concept or a complicated version of an old concept? The answer is not as important as seeing that mental methods of representation help us manage complexity wherever we encounter it.

Children's Mental Leaps and Ours: Ordering Higher-Order Operations

To make sure that a child's dignity does not slip away from our psychological imagery, it is wise to remind ourselves of how much humanity simple acts entail. Just saying "Hi" implies a complex relation among human beings, even though it is not easily delineated with available scientific notions. Likewise, we have seen that what is involved in conscious rumination, giving rise to errors detected in false belief experiments, may be less sophisticated than what our minds carry out implicitly and unconsciously. The experimental false belief tasks are really testing a higher-order operation rather than simply false belief: a further judgment made on top of a false belief representation, the assumption of another point of view in order to answer a question. It is like putting false belief on a blackboard, or using zeroes, to create a fixed object from which to make a further judgment. The invention of the term *false belief* is just such a further operation on such situations, which we also expect to be beyond the ability of a nursery school child.

These speculative remarks are just that—quite speculative. We remain a long way from having secure representations for cognitive activities. Without them, we must remain cautious about every assertion with respect to how thinking works. We know what thoughts look like once expressed, but the crucial representations that precede expression—where thinking really happens—remain elusive. What is the representation that allows us to choose the words that go into our sentences? We readily take the look on someone's face as an avenue to her true thoughts. What is the thought behind the look on someone's face, which we may interpret, but of which he may be unaware? If we see ambivalence in someone's eyes, how can we state the state of mind behind it? Is it made up of two incompatible representations, both feeding into one face? The mind behind an odd look on a person's face could be as complex as the one behind a discussion of sophisticated scientific theories. We really do not know.

These speculations may be wrong; they are surely incomplete. Nonetheless, they show that we need an expansive model—not a minimized model—of all kinds of thinking in order to see what children are doing in a way that does not diminish them unfairly. Older people too may lose particulars too rapidly, but they retain plenty of human wisdom about other people and therefore other minds. Ironically, it is the same habit of easy abstraction that allows psychologists to overstate children's mental limitations (by attributing egocentricity to them—unfairly, it is now commonly believed). To be a bit harsh about this, the weakness that some researchers wish to attach to children may better describe their own. In fact, in my casual observations, it has been precisely those parents who have difficulty seeing several points of view in a discussion who may say or insist that their children are "egocentric."

The same danger exists in the study of false belief. How can we be careful not to abstract too quickly, to make sure that a claim about one module of mind is not instantly applied to the whole person? We all make simple abstractions about the nature of thinking because we cannot keep its full complexity in mind.

Once again, we arrive at the view that we must be vigilant about not underrating human beings, children in particular, in our effort to find simplifying insights. This whole discussion of how language and thought connect is built upon the idea that children may fail to compute a representation properly without failing to have concepts (whatever they are—a topic that philosophers quarrel over constantly). Principles can be expressed differently in different mental domains, with very little translation. The distinction between conceptual problem and computational problem is important not only for how we treat children but also for how we think about them. If we regarded grammar the way we regard vision, then we would be no more tempted to treat *I don't got none* as a mistake in thinking than we would consider an inability to see a faraway object to be a mistake in seeing. Without a better understanding of grammar, we must constantly fight an inevitable inclination to overstatements about children's minds, which really pose a challenge to their dignity. As I will argue in the next chapter, the modular perspective (though not without its own problems) is the key to this ethical challenge.

The Ideas behind the Concept of "Idea"

What is the connection between language and mind? We have focused on the details of grammar, but how about plumbing the depths more deeply, asking the big questions about human nature?

In this chapter, we explore what the concept of "idea" itself is—to what extent conscious, to what extent unconscious—and where other notions of mind come in: our quirky beliefs, our shifty points of view, our capacity to build abstractions, legitimate and illegitimate, and our nonlinguistic thoughts. They all reverberate in language differently. By seeing how far language fails to capture mind, we get more insight into mind.

When we think about the child's mind growing, it is too easy to think of it as full of ideas. If we turn a spotlight on that word *ideas*, it starts to break down into many more interesting notions that make consciousness seem like a shadow-and-light theater where ideas are only half-visible.

You may feel a bit uncomfortable about the discussion to follow. I will not be completely clear about what I mean by *thought, emotion, belief,* and *nonlinguistic concepts.* I will lean a lot on examples. That is, however, the best I can do. Real science is loaded with unclarities and half-articulated ideas. So you should not blame yourself (or me, for that matter) for the many tremors of uncertainty that remain in this discussion.

Implicit Ideas

Grammar is famously the domain of "innate ideas," as Chomsky has described them. Being innate means that they are a tacit, or implicit, part of our unconscious. What about implicit ideas outside grammar?

An *implicit* idea can, at times, be evident to a child even when an *explicit version* of the same idea is still incomprehensible. This seems paradoxical at first but quickly becomes self-evident. Most children do not understand a term like *infinity* until they are in grade school. Yet even a three-year-old may resolutely use the term *never* ("I'll never eat carrots!")—a term that has its emotional thrust precisely because it entails the *notion* of infinity. Thus, words seem to make our ideas explicit, but they contain hidden implications as well, which are not explicitly conscious. Likewise, the concept of causation and terms like *cause* and *causation* are not acquired until the teenage years, but seemingly more complex words—like *because*, which entails both the idea of causation and an attribution of cause—are available to four-year-olds.

These linguistic facts imply that children grasp things in bundles, where the whole is evident and genuinely entails its parts, but the child cannot yet sift out the parts. This by itself indicates that the acquisition of knowledge is not fundamentally incremental. Children are oriented to larger units, patterns, whose parts are more remote than the whole. It is just like the fact that we humans can perceive in three dimensions more easily than in two.

So children are very often capable of the right idea, but they fail at some aspect of grammar or word meaning. They can easily seem to misunderstand adults more fundamentally than they actually do. Piaget famously claimed that children do not understand reciprocity. One boy, for example, when asked about the boy next to him, said, "He is my brother"; however, when asked "Does your brother have a brother?," he answered, "I don't know." From cases like this, Piaget and others have concluded that children lack the notion of reciprocity, and typically this lack is attributed to egocentrism.[1] But three-year-olds easily understand *each other* in cases like *The children are kissing each other*, and may extend reciprocity to other cases even when the words themselves are not actually present, like *The boys are fighting*. At an implicit level, reciprocity is very much present. Similarly, children with imperfect knowledge of passive may not grasp that there is an implicit agent in *The ball was dropped*, but surely they have the notion of agent elsewhere. What is in the child's mind is hard to say, but the best guess is that it is not the core notion of reciprocity that is lacking in young children, but whatever special requirements are needed for being verbally conscious of it—whatever higher form of knowledge is involved in understanding the word *reciprocity* itself. In any event, if we wish to keep the dignity of the child in mind, it is important that we do not casually assert that a child has no understanding of reciprocity when, as Jerome Bruner has shown, mere eye gaze is full of reciprocal awareness.[2]

Perception in Humans and Animals

We are not the only ones who live in a world of implicit ideas. All creatures do. Consider the epistemology of a frog. Its vision system distorts everything it sees so it can catch flies. The system makes flies look larger than they are, so the frog's tongue can grab one. If flies are disproportionately large for a frog, then the vision system distorts reality in one sense, but it serves the purposes of a frog just fine—and gives him something to eat. So distorting reality gives the organism advantages and therefore may serve an evolutionary purpose.

Our ears work the same way. Whispers are exponentially enhanced, given their actual volume (measured by machine), so we can discern their details. So we arrive at a nifty paradox: it is the distortion of reality that enables us to deal with reality. All of our senses involve a kind of magnification in order to achieve perception. Perception involves rejecting most of the possible points of focus in our environment. Autistic children seem to choose a different range of foci, which radically alters their capacity for finding the perceptions that are shared in most social situations.

Infinities Again

At any moment, there is an infinite set of ways a biological organism could perceive its immediate environment. Our human mind automatically selects a few that serve the intentions of human beings. If we look at an empty coffee cup in the evening, it may be a symbol of a pleasant conversation. In the morning, the same cup just feels like something to clean up. And that "gotta clean it up" feeling is different if you are about to go to work, and the feeling may vary in intensity with distance (a nearby cup may seem to need washing more than one that is twenty feet away). So, moment to moment, we are manipulating an infinite range of ways to focus on objects, combining an inherent heterogeneity of perception and attitude that comes from the fact that utterly different parts of mind contribute to every moment. Still, all these factors come highly orchestrated by the biology we have inherited.

The Epistemology and Logic of Animals

Now animals also have intentions which utilize limbs that embody abstract principles and infinities. That is the biology they have inherited. Scientists need to characterize it. Ray Jackendoff has argued that we have to attribute "if-then" logic to animals in order to explain what evolution has delivered.[3] If a monkey reaches for a banana, it will get something to eat, but only if it takes off the skin. We cannot really explain what the monkey does if we do not represent that "if-then" relation somewhere: only if I take off the skin, do I then get something to eat.

Evolution—guided in ways we do not understand—has clearly led to organisms which control physical systems that fulfill a complex array of linked "ideas," the same in some sense as a physical principle like gravity, but much closer to the sorts of ideas we associate with organic and ultimately human nature. If a child is born with an attachment to and trust in a parent, then that attachment entails many principles that the child will not have consciously and may not exhibit in other arenas. There is genuine altruism in the mother cat who risks and perhaps loses her own life fending off a predator to save a kitten. Why should we say her action is anything less, any less noble, just because it has fixed biological origins? Our human, more ruminative sorts of altruism may have the same kinds of origins with a few degrees of freedom added in. Those few degrees of freedom make a huge difference in our lives, but from a deeper biological perspective, animals are not so different.

Marc Hauser argues that moral perceptions are sharp and immediate, just like any others.[4] Suppose one child sees an infant about to fall and instinctively reaches out to prevent the accident. That instinctive action, I believe, calculated in milliseconds, entails an ethical and altruistic attitude built into the mind and muscles that make an arm reach out. The same child might completely neglect the infant's needs in other situations, because of either ignorance or indifference, but that hardly means that children are born devoid of moral dispositions.

Amoral Principles and the Modules of Mind

Inborn ideas, produced by biological principles, give the child his instinctive apprehension and avoidance of danger, moral principles, and amoral principles as well. What could an amoral principle be? Let's construct an example. Suppose a mother and her son fall through thin ice. As both are instinctively flailing around, the mother might unintentionally but uncontrollably hit her son in the head, causing his death. If instinctive behavior were under control of other moral perspectives, the mother might gladly restrain her flailing and sacrifice her own life for her son's, but those instinctive flailing actions are unable to integrate moral perspectives coming from another module of the brain. Therefore, the mother cannot reprogram her instinctive efforts to stay afloat with the moral imperative to save a child, even if in another realm of mind, granted more time, that is precisely what she would do. So the fatal slap was not truly an "accident"; it was an instinctive move immune to moral influence.

And, actually, our legal system will honor the diversity of mind that leads to such events, not accusing the mother of murder. No parent would be jailed because he or she did not save a child when both were instinctively trying to keep their heads above water.

The situation is reminiscent of the actions of certain kinds of split-brain patients who will button a shirt with one hand and unbutton it with the other. In a sense, we have many splits in our brains, largely independent modules that dictate different actions for the same situation. Resolving competing urges is a daily affair, and involves our personality modules as well. Most of us feel, at any moment, that perhaps we should be doing something else—our urges are competing in a hidden war.

The Concept of "Concept" Is a Poor Concept

The discussion to follow constructs a little logical scheme. In summary form, here is where we are going:

1. The mind has different modules.
2. What we think of as concepts (e.g., infinity, reciprocity) are represented in different ways in those different modules.
3. Translation between and within modules can be difficult.
4. As a result, saying that someone "has no concept of something" is an unfair generalization because the person may "have it" in some ways, just not the way we are thinking of.
5. Just because one of a person's modules is weak does not mean they all are.
6. So if a child or adult seems to be having trouble with a particular task, it may be because one particular module is weak or because translation between modules or even within a module is difficult or impaired.

Paul Churchland's observation quoted in chapter 12—that our notion of cognition must extend to our basic neurological organization—is both revealing and consequential. What is a concept? Our physical capacities are so quick—like 3-D perception—that we are unaware of how the concepts needed for vision are entangled in the particular cognitive map involved in seeing. The way our eyes unpack color and light is a far cry from the way an artist contemplates color and light, although we misleadingly use the same terms to describe them both.

The term *concept* and other conceptual words mislead us. Expressions like *good behavior* or *He has no concept of helping others* just cover too much cognitive territory—and even terms like *attention deficit syndrome* implicitly deny the diversity of factors that contribute to behavior.

Translation across modules is not always possible, nor do we yet understand how the translation works. For some people, the translation between seeing and finger strokes allows them to effortlessly sketch with great accuracy, whereas for others, no amount of training enables them to do it. To say "You see an oval, so draw an oval" is no help to any hapless, wannabe artist. All of geometry can be algebraically expressed, but for some people the translation between a visual and a numerical representation is harder than for others. Rather than talking about "the concept of X," we need to understand the particulars of how each module where X is represented works; and we need to understand those particulars before we can begin to understand the translation between modules. The term *concept* just gets in the way. It is useful as a starting point in academic discussions of this kind, but ideally we would state such concepts in ways that fit the modules they are embedded in. Reciprocity in eye gaze and in friendship are related, but stuffing them into one word distorts how differently they are represented in the mind.

Surely when we say a child has a concept, we do not mean the concept at the level at which academics talk about it. If I assert that a four-year-old understands the concept "cause and effect" when she asks "Why?," it does not mean that I think I can instantly expect her to understand the word *effect* or a physics formula that expresses it. "Cause and effect" is not one mental concept, but many, which is why it is discussed in high school science and not nursery school. It is an abstraction that crosses many mental domains and that is expressed differently in each.

The Evils of Unmodularity

We have other "concepts"—and lousy, unfair ones they are—that we toss around to inaccurately allude to what we mean, like "He's not very smart." To escape the broad psychological smear, we invent terms like *learning disabled*, which are not much of an improvement in their effect on our sense of dignity.

We cannot be fair to one another without accepting the modular independence of many aspects of mind. We know that hard-of-hearing does not mean "hard-of-thinking," but we do not easily make the same distinction within the mind itself: we have trouble seeing that hard-of-algebra does not mean hard-of-geometry.

Little breeds more trouble in the world of psychology than the concept "concept," which is so open that it can become a depository for ideology. The notion "egocentric," which is cavalierly loaded onto the image of children, nicely fits the wishes of those who ideologically expect their children to be selfish and competitive. One day I was sad to hear a parent exclaim with surprise that she was amazed how much her two- and four-year-old children loved each other. Her expectations had been programmed by modern notions of egocentricity to suppose that sibling rivalry was the only possibility. A three-year-old can be as quick as his mother to attend to a crying two-year-old. Three-year-olds are full of sympathy if we let ourselves see it.

When people say that others "have no concept of X," the statement is often justified by a link to language. A PBS program blithely asserted that members of a South American Indian tribe always say the equivalent of "The bowl broke" rather than "I broke the bowl." From this linguistic preference, the anthropologists and writers of the program were led to conclude that the culture had no "concept of responsibility," since no agent is expressed in sentences like *The bowl broke*—as if a preferred description of a dropped pot implies, for instance, that the tribe's members will be neglectful parents. It is rare that the locution *has no concept of* does not overstate something.

How do we develop a more refined view of the peculiarities of translation paths between different parts of mind? It is a huge challenge. Until we solve it, we need to collectively find more benign ways of talking about each others' minds.

Modules inside Modules

Translation may be difficult even within what looks like a single module. An interesting example is handwriting, or handedness of any kind. I know how to write my signature quickly and distinctively, but only with one hand. If I have "the concept," why am I unable to carry it out with both hands? Each hand does hundreds of things with equal neurological dexterity. It is not muscle tone that is making the difference. It is something we will eventually have to say about properties of writing knowledge that it does not easily transfer from one hand to another. That is, one hand, at some level, is able to follow an articulated cognitive map—a partly aesthetic representation—that the other hand can execute only in a gross fashion. In a sense, then, the mind of our dominant hand is actually different from the mind of our other hand.

At a subtler level, soccer players have to know how to kick goals with both feet. Yet they are always "better" with one foot. Wherein does the "betterness" lie? It is somehow bound up in subtle degrees of accuracy, eye-foot coordination, and translating between visual and tactile maps. Behind that "coordination" are mental maps full of what we are tempted to call "concepts," not just physical wiring. But the knowledge, though roughly transferable, is not *easily* transferable. There seem to be mini-modules inside modules that resist translation as well, a right-foot module distinct from a left-foot module inside our foot module (assuming we have a foot module).

Are Ideas the Right Idea?

A deeper philosophical question arises about the nature of ideas. We have decomposed the idea of an "idea" to the point where it no longer fits our intuitions. Maybe it is time for the term *idea* to die as we look more closely at it, to be replaced by terminology that covers the organic and inorganic world in a more coherent way.

This is not an uncommon development in science. In the nineteenth century, "life force" was an important scientific concept, and discovering it was a goal for biologists. However, the term *life force* lost coherence when microbiology came to dominate the field, and it has only literary currency today. Whatever the source of life, it has to be expressed in the terminology of microscopic entities, a task that is still dazzlingly difficult.

Our ultimate goal should be, I think, to show that the concepts in the human mind and the principles in the physical world belong to a common set. I will just take a few steps in that direction. Many philosophers, among them John Searle, hold that an idea is an inherently conscious phenomenon and not a property of a physical object.[5] In their view, if we embed the notion of "idea" in physical objects, we seem to obscure the notion itself of what an "idea" is. Where are ideas?

As an exercise, let us leap to the radically opposite view: physical objects in a real sense contain ideas. We describe physical relations in terms of physical principles that are both objects in our imagination and true statements about inanimate objects. The sun does not have the idea of "circularity," but the sun does describe a circle, and many physical consequences in astronomy can be attributed to its circularity. The counterintuitive aspect here is not in the notion of intrinsic "idea" but in the phrase *have an idea*. Does a bicycle have the idea of forward motion? If I break my arm, I have not lost the idea of what an arm is. But what have I lost? I have broken or lost a link (a crucial bone) in a system of coordination that carries out sophisticated ideas, needing a mathematical representation of how muscles and bones are temporally coordinated. Under this perspective, a full explanation of a broken arm will arrive at the conclusion that a kind of "physical idea is interrupted." There are plenty of philosophical niceties we could discuss at this point, but I hope the core perspective is relatively clear. This approach deserves respect if we are to understand our relation to physical systems. The biological aspect of organic systems and "ideas" will require some more philosophical precision before we see it clearly.

A Brief Glance at the Mind/Body Problem

The next paragraphs are a digression in philosophy for those who sense that some fairly radical ideas are afoot here. Let us push these arguments to their logical extremes and see where they go. They remain pertinent to how we see ourselves and our children. They are, once again, one scholar's views—not a representative view of developmental psychologists. Actually, they might be seen as a critique of representative views, were those views articulated and not just implied, as is usually the case.

My conclusion so far is this. The hardware of neurology will eventually be defined by the software (grammar) that it is designed to carry out. Likewise, the hardware of vision (retina) will eventually be defined by the software it is made to carry out (3-D interpretation). This train of thought leads to saying that, ultimately, the mind (software) will define what the body is (hardware) and not the other way around.[6] Labels for parts of neurology will come from mental descriptions, and quite likely there will be no independent notion of learning, or memory, or physical motion.

This may seem extreme, but in a way it is common sense. The explanation for why we have two eyes put right where they are—slightly separated—lies in the concept of stereoscopy, the use of two perspectives to determine distance. A measurement—your eyes are a couple of inches apart—does not capture this abstraction. And stereoscopy is not an accidental product of this physical relation—it is the explanation of why the physical relation is the way it is. Similarly, mind—contrary to many academics' views—is not an accidental by-product of the brain. Mind is the brain's purpose, so the brain cannot be adequately described without including its purpose. Furthermore, in order to capture the concept of stereoscopy, one must include principles of geometry. But now concepts used by the mind are playing a role in a physical description. The mind/body problem then reduces to the mind, not the other way around.

The Nonexistence of Learning

If abstract principles are at work, we should not conclude that the most abstract concept is the most correct concept. It is likely that there will be no separate biological concept of "motion" that captures the movement both of legs and of eyes. They are too different. Biological principles will not simply be principles of physics; rather, they will be linked to a definition of the kinds of motion that a leg or an eye can undertake.

In the same vein, visual learning and verbal learning are so different that any overarching theory of learning will miss many particulars. The level of abstraction required might obscure as much as it illuminates. We can say that a person must "discriminate" both sounds and images, but the term *discriminate* just avoids the mechanisms of visual and auditory perception and the fact that the kinds of information in hearing and seeing are so different. The concept "discriminate" as a generalization (though it was dear to Piaget) may not be useful.

Moreover, the mechanisms are inherently nonintentional, though their uses may be highly intentional. We may turn a key deliberately in order to start a car, but from then on the mechanism operates automatically. Language acquisition is in part the result of hearing, which is involuntary, more than of listening, which is deliberate. We have eyelids, but no earlids, so the sound just comes in and gets automatically organized. The same holds for syntactic organization at a higher level. While there are intentional acts—desires to communicate—that initiate the linguistic system, much of the rest is a mechanism immune to intention. Thus, it is a mistake to seek to define grammar in terms of communicative intentions, just as it would be a mistake to try to define a car's motor in terms of the human desire to go somewhere.

In a fully articulated theory of biology, the term *learning* may disappear altogether. It would be an odd thing to say that "trees learn to drop their leaves in the fall," but if we insisted on extending the notion of learning to trees, then we would end up with such a formulation. In fact, extending biological metaphors in the opposite direction may be more helpful. Language acquisition happens to a child more like a tree acquiring and losing leaves than like a person deliberately learning to do mathematics.

This is why many of us in linguistics prefer the term *language growth*, to indicate that language develops like an internal organ, to use a metaphor developed by Noam Chomsky.[7] This is a strong mentalist perspective—mentalism being the claim that one cannot adequately describe an object without using mental vocabulary. This view contradicts the claims of modern connectionist learning models that seek overarching abstractions to cover all types of "learning." Much could be added to these brief remarks. They are, at least, logical extrapolations of the strong mentalist perspective.

Just where has this discussion come to rest? We have resolutely pursued extrapolations from language to the whole human mind, despite frequent uncertainty. We have found plenty to say about the diversity of modules and the question of how the mind achieves translations. What remains is perhaps the biggest mystery of mind: how do we consult and integrate impulses from diverse modules to decide upon a single action at a single moment? We will need to imagine more architecture—more abstract principles—before we really understand how the mind works. Understanding the principles behind hand-eye coordination may capture more of the essence of the human mind than understanding the principles behind just hands or just eyes.

How do the connections between modules grow and mature? What should we imagine transpires within the growing mind? Approaches to these questions—in both academic and popular psychology—remain pitifully crude beside the reality of how the mind grows. Every intellectual claim has an ethical reflex. How we speak to our children should respect the modular complexity they embody, which is the topic of the next chapter.

15 In Defense of Dignity

We have looked at the nature of ideas philosophically, and at how they penetrate children's language and even our notion of what children are like.[1] Now we turn to the ethical implications of this perspective on language for how we regard children and for the responsibility of adults, particularly intellectuals.

The key question is, how can we assume responsibility for ourselves and others when we can never understand others fully—including children—and when many of our most important ideas about human nature are not secure and solid? In other words, how can we develop an ethical philosophy that uses our incomplete knowledge in a responsible way? I will argue that ideas have not been used responsibly and that we need to fashion a new intellectual culture where our ethical benchmarks are easier to see. I suggest a simple one: be suspicious of all judgments that denigrate human nature. This is particularly important with respect to how we judge children and when we should feel entitled to judge them.

The Instant Impact of Imperfect Ideas

While some people think that ideas are just ideas until they are "implemented," I have pursued a different assumption here: all ideas have an instant impact on our lives, though often unconscious. Can we see the impact? I think, for instance, that the parent who playfully reprimands a child while muttering, "You little monkey," has been influenced by Darwinist theory. (It would be interesting to know what parents long ago—say, in the deistic fourteenth century—said in a moment of playful irritation to their children.) The impulsive criminal who says, "I just don't know what made me rob the store," has experienced a trickle-down version of the idea that free will is an illusion. The teen who defends his unpopular views by saying, "It all depends on how you look at it," is the beneficiary of relativistic popular culture, which itself is unconsciously boosted by relativistic physics. Ideas filter down to the tiniest gestures. Parents use both body language and their inherited culture of ideas to interpret and respond to the gestures even of infants. The judgments "She just wants attention" or "She likes to be near her brother" contain very different dispositions toward human nature. We sometimes measure each other's sense of self-esteem in the first milliseconds that our eyes meet. Commentators have noted that despite all the words and actions that manifest George W. Bush's sense of confidence over the years, sometimes his eyes have a fearful "deer in the headlights" look—and for some, the image flashed in those milliseconds weighs as much as many years' worth of decisions and speeches. And even such fleeting impressions can incorporate bias. Republicans and Democrats judge the famous Bush "smirk" in different ways.

The blending of seemingly incompatible ideas may be beneficial. Think of the long-running debate over using the whole-word method or phonics to teach reading.[2] Many reading teachers have the intuition that they should take a middle path and teach both, to the dismay of the partisans. Perhaps these teachers are carrying out an intuition that is actually far ahead of science. Perhaps there is a sophisticated algorithm that mediates between whole words and phonetics in ways that are not yet understood, just as has been argued for other cross-modular formulas.

Imagine another era. The mother in a slave-owning family whose child played with black children might, with a commitment to her child, have been able to see that the black child was the one who understood numbers best or was her child's best friend, despite the ideology of inferiority. The mother's attitude would have been a combination of a crazy and mean-spirited ideology and a simple, benevolent perception of what was best for her child and true about her child's friend, despite the contradictory nature of the ideas. We are fortunate that our attitudes are shaped not only by current intellectual trends but also by undeniable human perceptions.

Nevertheless, we are all caught in a web of partial truths, somewhat contradictory ideas, and perceptions of daily life. Most parents are in the same boat as the slave owner, encompassing views determined by both ideology and everyday perceptions. Is my child driven by love, hormones, justice, rewards, group-think, God, karma, bad genes, or what? These alternatives reflect philosophical differences over what it means to be a human being. Such alternatives can be present while unresolved—when we glance at a sleeping child or try to influence a teenager. Our success as parents may depend as much on how we grasp the world of ideas we live in as on offering love. And seeing that world clearly means realizing that we are all standing in a forest of conflicting views about what a child or a human being is. Professing belief in one theory or another does not fully free us from the influence of discredited ideas or ones we reject ourselves.

This book contains a plea for recognizing the personal and intellectual uniqueness and inalienable dignity of each child. That idea seems to be—and is—just common sense, but it is common sense that can be hard to maintain. Modern communication means that we are exposed to more contradictory thinking, more incompatible ideas, than human beings have ever faced before. If each idea, right or wrong, has some impact, then we live in a universe, not only where science makes steady progress, but also where it is unusually difficult to see oneself and others with clarity.

Intellectual Responsibility

Though we have no way to fully fathom how ideas affect us, somehow the impact of ideas should be a part of the moral calculus of those who promote them, whether intellectuals, teachers, or parents, particularly when it is obvious that only "partial truths" are available. For instance, a Darwinist may object to my forging a link between evolutionary ideas and the parenting style of those who laughingly call their child "little monkey." Some protest (though not the sociobiologists) that biologists are only talking about insects and mice when they talk about insects and mice and that no extrapolation to people is intended; Darwinism need not lead to neglect of poor people. Such disclaimers are really inadequate moral evasions: the emergence of social Darwinism is an inevitable and logical extension of the fitness concept, and therefore its inhuman consequences are partly the responsibility of intellectuals who invite, deliberately or not, extrapolations from animal behavior to human behavior. The consequences of ideas extend from what a mother's glance contains to a politician's decision to approve ethnic cleansing.

It is important to realize that most sciences of the human being, including much of medicine, remain in a "pretheoretical" state. The term *pretheoretical* is used for those early-stage sciences based on models where central terms have no rigorous definition and where ordinary intuition is ahead of science in its subtlety of insight. I think that no approach to the human mind can extract a subpart of human ability without distorting the overarching "self" that organizes our actions. For scientists to exhibit humility before the complexity of human nature is a virtue and not a failure. It means simply that we should prevent any crude science from displacing sophisticated kinds of human intuition when real human beings are involved. "Scientific" wisdom is nowhere near human wisdom.

Many intellectuals realize the limits of their own ideas, but they may not see that those limitations are not evident to the public. I once heard an anecdote about an economist who promoted the theory of "rational expectations." He was contemplating a sabbatical abroad with considerable uncertainty. A friend said he should just use his rational expectations model and measure the pros and cons mathematically. He replied, "Oh, be serious, this is the real world." In effect, he was confessing that the model really did not apply very well. Such truths are often kept for friends, not included as part of one's public posture.

Ideas and Dignity

How, then, should we proceed? Once again, I think it is fair to say that our deepest intuition about human nature is that all people should respect each other's dignity, and especially each child's dignity. If so, the goal of humanitarian science should be to honor that notion in a scientifically respectable way. Dignity is the core of our sense of self, but it is easily undermined. I think efforts to subdivide human abilities lead to primitive definitions of human nature that inevitably damage our sense of mutual regard.

How can we recapture and preserve human dignity in science? It is a very difficult task because science must begin with simple models, yet it is precisely the inherent oversimplification of our models that endangers our respect for one another. The problem is not confined to psychology; it arises in physics and biology as well, which also have implications for our vision of human nature. The way to minimize the problem is to articulate the goal of psychological research in a way that does not avoid mysteries, but highlights them as the domain in which to seek the deepest principles of human nature. We must try to project what a fully articulated theory of self and intelligence must entail, so that it is very clear that we have not yet attained it.

An Ethical Benchmark

The critic and essayist Dwight MacDonald once said wisely that if something "feels wrong, then it is wrong," even if we are not sure why.[3] Perhaps we should be asking about every theory, "How does it feel?" Many parents rely on Dr. Spock because he tells them to trust their own feelings and intuitions more than the popular experts.[4] Skepticism of both academic and popular theories is probably the best stance. (Skepticism about the inevitable truth of one's feelings is, of course, just as important.)

In that spirit, let us carve out a rough principle:

A full theory of mind will leave our sense of personal dignity intact.

The right theory of mind will be one that is gratifying to know and does not diminish our sense of ourselves. All theories that demean human beings should be treated with suspicion. Wittgenstein articulated the same perspective when he observed about physicalist theories, "It is humiliating to have to appear like an empty tube, which is simply inflated by a mind."[5]

How should we formulate an ethical benchmark? The law has a dictum, "Innocent until proven guilty"; medicine, the dictum "First do no harm." Science has shown very little awareness of the impact of imperfect ideas, so it has no dictum. Demeaning ideas about human nature are put forth with the implicit notion that we have to "accept the grim truth," even when the truth remains quite uncertain. Even recognition of past errors rarely leads to remorse among intellectuals. The behaviorist model was built upon repetition, reward, and punishment, with no room for any sort of mind. Many children were mistreated and suffered in ways we cannot measure because the behaviorist model was imposed upon education and curricula. In fact, much of public discourse carries the leftover rhetoric of behaviorist psychology, which made the ultimate claim that we are environmentally controlled by forces beyond ourselves or by physical forces within ourselves.

Although people often feel remorse over political ideas they have held (racism or sexism or some other attitude they later regret), one virtually never hears of intellectuals expressing sorrow about the harm done by ideas they have defended and later discarded. We do not often hear of former behaviorists who express chagrin over the fact that thousands of children have suffered (and still do) from antimentalist doctrines in education. Nor do those who once used intelligence tests (which have not acquired any respectable intellectual foundation over the course of seventy years) express regret over children whose poor scores left lifelong scars, because their particular formula for intelligence is not officially recognized.

Stanley Milgram is famous for experiments that manipulated people into thinking it was all right to give electric shocks to others. What effect did it have on the participants to realize that they had participated in torture? Theodore Kaczynski, the "Unabomber," who later killed three people and injured twenty-nine, took part in a related experiment by Henry Murray at Harvard. Murray subjected his unwitting students, including Kaczynski, to intensive interrogation—what Murray himself called "vehement, sweeping, and personally abusive" attacks, assaulting their egos and most-cherished ideals and beliefs. And what responsibility has the academic community taken for allowing this kind of unethical manipulation of subjects? We now have human subjects review committees, but are they adequate? Every personal question can have unwanted consequences ("Do you like one friend more than all the others?").

In a recent *New Yorker* article, Jane Mayer reported extensively on how a man with a doctorate in social psychology used his knowledge to assist in torture by explaining humiliation techniques he had learned.[6] No ethical code, like a Hippocratic oath, hindered him. No collective response from the intellectual community that grants doctorates has been forthcoming.[7] There is no indication, at the time of this writing, that these activities have stopped.

When challenged about negative aspects of their ideas, intellectuals usually retort that all theories are complex and their downside is simply not evident at first. But every theory has an impact on the public via its headlines—the soundbite version of the theory—and these can be subjected to introspective evaluation. Intellectuals should not be mere "bystanders" when academic knowledge is applied. How simplistic ideas extrapolate to the whole human being is not usually hard to see. Is it true that people act only in terms of rewards and punishments? Is it plausible that children have difficulty with reading only because they lack self-esteem? As a reader, of course, you should demand the same of me: what is the downside of modularity? We will look at this question soon.

In sum, when dealing with human beings, we need some failsafe approaches that prevent the overapplication of simplistic ideas. The suggestion from the arguments made here would be "Always imagine, discuss, and see some responsibility for how ideas can be illegitimately extrapolated." As noted earlier, it is interesting that Einstein rejected a plausible theory of the universe, the big bang theory, because of its social implications. Perhaps it is just as well that the idea emerged a few decades later, rather than in Einstein's day.

The Legitimacy of Humanism

Criticism of "scientific psychology" is nothing new—humanistic disciplines have usually been opposed to and offended by most of the psychological concepts that modern work in psychology and artificial intelligence have produced, for just the reasons we have been looking at. There were those, like Bruce Maslow, who saw right from the outset that behaviorism diminished our sense of ourselves.[8] His championing of humanism is sometimes seen as sentimental more than scientific. My goal is to defend a rigorous and scientific approach to the mind but be clear about its limitations and biases and seek to limit its inappropriate public impact, particularly in the back-and-forth of early stages of research. The proposal I am advocating here is simply this: I believe that humanistic insights should be compatible with scientific ones; if they are not, the science is suspect. Mathematical representations of creativity are an important step toward bridging the gulf. Much remains unclear, but we should not lose sight of humanistic truths.

Free Will and Respect

If we view free will in the same light, then we should assume that free will must be real, unless we can prove otherwise, precisely because denying it contradicts our intuition about ourselves. Any explanation that leaves us feeling impoverished is not the right explanation. The notion of creativity in linguistics has the automatic virtue that it surely enhances human dignity. Chomsky has distinguished human language from bee language precisely on the grounds that it is free and not controlled by an external stimulus.[9]

Once again, the resigned view that "it's all in the physics" has precisely the defect that it implies that our sense of dignity is a sham, a deceptive image in a mirror, and it undermines self-respect, personal resolve, and our faith in the legitimacy of our own ability to make decisions. The implications flow right up the line. If there is no free will, then children do not need to be persuaded, as if they can sympathetically understand adults and freely support them; rather, we must "manage their behavior." Then parents seek to control their children and teachers focus on discipline, as if children were nothing but a bundle of uncontrollable urges. Some psychologists have come to see that the many modern labels (Asperger syndrome, attention deficit syndrome, and so on) all deny or downplay that a person with free will lives within that label. A label that is intended to sympathetically identify a problem can still be demeaning.

Ethical Modularity and Integrity

I have argued that the mind is modular and that language, a module within the mind, has many modules too.[10] This view has led to an important ethical assumption about the mind:

If a child lacks knowledge in one module, do not assume that the knowledge is lacking in all modules.

For instance, I have argued that a child who does not understand the "variable" inside a question does not lack the notion of a set in all behavior. And I have argued for caution in interpreting the results of false belief tasks.

Another issue arises that has the opposite ethical implication:

If the mind is modular, how can we have a sense of integrity?

Freud's doctrine of the unconscious already contained an implicit challenge to the notion of "integrity," the idea that our actions are consistent and honorable, our promises real. If we do not know what our unconscious is doing, and our demeanor may therefore be full of not really conscious "mixed messages," then how can we ever feel integrity in ourselves or attribute it to others?[11] It has been too easy for some to adopt the supposition that "her lips say 'no,' but her eyes say 'yes,'" when others argue that integrity should be assumed ("*No* means *no*"). As this book has shown, these are not just abstract philosophical issues, but ones present in our daily lives.

How often do parents deny the integrity of their children? If we say to a child, "You say you don't want to go on the merry-go-round, but I think you do," or "You shouldn't say you hate your grandma, because you really love her," what does this verbal style tell the child about the integrity of her own feelings and those of others? It is a verbal style that makes different assumptions than a statement like "Well, today you are mad at your grandma, but you had a good time with her yesterday. Do you think maybe you will again tomorrow?"

The notion of an unconscious warns each of us that we should try to be sure that our unconscious motives are not different from our conscious ones. Is there any way we can do that? Since we have only the dimmest idea right now of where a sense of integrity comes from, these speculations are rough, shaky, and unconvincing. Yet that is a limit on our knowledge of human nature. It should not limit the importance of what we recognize to be integrity in others or ourselves.

The Bias of Linguistics

My rhetoric has been respectful of children, but perhaps the ideas expressed here actually run the other way. I need to put the ethical spotlight on my own claims. The truth about ideas is, of course, hard to see in the moment being lived.

One bias in the approach taken here, even though I fight it, is that it is still heavily influenced by mechanical, inorganic computer imagery. Centuries ago, political language was dominated by organic biological imagery ("the tree of government"), whereas now it is modeled on the inorganic ("the Chicago political machine"). Though we have the idea that the "organic" machine is the same as the inorganic one, I believe that if we understood life better, we would see flexibility in organic situations that inorganic machines do not have, whether we are looking at human beings making up their minds or vines seeking the sun.

The image outlined here of grammar in the life of a child has been structured by the modern concepts of innate ideas, modularity, and computer-like machines working in a fast, deterministic way. Can notions like free will, integrity, and creativity fit in?

Slow Thought and Integration of the Mind

What *are* we doing when we think slowly, ruminate, let notions settle for a few days? This is the realm of slow thought—which, though it bubbles to the surface now and then, remains a largely unconscious activity.

When we think slowly, perhaps we are undertaking exactly what modularity denies: we are trying to take information from everywhere to see if it is consistent. This is known as the "frame problem" in computer science. How does our mind accommodate almost any set of factors in a given situation (like cooking dinner) to create a "framework" in which they can be organized?

To have self-respect, we must believe that our decisions are made not by some secret unconscious self with devious purposes (as a version of Freud's ideas would suggest), but by our selves—selves with rich enough connections to unconscious realms that we believe that our decisions are decent for both our conscious and our unconscious selves, our society, and the world we inhabit. In other words, though not conscious of everything in ourselves, our internal surveying device may seek to guarantee that everything important to us has been unconsciously consulted. This is evident in everyday life, though we are not aware of it. If we say, before buying a toy, "Let me think if it is the best present," we do not consciously consult every corner of concern, but we feel that we have unconsciously done so. And it is as a result of that process that we maintain a sense of integrity in action.

The claim that ideas permeate our minds seems to run against modularity. As Jerry Fodor has discussed, the judgment that the mind is modular must be supplemented by something, though it is not clear what, that organizes the modules.[12] It remains somehow true that ideas "affect" everything in our minds, but not necessarily in a logical, consistent, or advantageous way. The mind as a whole is so mysterious that one hardly knows how to begin thinking about it. It reflects whatever slow thought is up to. It is the true hidden algebra of mind.

The notion of creativity in linguistics has the virtue that it enhances human dignity. It does not simply reduce what we know to a common human pattern; instead, it says that although patterns exist, they are "generative," and that the capacity to create stunning new sentences gives an individual a tool that can instantly remodel or redefine a whole situation, just as a whiff of cognac can shake our sensibility. The notion of creativity in grammar is partway to a notion of free will, but the two are still logically distinct.

Although no one is in a position to prove the correctness or incorrectness of what has been argued in this chapter, it seems to me that moral perspectives should guide how new theories are greeted from the outset. It is possible that unsettling claims about human nature are true, but until a solid theory of human nature is in hand, negative views of human nature should be viewed with suspicion. This is another reason why parents need to trust their full impression of their children rather than what any narrow theory articulates.

Language Is Not Thought

In this book, I have vehemently denied that a person fails to think if the thoughts are not in words. There are many scientifically remote valleys of mind beyond language—where thought occurs with great personal immediacy.

Nothing is more important than avoiding the misperception that thought must be in language, since it readily feeds prejudice in our society every day. Here's another example. In December 2000, Supreme Court Justice Clarence Thomas was asked by visiting schoolchildren why he is so often silent in court proceedings. He answered (roughly quoted), "When I was a child, I grew up in an area where the Gullah dialect was spoken, and I was made fun of at school. So I got into the habit of listening carefully without speaking. I was still thinking in Standard English but it came out in a strange dialect."[13] Here we have another sad case of silence imposed by dialect—silence that persists throughout the life of even an extraordinarily successful man whose profession requires sensitivity to the nuances of legal language. While he is aware of that unfair consequence of his origins, he promotes dialect prejudice at the same time. I would submit that his notion that he "thought in Standard English" is just an effort to make himself acceptable to the prejudices of his audience and unfortunately to anchor, in a false form of language legitimacy, an illusion about how he thinks himself. As a child he was, of course, just thinking in his mind with the full range of human influences upon him, with perhaps a word or a few phrases coming to mind. While language may help hold a thought, the real thinking must take place prior to language.

Clarence Thomas's childhood dialect, like any dialect, is adequate to expressing anything, so were he to be thinking in language, it could as well be dialect. Fully expressing any idea in any dialect requires at most borrowing a few words (such as legalisms) from another dialect, just as all speakers take words from other languages when they need them (think of words like *schlep*, *chutzpah*, and *bon voyage* borrowed into English from other languages). Clarence Thomas provides another case where the doctrine that we think only in language is damaging to human dignity.

The Last Word

The journey through this book may have been a real roller-coaster ride. We have touched on dozens of empirical and philosophical issues. Though it should be clear that many intellectual issues remain tumultuous and unresolved, I hope to have arrived at a few quiet insights and deeper truths that remain constant. My goal has been to show that the smallest utterances have deep principles of grammar buried within them: creativity, infinity, and abstract structures; that the same principles are found in all activities of the mind; that these ideas are part of how we contemplate who we are; and that the defense of human dignity lies in part in recognizing the kinds of formal creativity that underlie our sense of free will.

All of this has been undertaken with an accent on the question of how children acquire language, what is known about it, and how anyone can find out more. I have tried to make it clear that society has a role in defining intellectual problems, using the various kinds of partial knowledge already available, and maintaining a positive view of human nature. Ideas have consequences every moment of our lives, both those we entertain and those unshakably built into us.

Afterword

I would like to dedicate this book to my extended family, its pedagogical traditions, and the community of children, teachers, alumni, administrators, and friends who carry that tradition forward in many different schools. It began with my grandfather, Max Bondy, who had a commitment to a democratic school community, and my grandmother, Gertrud Bondy, who worked with Sigmund Freud and adopted his vision of human individuality. They championed these ideas in Germany in 1920 by founding the Schule Marienau (which still exists). Driven from Germany by the Nazis in the 1930s, they moved to the United States and started the Windsor Mountain School in Lenox, Massachusetts. In 1941 my parents, George and Annemarie Roeper, founded the Roeper School in Bloomfield Hills, Michigan, which also continues to thrive. In my estimation, these schools (captured in the documentary "Across Time and Space: The World of Bondy Schools") remain unmatched in their capacity to respect individuality within community. I like to see this book as my small contribution to that tradition.

I have always felt that a real perception about human nature underlay my grandparents' and parents' respect for creative individuality. It was always my dream to seek a rigorous scientific view of the mind that would reflect their insight and make it something more than a sentimental truism. The subtle and systematic image of mind I see in generative grammar offers a path to that goal.

When my parents retired, I asked each of them separately what they would miss most. My father said, "Talking with children," and my mother said, "Listening to children"—which, at age 88, she continues to do in private practice. This book is just another way of listening to what children say—but far from the most important way.

Notes

Chapter 1

1. This entire book is an outgrowth of both early and recent proposals about language and mind by Noam Chomsky (see, for example, Chomsky 1965, 1995), together with new thrusts that come from modern work in acquisition, parsing, and semantics.

Modules are a central feature of human language. Their role in all mental activity has been championed and carefully articulated by Jerry Fodor in a series of books (most recently Fodor 2000).

The book *Chomsky and His Critics* (Antony and Hornstein 2003) provides a good overview of current philosophical controversies and Chomsky's position on them. My position is that once we acknowledge clearly what we do not know, then it is clear what we do know. I will present a simple view of mental capacities, the need for representations, and the case for modularity, which is not overturned by remaining questions about what the term *representation* entails. Chomsky's replies in Antony and Hornstein 2003 emphasize that the core claims of mentalism are clear and relatively uncontroversial.

The Platonic philosophical tradition is essential to these perspectives and leads to the advocacy of mentalism. It links Leibniz, Descartes, and the Continental tradition of Kant to Chomsky. Blackburn 1999 is a good introduction to many issues discussed here. I am indebted to the philosopher Robert Sleigh for his insights into Leibniz and their relevance to modern images of mind.

Ideas about looking at children's statements through a philosophical lens can be found in Matthews 1994 and in the pedagogical movement toward discussing philosophy with children that Matthews's work has engendered (see www .philosophyforkids.com).

2. Good overviews of acquisition can be found in O'Grady 1997 (particularly for students) and Golinkoff and Hirsch-Pasek 2000 (particularly for parents). Other general books on acquisition and mind include Pinker 1994 and Jackendoff 2002; for more technical discussion, see Crain and Thornton 1998 and Guasti 2002.

3. Arenson 2001, 9.

4. Blackburn 1999, 105.

5. See similar cases in Bowerman 1982.

Throughout the book, I frequently use real examples. Many of them are from the diaries I kept of my own children's language development; others were reported to me by friends, colleagues, and students over the years; still others come from books. When possible, I credit the child (although in some cases I've chosen not to reveal the source of a particular comment); and of course, the published sources are duly noted.

By far the largest reservoir of child language is the extensive electronic archive housed at Carnegie Mellon University, the Child Language Data Exchange System (CHILDES). CHILDES was originally funded in the 1980s by the MacArthur Foundation and developed by Brian MacWhinney and Catherine Snow. MacWhinney has served as its director since its inception. A thorough description of the system and how to use it may be found at childes.psy.cmu.edu or by consulting MacWhinney 2000. Material cited from the CHILDES database includes a print reference associated with the file.

6. O'Neil 1998.

7. Extensions of this book, a three-part discussion of how language creates an interface to aspects of meaning, including more explorations, can be found at www.umass .edu/linguist/people/faculty/roeper/roeper.html. "How to Manage Meandering Meaning" looks in depth at passives and how an agent can be implicit and linked to other implicit agents. "Time" looks at unusual uses of the past tense to refer to the present (*What did you say your name was?*). "Possession" explores how possessives range over meanings (*John's picture* = "picture of, by, or owned by John") and how children's acquisition of possessives develops.

8. Satoshi Tomioka brought the ellipsis example to my attention. See Tomioka 2001.

9. Seymour, Roeper, and de Villiers 2003, 2005; Seymour and Pearson 2004.

10. In fact, many of the proposed explorations could turn into important dissertations if they were carefully researched. I urge anyone who would like to research one of them to contact me, because there is much more to be said about how to approach each one.

11. I rely upon the physicist David Griffiths (personal communication) for this judgment.

12. See, for example, Baddeley 1999.

13. See Borer and Wexler 1987; Babyonyshev et al. 2001.

Chapter 2

1. Blackmur 1989.

2. The mind/body "problem" is a traditional philosophical issue. My perspective reflects remarks that Noam Chomsky has frequently made (see especially 1968, 2000).

3. Ekman 2003; Ortony, Clore, and Collins 1988.

4. See Meltzoff and Moore 1977. For a more recent summary of work in this area, see Meltzoff and Moore 1997.

5. This view can be taken as the logical extreme of Gardner's (1983) proposals about multiple intelligences.

6. Jerry Fodor (personal communication) attributes this example to Ken Forster.

Chapter 3

1. Markman 1991.

2. David McNeill, personal communication. For more on the social use of language by chimps and tamarinds, see Elliot 1981.

3. See Clark 1993, from which the following series of examples is drawn. See also Braunwald 1978 and discussions of the one-word stage in acquisition textbooks.

4. Kulikowski 1980.

5. Kratzer 1999; Potts 2005.

6. See Elliot 1981.

7. To study children's use of pronouns, students searched the CHILDES database (MacWhinney 2000).

8. Higginson 1985 (CHILDES database).

9. Brown 1973 (CHILDES database).

10. Higginson 1985 (CHILDES database).

11. Schafer and Roeper 2000.

12. Wijnen, Roeper, and Van der Meulen 2004.

13. Sarah corpus (Brown 1973; CHILDES database), reported in Wijnen, Roeper, and Van der Meulen 2004.

14. Brown 1973 (CHILDES database).

15. These views depart from those expressed in well-known works like Vygotsky 1962 and Piaget 1959.

16. See Astington 1993 for an overview of how children's knowledge and processing of false beliefs differ from adults'.

17. "Hi table" example from Roeper diaries.

18. Elizabeth Rezendes used the words *giantic* and *housepitality*.

19. Lisa Matthewson provided the *neath* example from her son Merlin.

20. Jennifer Griffiths is the author of *sq-worm*.

21. Harry Seymour first pointed out to me that *hi* and *hello* mean different things.

Chapter 4

1. The *Daddy's sneakers* example is drawn from the work of Lois Bloom (1973), who did much of the pioneering research on one- and two-word utterances. See also O'Grady 1997; Golinkoff and Hirsch-Pasek 2000; Guasti 2002.

2. The *coat* example is from Patricia Greenfield (personal communication).

3. Marc Hauser's work shows that animal cognition is much more sophisticated than previously thought (see Hauser 2000).

4. Children sometimes utter two words with a pause in between that might seem like a conjoined phrase ("Knife (pause) fork"), but I take constructions like this to be merely sequences of words, not conjunctions.

5. The concept of merger is central to the current linguistic theory known as *minimalism* (Chomsky 1995, 2005). It has many connections to work in semantics and mathematics (see Partee 2004). The notion of one element dominating another reflects the concept of function-argument. Here, the important point is not the technical formulation but the claim that the dominance relation distinction is psychologically real.

6. See Chomsky 2005, 2006; Hauser, Chomsky, and Fitch 2002.

7. Examples from the CHILDES database: Bloom 1973 (Allison), Brown 1973 (Sarah) (ages given in years and days).

8. Examples from Snyder and Roeper 2004; see also Hiramatsu et al. 2000.

Chapter 5

1. On the acquisition of gender, see Mills 1986.

2. See Gleitman 1990.

3. Annemarie Roeper made this observation about how nursery school teachers-in-training point at things.

4. Thanks to Ed Gettier for the *Moby-Dick* example.

5. Thanks to James Higginbotham for the example of how the word *understand* is used with respect to a storm.

6. See Maratsos 1976. The Diagnostic Evaluation of Language Variation (DELV; Seymour, Roeper, and de Villiers 2003, 2005) uses many similar tests of definiteness and indefiniteness to assess language disorders.

7. For details of determiner use in Salish, see Matthewson 1998.

8. See Matthewson, Bryant, and Roeper 2001.

9. See Schafer and de Villiers 2000.

10. See Schafer and Roeper 2000 for extensive theoretical discussion.

11. From the CHILDES database: June and April (Higginson 1985); Adam and Eve (Brown 1973); Naomi (Sachs 1983); Peter (Bloom, Lightbown, and Hood 1975).

12. Discussion of multiple deictics in Chris Potts's seminar helped clarify these examples.

13. There is a huge literature on the acquisition of negation. On semantic properties of negation, see Drozd 2002; on syntactic factors, see Déprez and Pierce 1993.

14. See Bellugi 1967.

15. See Roeper 1982.

16. These results come from Roeper and Matthei 1975. Since then, a great deal of experimental work has been done on negation and quantification. See the following, among others, for extensive discussion: Crain et al. 1996; Drozd 2001; Lidz and Musolino 2002.

17. See Roeper and Matthei 1975.

18. From Bellugi 1967.

19. Roeper and de Villiers 1993; Avrutin and Thornton 1994; Philip 1995. For an entry point to the considerable literature on semantics, see Heim and Kratzer 1998.

20. See, for example, Fromkin and Rodman 1998.

21. Example from Roeper 1965.

Chapter 6

1. Examples from my own diary studies (unpublished).

2. Hauser, Chomsky, and Fitch 2002, 1569, 1571, 1574. Recursion is widely discussed in mathematics and computer science and is perhaps one of the most influential concepts of the twentieth century.

3. For more discussion of acquisition and recursion, see Snyder and Roeper 2004; Roeper and Snyder 2004, 2005.

4. From Bellugi 1967.

5. Mohawk commentary from Mark Baker (personal communication). See Baker 2001.

6. Tim Roeper (Roeper corpus).

7. See Gentner et al. 2006.

8. These figures are from a search of the CHILDES database carried out by Mari Takahashi.

9. For discussion of restrictions on possession, see Eisenbeiss 2002; and for further references, see Roeper and Snyder 2005.

Anders Holmberg (personal communication) observes that, according to traditional grammars, a single prenominal possessive is possible with nonagents in Swedish, but more than one is not possible.

10. Let's see if we can create a comparable impossibility for English speakers, to get a sense of the problem double possessives pose for nonnative speakers. Suppose we try to make indirect objects recursive:

I gave help to Mary to John to Bill.

This is all right if I helped three people, but suppose the meaning we are trying to get across is this:

"I helped Mary help John help Bill."

If that is the case, then we have to put in a new verb each time; we cannot just use recursive *to* phrases. So maybe recursive possessives feel to nonnative speakers of English the way recursive *to* phrases would feel to native speakers.

11. See Galasso 1999.

12. CHILDES transcripts: Sarah (Brown 1973).

13. From the CHILDES database: childes/DATABASE/ENG/MACWHIN/ROSS/ROSS42.CHA.

14. From the CHILDES database: childes/DATABASE/ENG/DEMETRA/WORKPAR/E_MOT04.CHA.

15. From Armstrong 2001.

16. From Armstrong 2001.

17. See Gentile 2000.

18. See Matthei 1982. Also see Crain and Thornton 1998, where it is suggested that cognitive complexity can contribute to children's choice of a default coordination.

19. See Bryant 2006.

20. See Randall 1982 for an extensive discussion of the acquisition of *-er* and its phrasal nature.

21. *Look at the one in the middle's fur* was written by Emily Riddle at age 7.

22. This exploration scenario comes from a pilot study by Harry Seymour and Janice Jackson at the University of Massachusetts, Amherst.

23. See Akmajian and Heny 1975 for a nice presentation.

You can explore phrasal possessives with a child either by using Seymour and Jackson's boy/tree/hat scenario or by setting up a situation where you and the child are looking at four things in a row, two of which are the same. For example:

your mother   chair   man   chair

In this case, you would first point to the relevant chairs, saying,

"This is my mother's chair, and this is the man's chair."

Then you would ask,

"Show me the man next to my mother's chair."

Does the child point to the man, who is next to your mother's chair, or to the chair (of the man next to your mother)?

Chapter 7

1. The phrase *The Structure of Silence* used as the chapter title is half borrowed from Merchant 2001.

2. This dialogue is from the CHILDES database (Brown 1973).

Discussion with Luisa Marti and François Recanati has enabled me to see how verbs vary pragmatically. If you come up to me while I am eating cherries and I ask, "Have you eaten?," your reply "Yes, I had a doughnut" makes sense, but if you come up to me while I am standing next to a chessboard and I ask, "Do you play?," you cannot say, *"Yes, I love soccer." *Play* is transitive even if the object is invisible, while *eat* is intransitive, allowing us to freely infer what is eaten.

3. From the CHILDES database (Kuczaj 1976).

4. Frazier and Clifton 2001.

5. From the CHILDES database (Brown 1973).

6. In ongoing work, Kathy Hirsch-Pasek, Meredith Jones, Robin Golinkoff, and I have tried this experiment with three-year-olds, showing them pictures on a TV screen and monitoring their screen-watching behavior to judge their responses. First we said to them,

"Here's some dirty socks. Do you want some?"

Then we showed them either a picture of someone eating dirty socks or a picture of someone eating food. Judging by their responses, a first impression is that the three-year-olds seemed to know that *dirty socks* must be filled in after *some*, unlikely though that interpretation is.

7. Karmiloff-Smith 1980.

8. The experiment was carried out by Deanna Moore, working with the University of Massachusetts Language Acquisition Lab. Laura Wagner, Kristen Asplin, and Ayumi Matsuo were also involved in this study.

9. Karmiloff-Smith 1980.

10. See Frazier 1999; Wijnen, Roeper, and Van der Meulen 2004. Also see Frazier et al. 2003.

11. For an introduction, see Radford 1997 or Haegeman 1994; for more detail, see K. Johnson 1996, 2001.

12. The large body of acquisition work on coreference and ellipsis is represented by Abdulkarim and Roeper 1997, Matsuo and Duffield 1997, Foley et al. 1999, Thornton and Wexler 1999.

13. See Abdulkarim and Roeper 1997.

14. Again, see Abdulkarim and Roeper 1997.

15. Matsuo and Duffield 2005. Research under the direction of Sergey Avrutin at Utrecht University is also pursuing these issues.

16. African-American English judgment provided by Tim Bryant, University of Massachusetts, Amherst.

17. Jill de Villiers, personal communication.

18. These comments are right at the cutting edge of current research, and much is unknown. For instance, we do not know if children's production of ellipsis allows a wider range of interpretations.

19. See Potts 2005. Epithets are treated in Potts and Roeper 2006.

20. For further discussion, see Moore, in preparation.

21. I have asked people this question informally, and others may well have also investigated the interpretation of such sentences formally.

22. Tavakolian 1981.

23. William Snyder, Ken Wexler, and Dolon Das have also shown that children have difficulty with sentences like this that involve two simultaneous comparisons, which are excluded in many languages (see Snyder, Wexler, and Das 1995):

John wants to visit Bill's house more than Fred Martha's.

= more than Fred *wants to visit* Martha's *house*

This sentence involves two discontinuous restored phrases.

24. Chomsky 1972.

25. The discussion in this section has roots in philosophy and logic. For some acquisition studies, see Noveck and Chevaux 2002 and Bryant 2006.

26. Experimental results here are contradictory. Some have found that children will drop the temporal reference when it is implied. See Noveck and Chevaux 2002.

27. Barbara Schmiedtova (2004) showed in a series of subtle experiments that German-speaking children were able to understand the word *gleichzeitig* ("at the same time"). In other words, she has shown that children are sensitive to the fact that events are simultaneous.

28. See Bryant 2006 for results and discussion.

29. Children's Storybooks Online (www.magickeys.com/books/; accessed 12/16/04).

30. Children's Storybooks Online (www.magickeys.com/books/).

31. Jill de Villiers, personal communication.

32. Massachusetts Comprehensive Assessment System test help (www.mcasmentor .com; accessed 12/16/04).

33. *Richard III*, act V, scene ii.

Chapter 8

1. From my diaries of my children and their friends.

2. There is a vast literature on plurals. Introductory discussions can be found in semantics textbooks. For a classic discussion, see Carlson 1977; a more recent one is Landman 2000.

Cases like *Unicycles have wheels* first became prominent in Barbara Partee's (1973) discussion of Montague grammar.

3. The notion of distributivity is discussed from the standpoint of acquisition in Roeper and de Villiers 1993 and in many other works, such as Philip 1995, 2004, Avrutin and Thornton 1994, and Drozd 2001. See references therein for background articles on semantics and philosophy. Piaget (Inhelder and Piaget 1964) and Bever (1970) have discussed the phenomenon under the assumption that language and cognition are the same.

4. Pérez-Leroux and Roeper 1999.

5. Miyamoto 1992.

6. For Vainikka's results, see Roeper and de Villiers 1993. For Sauerland's results, see Sauerland 2003; also see Sauerland, Anderssen, and Yatsushiro 2005.

7. See Sauerland, Anderssen, and Yatsushiro 2005 for discussion.

8. Uli Sauerland, personal communication.

9. Roeper and Matthei 1975.

10. See Kouider et al. 2006.

11. See Drozd 2001 for related work.

12. Search engines allow us to combine diverse phenomena rapidly, but it is unlikely that the human system and the computer system are really alike, though there are suggestive connections in computer architecture.

13. Higginbotham 1993.

14. In this line of research, Zvi Penner, Petra Schulz, Barbara Pearson, Jill de Villiers, Peter de Villiers, Uri Strauss, Denise Finneran, Jürgen Weissenborn, and I were all directly involved at various stages. Much of this work is described in Finneran 1993, Roeper et al. 2002, and Strauss et al. 2003. Also see Roeper 2004 for extensive discussion of the singleton interpretation phenomenon from the perspective of language disorders.

15. Roeper et al. 2002.

16. Roeper et al. 2002.

17. In addition to introductory textbooks such as Heim and Kratzer 1998, see Chierchia 1992–1993. *Who bought what?* was initially explored from an acquisition standpoint by Jill de Villiers and me. Later, together with Jürgen Weissenborn (Weissenborn, Roeper, and de Villiers 1990), we addressed another question: why does English not allow *What did who buy?*, whereas German does allow the equivalent of the same sentence? We found that four-year-old English-speaking children adamantly refused to produce "What did who buy?," whereas German-speaking children readily produced the German counterpart.

18. DELV: Seymour, Roeper, and de Villiers 2003, 2005. An extensive report on the tryout pilot results for the DELV can be found in Seymour et al. 2002.

19. Seymour et al. 2002; also Roeper 2004.

20. Seymour et al. 2002.
   These statistics refer only to children with a language disorder known as Specific Language Impairment. Many other children have other types of language disorders; they are excluded here because they show cognitive problems of other kinds. Children with severe retardation, for example, can be limited to a vocabulary of just fifty words with no combinations. Therefore, the predominance of singleton grammars is

probably much greater among children with language disorders than these numbers suggest.

21. See Pérez-Leroux 1993.

22. Nishigauchi 1999.

23. Roeper, Strauss, and Pearson 2006.

24. Merchant 2005.

25. Philip 1995; Strauss 2006. For background on the DELV database, see www .umass.edu/aae.

26. Strauss et al. 2003.

27. Philip 1995; see Philip 2004 for further references.

28. These results and arguments about the acquisition path are discussed in Roeper, Strauss, and Pearson 2006.

29. Roeper and de Villiers 1993; Roeper, Strauss, and Pearson 2006. This syntactic approach fits the semantic representation articulated by Herburger (1997), who explains how "focus" and "weak" quantifiers involve objects if the quantifier alone is attached higher as proposed here. See Smits, Roeper, and Hollebrandse 2006 for new evidence and discussion of the "weak" quantification alternative.

30. There is an extensive literature on children's acquisition of quantification. For a comprehensive overview, see the forthcoming issue of *Language Acquisition* devoted to this topic.

31. Stickney 2003.

32. It is possible that the missing quantifier here is not exactly *each other* or that it could be indirectly captured in a meaning representation.

33. Thanks to Tim Roeper for this insight.

34. Takahashi 1991.

35. Inhelder and Piaget 1964.

36. See the discussions of vision in, for example, Kosslyn 1994 and Pinker 1984.

Chapter 9

1. These next chapters are more informal and reflect to a greater degree my personal experience of the concepts I discuss. Often I am not sure of the source of the stories I report, but their existence in the popular culture shows the impact they have on us. When possible I have credited colleagues' work in this area, but for the most part the feelings and opinions represented are my own. Nonetheless, I hope they give a clear impression of the social side of dialect.

2. Max Weinreich is generally credited with the first print citation of this expression (in Yiddish) in *Yivo-bleter* 25.1, 13. See www.edu-cyberpg.com/Linguistics/armynavy .html (accessed 12/20/04).

3. Janice Jackson, personal communication.

4. Dyer and Callanan (2003) found similar results. Their work also suggests that even four-year-olds hear and understand *explicit* irony.

5. A good overview of children's acquisition of formal and informal modes of speech is Andersen 1990.

6. Siegel 2002.

7. The Linguistic Society of America's statement on the Ebonics controversy can be found at linguistlist.org/issues/8/8-57.html (accessed 12/20/04).

8. Walt Wolfram, personal communication.

Chapter 10

1. Randall 1980.

2. See Kroch and Taylor 1997; Roeper 1999, 2003; Yang 2003.

3. From www.wired.com/news/mp3/0,1285,53342,00.html; www.starwars.com/gaming/ other/rpg/news20040614.html.

4. Akmajian et al. 2001, 307.

5. From a *National Geographic* article.

6. Huang 1982.

7. V. Johnson 2001.

8. See Kratzer, to appear.

9. Benjamin Whorf (1956) made this type of language famous through his discussions of the inflectional system of Hopi, which (in simplified terms) allows a vast range of ways to describe the style and content of events and the intermixture of time and space.

   Whorf is associated with the hypothesis that language affects how people perceive their reality, that language in effect coerces thought.

10. Van Hout 1995. On the completive properties of particles—the impact of "upness"—also see Jeschull, in preparation.

11. Terada 1991.

12. Barbara Schmiedtova devised these sentences for an experiment in progress, conducted at the University of Massachusetts, Amherst, and the Max Planck Institute.

Chapter 11

1. McWhorter 1998.

2. See, for example, William Labov's (1970) seminal article. For a more sophisticated discussion of how ellipsis works, see K. Johnson 2001.

3. Deevy 1999.

4. See John Baugh, "Housing Discrimination Based on Speech," www.stanford.edu/ ~jbaugh/service.html (12/20/04).

5. See Green 2002; Terry 2004. For work in the important tradition of Labov and Wolfram, see Rickford 1999.

   Very subtle work on children's acquisition of AAE has been undertaken at the University of Massachusetts, Amherst. See, for example, Wyatt 1991; Bland et al. 1998; Coles 1998; Jackson 1998; Burns 2004.

6. Terry 2004.

7. The second and third sentences are attested examples from Green 2002, chap. 2.

8. Green 2002, chap. 2.

9. Jackson 1998.

10. For general remarks, see Rickford, n.d. For more detailed discussion, see Asante 1990.

11. See V. Johnson 2001 for discussion of rules for lexical items that are dialect sensitive.

12. Green 2002, 77.

13. For discussion of aspectual *do*, see Green 2002.

14. Hollebrandse and Roeper 1996; Davis 1987.

15. Eliane Ramos, personal communication.

16. Zvi Penner, personal communication.

Chapter 12

1. See Phillips et al. 2000.

2. Jay Garfield brought this reference to my attention, through his web site. For more discussion of the concept of representation (which I continue to see as viable, although it presents many interesting challenges), see www.smith.edu/philosophy/ jgarfieldintention.htm.

3. Weinberg 2001.

4. Steele 1997.

5. Gladwell 2005.

6. Bridge laws are commonly invoked by philosophers of science. See, for example, Fodor 1974.

Chapter 13

1. Chomsky 2006.

2. Jill de Villiers has done a variety of experiments that explore this possibility. For a general review, see de Villiers and Pyers 2002.

3. Many philosophers have addressed the intricacy of conversation; see, for example, Searle 1969.

4. From the CHILDES database (Brown 1973).

5. For a linguistic approach that deals with just these questions, see Gunlogson 2003.

6. From the CHILDES database (Brown 1973).

7. Regarding tones of voice, see Levinson 1983.

8. Jill de Villiers, personal communication.

9. This perspective is much indebted to discussions with Bart Hollebrandse, Jill de Villiers, Peter de Villiers, and Peggy Speas, but it should not be taken as a representation of their views.

10. Example from Orin Percus, personal communication.

11. This research stems from Tavakolian 1981; see also Lebeaux 2000.

12. Is the word *that* innocuous? Surely it has a meaning. In fact, children consistently delete it at first—as German-speaking and French-speaking children delete its counterpart, although it is obligatory in those languages. Perhaps it means something like "Form a proposition." It indicates to the listener a difference like the one between

I see a red ball.

and

I see that the ball is red.

The property expressed in the latter sentence stands in contrast to an infinite set of other properties that could be attributed to the ball.

Exactly what goes into the meaning of *that* and how a child acquires it is an interesting topic that goes beyond what we can discuss here.

13. Hollebrandse 2000.

14. Tanz 1980.

15. See Pinker 1997 for a comprehensive discussion of thinking.

16. Horgan 2004.

17. Luria 1968.

18. There is a kind of memory that goes the other way: what has been called "flashbulb memory," where every detail is locked into an event. If our minds usually decompose events into details, but flashbulb memories are tightly integrated, it should be more difficult to include flashbulb memories in generalizations. That is, if you were eating curry the moment John F. Kennedy was shot, and someone later asked you how often you generally ate curry that year, you might recall all the other times you ate curry more easily than the time you ate it on the day of Kennedy's assassination, just because the other times were not deeply embedded in a flashbulb experience and were therefore easier to extract from minutiae.

19. Thanks to François Recanati for discussion of the idea of simplifying opaque propositions by omitting definite reference.

20. See Matthewson, Bryant, and Roeper 2001.

21. See Matthewson, Bryant, and Roeper 2001.

22. See Gelman 2003.

23. Karen Searcy, personal communication.

24. See, for example, Spelke 2002.

Chapter 14

1. See Piaget 1995.

2. Bruner 1977.

3. See Jackendoff 2002 for discussion of animal cognition.

4. Marc Hauser, personal communication.

5. See Searle 1995.

6. Chomsky 1968.

7. Chomsky 1986.

Chapter 15

1. This chapter is partly adapted from an essay in a volume devoted to the works of John Searle (see Roeper 2002).

2. For a discussion of the debate between whole-word and phonics, see Lemann 1997.

3. Nick MacDonald, personal communication.

4. Spock 1968.

5. Wittgenstein 1978, 11.

6. Mayer 2005.

7. There is now an effort at the University of Massachusetts, which I participated in initiating, to link an ethical code to the granting of doctoral degrees.

8. Maslow 1954.

9. Chomsky 1968.

10. For a debate on this issue, see Pinker 1997 and Fodor 2000.

11. On the conscious/unconscious divide, see Searle 2005.

12. See, for example, Fodor 2000.

13. Milloy 2000.

References

Works marked with an asterisk underlie the whole book more generally.

Abdulkarim, L., and T. Roeper. 1997. Economy of representation: Ellipsis and NP reconstructions. In A. Sorace, C. Heycock, and R. Shillcock, eds., *Proceedings of GALA 1997*, 1–6. Edinburgh: University of Edinburgh, Human Communication Research Centre.

Akmajian, A., R. A. Demers, A. K. Farmer, and R. M. Harnish. 2001. *Linguistics*. 5th ed. Cambridge, Mass.: MIT Press.

Akmajian, A., and F. Heny. 1975. *An introduction to the principles of transformational syntax*. Cambridge, Mass.: MIT Press.

Andersen, E. 1990. *Speaking with style: The sociolinguistic skills of children*. London: Routledge.

*Antony, L. M., and N. Hornstein, eds. 2003. *Chomsky and his critics*. Oxford: Blackwell.

Arenson, K. W. 2001. Bulletin board: Paper to focus on discrimination's toll. *New York Times*, August 22, Late Edition Section B.

Armstrong, T. 2001. Research report, University of Massachusetts, Amherst.

Asante, M. K. 1990. African elements in African-American English. In J. E. Holloway, ed., *Africanisms in American culture*, 19–33. Bloomington: Indiana University Press.

Astington, J. W. 1993. *The child's discovery of the mind*. Cambridge, Mass.: Harvard University Press.

Avrutin, S., and R. Thornton. 1994. Distributivity and binding in child grammar. *Linguistic Inquiry* 25, 165–171.

Babyonyshev, M., J. Ganger, D. Pesetsky, and K. Wexler. 2001. The maturation of grammatical principles: Evidence from Russian unaccusatives. *Linguistic Inquiry* 32, 1–44.

Baddeley, A. 1999. *Essentials of human memory*. Hove, England: Psychology Press.

Baker, M. 2001. *The atoms of language*. New York: Basic Books.

Bellugi, U. 1967. The acquisition of negation. Doctoral dissertation, Harvard University.

Bever, T. 1970. The cognitive bases of linguistic structures. In J. R. Hayes, ed., *Cognition and the development of language*, 279–352. New York: Wiley.

Blackburn, S. 1999. *Think*. Oxford: Oxford University Press.

Blackmur, R. P. 1989. *Outsider at the heart of things*. Urbana: University of Illinois Press.

Bland-Stewart, L., H. N. Seymour, M. Beeghley, and D. Frank. 1998. Semantic development in African-American toddlers exposed to cocaine. *Seminars in Speech and Language* 19, 167–187.

Bloom, L. 1973. *One word at a time: The use of single-word utterances before syntax*. The Hague: Mouton.

Bloom, L., P. Lightbown, and L. Hood. 1975. Structure and variation in child language. *Monographs of the Society for Research in Child Development* 40 (Serial No. 160).

Borer, H., and K. Wexler. 1987. The maturation of syntax. In T. Roeper and E. Williams, eds., *Parameter setting*, 123–172. Dordrecht: Reidel.

Bowerman, M. 1982. Reorganization processes in lexical and syntactic development. In E. Wanner and L. Gleitman, eds., *Language acquisition: The state of the art*, 319–346. Cambridge: Cambridge University Press.

Braunwald, S. 1978. Context, word, and meaning: Toward a communicational analysis of lexical acquisition. In A. Lock, ed., *Action, gesture, and symbol: The emergence of language*, 285–327. London: Academic Press.

Brown, R. 1973. *A first language: The early stages*. London: George Allen & Unwin.

Bruner, J. 1977. Early social interaction and language acquisition. In H. R. Schaffer, ed., *Studies in mother-infant interaction*, 271–290. New York: Academic Press.

Bryant, D. 2006. Koordinationsellipsen im Spracherwerb: Die Verarbeitung potentieller Gapping-Strukturen. Doctoral dissertation, Humboldt University, Berlin.

Burns, F. 2004. Elicited and open-ended narratives in African American children. Doctoral dissertation, University of Massachusetts, Amherst.

Carlson, G. 1977. *Reference to kinds in English*. Amherst: University of Massachusetts, Graduate Linguistics Student Association.

Chierchia, G. 1992–1993. Questions with quantifiers. *Natural Language Semantics* 1, 181–234.

Chomsky, C. 1972. Stages in language development and reading exposure. *Harvard Educational Review* 42, 1–33.

*Chomsky, N. 1965. *Aspects of the theory of syntax*. Cambridge, Mass.: MIT Press.

*Chomsky, N. 1968. *Language and mind*. New York: Harcourt, Brace.

Chomsky, N. 1986. *Knowledge of language*. New York: Praeger.

*Chomsky, N. 1995. *The Minimalist Program*. Cambridge, Mass.: MIT Press.

*Chomsky, N. 2000. *New horizons in the study of language and mind*. Cambridge: Cambridge University Press.

*Chomsky, N. 2005. Three factors in language design. *Linguistic Inquiry* 36, 1–22.

Chomsky, N. 2006. Turing's thesis. Lecture delivered at "Interphases: A Conference on Interfaces in Current Syntactic Theory," Cyprus.

Clark, E. V. 1993. *The lexicon in acquisition*. New York: Cambridge University Press.

Coles, D. R. 1998. Barrier constraints on negative concord in African American English. Doctoral dissertation, University of Massachusetts, Amherst.

Crain, S., and R. Thornton. 1998. *Investigations in Universal Grammar: A guide to experiments on the acquisition of syntax and semantics*. Cambridge, Mass.: MIT Press.

Crain, S., R. Thornton, C. Bosta, D. Lillo-Martin, and E. Woodams. 1996. Quantification without qualification. *Language Acquisition* 5, 83–153.

Davis, H. 1987. The acquisition of the English auxiliary system and its relation to linguistic theory. Doctoral dissertation, University of British Columbia.

Deevy, P. 1999. The comprehension of English subject-verb agreement. Doctoral dissertation, University of Massachusetts, Amherst.

Déprez, V., and A. Pierce. 1993. Negation and functional projections in early grammar. *Linguistic Inquiry* 24, 25–67.

de Villiers, J., and J. Pyers. 2002. Complements to cognition: A longitudinal study of the relationship between complex syntax and false-belief-understanding. *Cognitive Development* 17, 1037–1061.

Drozd, K. F. 2001. Children's weak interpretation of universally quantified sentences. In M. Bowerman and S. Levinson, eds., *Language acquisition and conceptual development*, 340–376. Cambridge: Cambridge University Press.

Drozd, K. F. 2002. Negative DPs and elliptical negation in child English. *Language Acquisition* 10, 77–122.

Dyer, J. R., and M. A. Callanan. 2003. Parents and children talk about irony: A work in progress. Paper presented at the Cognitive Development Society meeting, Park City, Utah, October.

Eisenbeiss, S. 2002. Merkmalsgesteuerter Grammatikerwerb: Eine Untersuchung zum Erwerb der Struktur und Flexion der Nominalphrase (Feature-driven structure building: A study on the acquisition of noun-phrase structure and inflection). Doctoral dissertation, University of Düsseldorf.

Ekman, P. 2003. *Emotions revealed: Understanding faces and feelings*. London: Weidenfeld and Nicolson.

Elliot, A. J. 1981. *Child language*. Cambridge: Cambridge University Press.

Finneran, D. A. 1993. Bound variable knowledge in language disordered children. Master's thesis, University of Massachusetts, Amherst.

Fodor, J. A. 1974. Special sciences: Or, the disunity of science as a working hypothesis. Reprinted in J. A. Fodor, *Representations*, 127–145. Cambridge, Mass.: MIT Press, 1981.

*Fodor, J. A. 2000. *The mind doesn't work that way*. Cambridge, Mass.: MIT Press.

Foley, C., Z. Núñez del Prado, I. Barbier, and B. Lust. 1999. Operator variable binding in the initial state: An argument from VP-ellipsis. In S. Somashekar, K. Yamakoshi, M. Blume, and C. Foley, eds., *Cornell working papers in linguistics 15*, 1–20. Ithaca, N.Y.: Cornell University, CLC Publications.

Frazier, L. 1999. *On sentence interpretation: Studies in theoretical psycholinguistics*. Dordrecht: Kluwer.

Frazier, L., and C. Clifton. 2001. Processing coordinates and ellipsis: Copy α. *Syntax* 4, 1–22.

Frazier, L., C. Clifton, K. Rayner, P. Deevy, S. Koh, and M. Bader. 2003. Interface problems: Structural constraints on interpretation? Ms., University of Massachusetts, Amherst.

Fromkin, V., and R. Rodman. 1998. *An introduction to language*. 6th ed. Fort Worth, Tex.: Harcourt Brace.

Galasso, J. 1999. The acquisition of functional categories: A case study. Doctoral dissertation, University of Essex.

Gardner, H. 1983. *Frames of mind: The theory of multiple intelligences*. New York: Basic Books.

Gelman, S. 2003. *The essential child: Origins of essentialism in everyday thought*. New York: Oxford University Press.

Gentile, S. 2000. On the acquisition of leftward-building recursive possessive structures in English. Honors thesis, University of Massachusetts, Amherst.

Gentner, T. Q., K. M. Fenn, D. Margoliash, and H. C. Nusbaum. 2006. Recursive syntactic pattern learning by songbirds. *Nature* 440, 1204–1207.

Gladwell, M. 2005. *Blink*. New York: Little, Brown.

Gleitman, L. 1990. The structural sources of verb meanings. *Language Acquisition* 1, 1–27.

*Golinkoff, R., and K. Hirsch-Pasek. 2000. *How babies talk: The magic and mystery of language in the first three years*. New York: Penguin.

Green, L. 2002. *African American English: A linguistic introduction*. Cambridge: Cambridge University Press.

*Guasti, M. T. 2002. *Language acquisition: The growth of grammar*. Cambridge, Mass.: MIT Press.

Gunlogson, C. 2003. *True to form: Rising and falling declaratives as questions in English*. New York: Routledge.

Haegeman, L. 1994. *Introduction to Government and Binding Theory*. Oxford: Blackwell.

Hauser, M. D. 2000. *Wild minds: What animals really think*. New York: Penguin.

Hauser, M. D., N. Chomsky, and W. T. Fitch. 2002. The faculty of language: What is it, who has it, and how did it evolve? *Science* 298, 1569–1579.

Heim, I., and A. Kratzer. 1998. *Semantics in generative grammar*. Malden, Mass.: Blackwell.

Herburger, E. 1997. Focus and weak noun phrases. *Natural Language Semantics* 8, 52–78.

Higginbotham, J. 1993. Interrogatives. In K. Hale and S. J. Keyser, eds., *The view from Building 20: Essays in linguistics in honor of Sylvain Bromberger*, 195–227. Cambridge, Mass.: MIT Press.

Higginson, R. P. 1985. Fixing-assimilation in language acquisition. Doctoral dissertation, Washington State University.

Hiramatsu, K., W. Snyder, T. Roeper, S. Storrs, and M. Saccoman. 2000. Of musical hand chairs and linguistic swing. In S. C. Howell, S. A. Fish, and T. Keith-Lucas, eds., *BUCLD 24: Proceedings of the 24th annual Boston University Conference on Language Development*, 409–417. Somerville, Mass.: Cascadilla Press.

Hollebrandse, B. 2000. The acquisition of sequence of tense. Doctoral dissertation, University of Massachusetts, Amherst.

Hollebrandse, B., and T. Roeper. 1996. The concept of *of*-insertion and the theory of INFL in acquisition. In C. Koster and F. Wijnen, eds., *Proceedings of GALA 1995*, 261–273. Groningen: Centre for Language and Cognition.

Horgan, J. 2004. A new kind of memory. *Newsweek* 10/25, 66.

Hout, A. van. 1995. Event semantics of verb frame alternations: A case study of Dutch and its acquisition. Doctoral dissertation, University of Massachusetts, Amherst. Published, New York: Garland, 1998.

Huang, C.-T. J. 1982. Logical relations in Chinese and the theory of grammar. Doctoral dissertation, MIT.

Inhelder, B., and J. Piaget. 1964. *The early growth of logic in the child*. London: Routledge and Kegan Paul.

*Jackendoff, R. 2002. *Foundations of language*. Oxford: Oxford University Press.

Jackson, J. 1998. Aspect in African-American English-speaking children: An investigation of aspectual "be." Doctoral dissertation, University of Massachusetts, Amherst.

Jeschull, L. In preparation. Acquisition of particle verbs and aspect. University of Leipzig.

Johnson, K. 1996. In search of the middle field (on gapping). Ms., University of Massachusetts, Amherst.

Johnson, K. 2001. What VP ellipsis can do, what it can't, but not why. In M. Baltin and C. Collins, eds., *The handbook of contemporary syntactic theory*, 439–479. Oxford: Blackwell.

Johnson, V. 2001. Fast mapping verb meaning from argument structure. Doctoral dissertation, Department of Communication Disorders, University of Massachusetts, Amherst.

Karmiloff-Smith, A. 1980. Psychological processes underlying pronominalization and non-pronominalization in children's connected discourse. In J. Kreiman and A. E. Ojeda, eds., *Papers from the Parasession on Pronouns and Anaphora*, 222–250. Chicago: University of Chicago, Chicago Linguistic Society.

Kosslyn, S. 1994. *Image and brain: The resolution of the imagery debate*. Cambridge, Mass.: MIT Press.

Kouider, S., J. Halberda, J. Wood, and S. Carey. 2006. Acquisition of English number marking. *Language Learning and Language Development* 2, 1–25.

Kratzer, A. 1999. Beyond "ouch" and "oops": How descriptive and expressive meaning interact. Comment on Kaplan's paper at the Cornell Conference on Context Dependency, March 26.

Kratzer, A. To appear. *The event argument and the semantics of voice*. Cambridge, Mass.: MIT Press.

Kroch, A., and A. Taylor. 1997. Verb movement in Old and Middle English: Dialect variation and language contact. In A. van Kemenade and N. Vincent, eds., *Parameters of morphosyntactic change*, 297–325. Cambridge: Cambridge University Press.

Kuczaj, S. 1976. *-ing*, *-s* and *-ed*: A study of the acquisition of certain verb inflections. Doctoral dissertation, University of Minnesota.

Kulikowski, S. 1980. A descriptive method for child language disability: The formal semantics, logic, and syntax of small languages. Doctoral dissertation, University of Massachusetts, Amherst.

Labov, W. 1970. The logic of non-standard English. In F. Williams, ed., *Language and poverty*, 153–189. Chicago: Markham.

Landman, F. 2000. *Events and plurality*. Berlin: Springer-Verlag.

Lebeaux, D. 2000. *Language acquisition and the form of grammar*. Amsterdam: John Benjamins.

Lemann, N. 1997. The reading wars. *The Atlantic Monthly* 280(5), 128–134.

Levinson, S. 1983. *Pragmatics*. Cambridge: Cambridge University Press.

Lidz, J., and J. Musolino. 2002. Children's command of quantification. *Cognition* 84, 113–154.

Luria, A. R. 1968. *The mind of a mnemonist: A little book about a vast memory*. Trans. by Lynn Solotaroff. Cambridge, Mass.: Harvard University Press.

*MacWhinney, B. 2000. *The CHILDES Project: Tools for analyzing talk*. 3rd ed. Hillsdale, N.J.: Lawrence Erlbaum. childes.psy.cmu.edu.

Maratsos, M. 1976. *The acquisition of definite and indefinite reference: An experimental study of semantic acquisition*. New York: Cambridge University Press.

Markman, E. 1991. *Categorization and naming in children: Problems of induction*. Cambridge, Mass.: MIT Press.

Maslow, B. 1954. *Motivation and personality*. New York: Harper.

Matsuo, A., and N. Duffield. 2001. VP-ellipsis and anaphora in first language acquisition. *Language Acquisition* 9, 301–327.

Matsuo, A., and N. Duffield. 2005. Paper presented at IASCL (International Association for the Study of Child Language) meeting, Berlin.

Matthei, E. 1982. The acquisition of prenominal modifier sequences. *Cognition* 11, 301–332.

Matthews, G. 1994. *The philosophy of childhood*. Cambridge, Mass.: Harvard University Press.

Matthewson, L. 1998. *Determiner systems and quantificational strategies: Evidence from Salish*. The Hague: Holland Academic Graphics.

Matthewson, L., T. J. Bryant, and T. Roeper. 2001. A Salish stage in the acquisition of English determiners: Unfamiliar "definites." In J.-Y. Kim and A. Werle, eds., *UMOP*

25: The proceedings of SULA 1, 63–71. Amherst: University of Massachusetts, Graduate Linguistics Student Association.

Mayer, Jane. 2005. The experiment. *The New Yorker*, July 11, 60–71.

McWhorter, J. 1998. *The word on the street: Fact and fable about American English*. New York: Plenum.

Meltzoff, A. N., and M. K. Moore. 1977. Imitation of facial and manual gestures by human infants. *Science* 198, 75–78.

Meltzoff, A. N., and M. K. Moore. 1997. Explaining facial imitation: A theoretical model. *Early Development and Parenting* 6, 179–192.

Merchant, G. 2005. Children's use of the quantifier *every*. Lab report, Smith College.

Merchant, J. 2001. *The syntax of silence*. Oxford: Oxford University Press.

Milloy, C. 2000. Good questions, bad answers from Thomas. *The New York Times*, December 17, C01.

Mills, A. E. 1986. *The acquisition of gender: A study of English and German*. Berlin: Springer-Verlag.

Miyamoto, Y. 1992. The collective and distributive interpretation in child grammar: A study on quantification. Ms., University of Connecticut, Storrs.

Moore, D. In preparation. Acquisition of comparatives. Doctoral dissertation, University of Massachusetts, Amherst.

Nishigauchi, T. 1999. Some preliminary thoughts on the acquisition of the syntax and semantics of *wh*-constructions. In *Theoretical and applied linguistics at Kobe Shoin* 2, 35–48. Kobe Shoin Institute for Linguistic Sciences.

Noveck, I., and F. Chevaux. 2002. The pragmatic development of *and*. In B. Skarabela, S. Fish, and A. H.-J. Do, eds., *BUCLD 26: Proceedings of the 26th annual Boston University Conference on Language Development*, 453–463. Somerville, Mass.: Cascadilla Press.

*O'Grady, W. 1997. *Syntactic development*. Chicago: University of Chicago Press.

O'Neil, W. 1998. Linguistics for everyone. Plenary speech at Annual Conference of the Australian Linguistic Society, Brisbane, July 3–5. www.cltr.uq.edu.au/als98.

Ortony, A., G. L. Clore, and A. Collins. 1988. *The cognitive structure of emotions*. New York: Cambridge University Press.

Partee, B. 1973. Some transformational extensions of Montague Grammar. *Journal of Philosophical Logic 2*, 509–534.

Partee, B. 2004. Compositionality. In *Compositionality in formal semantics: Selected papers of Barbara Partee*, 153–181. Malden, Mass.: Blackwell.

Pérez-Leroux, A. 1993. Empty categories and the acquisition of *wh*-movement. Doctoral dissertation, University of Massachusetts, Amherst.

Pérez-Leroux, A., and T. Roeper. 1999. Scope and the structure of bare nominals: Evidence from child language. *Linguistics* 37, 927–960.

Philip, W. 1995. Event quantification in the acquisition of universal quantification. Doctoral dissertation, University of Massachusetts, Amherst.

Philip, W. 2004. Two theories of exhaustive pairing. Ms., Utrecht Institute of Linguistics, OTS, Utrecht University.

Phillips, C., T. Pellathy, A. Marantz, E. Yellin, K. Wexler, D. Poeppel, M. McGinnis, and T. Roberts. 2000. Auditory cortex accesses phonological categories: An MEG mismatch study. *Journal of Cognitive Neuroscience* 12, 1038–1055.

Piaget, J. 1959. *The language and thought of the child*. London: Routledge and Kegan Paul.

Piaget, J. 1995. *Sociological studies*. Ed. by Leslie Smith. New York: Routledge.

Pinker, S., ed. 1984. *Visual cognition*. Cambridge, Mass.: MIT Press.

*Pinker, S. 1994. *The language instinct*. New York: William Morrow.

*Pinker, S. 1997. *How the mind works*. New York: Norton.

Potts, C. 2005. *The logic of conventional implicatures*. Oxford: Oxford University Press.

Potts, C., and T. Roeper. 2006. The narrowing acquisition path: From declaratives to expressive small clauses. In L. Progovac, K. Paesani, É. Casielles Suárez, and E. L. Barton, eds., *The syntax of nonsententials: Multidisciplinary perspectives*. Amsterdam: John Benjamins.

Radford, A. 1997. *Syntax: A minimalist introduction*. Cambridge: Cambridge University Press.

Randall, J. 1980. -*ity*: A study in word formation restrictions. *Journal of Psycholinguistic Research* 9, 523–534.

Randall, J. 1982. Morphological structure and language acquisition. Doctoral dissertation, University of Massachusetts, Amherst. Published, New York: Garland, 1985.

Rickford, J. 1999. *African American Vernacular English*. Malden, Mass.: Blackwell.

Rickford, J. n.d. *What is Ebonics (African American Vernacular English)?* Washington, D.C.: Linguistic Society of America.

Roeper, T. 1965. A study of grammar and style in the poetry of Donne and Herbert. Undergraduate thesis, Reed College.

Roeper, T. 1982. The role of universals in the acquisition of gerunds. In E. Wanner and L. Gleitman, eds., *Language acquisition: The state of the art*, 267–287. Cambridge: Cambridge University Press.

Roeper, T. 1999. Universal bilingualism. *Bilingualism: Language and Cognition* 2, 169–186.

Roeper, T. 2002. The hidden algebra of the mind from a linguistic perspective. In G. Grewendorf and G. Meggle, eds., *Speech acts, mind, and social reality: Discussions with John Searle*, 223–234. Dordrecht: Kluwer.

Roeper, T. 2003. Multiple grammars, feature-attraction, pied-piping, and the question: Is AGR inside TP? In N. Müller, ed., *(In)vulnerable domains in multilingualism*, 335–360. Amsterdam: John Benjamins.

Roeper, T. 2004. Diagnosing language variations: Underlying principles for syntactic assessment. In H. Seymour and B. Z. Pearson, eds., *Evaluating language variation: Distinguishing dialect and development from disorder*, 41–56. *Seminars in Speech and Language* 25(1).

Roeper, T., and J. de Villiers. 1993. The emergence of bound variables. In E. Reuland and W. Abraham, eds., *Knowledge and language*, 105–139. Boston: Kluwer.

Roeper, T., and E. Matthei. 1975. On the acquisition of "all" and "some." *Papers and Reports on Child Language Development* 9, 63–74.

Roeper, T., B. Z. Pearson, Z. Penner, and P. Schulz. 2002. The emergence of *wh*-variables: Cross-linguistic explorations. Paper presented at the IXth International Congress for the Study of Child Language (IASCL) and the Symposium on Research in Child Language Disorders (SRCLD), University of Wisconsin, Madison, July.

Roeper, T., and M. Siegel. 1978. Lexical transformations for verbal compounds. *Linguistic Inquiry* 9, 199–260.

Roeper, T., and W. Snyder. 2004. Recursion as an analytic device in acquisition. In J. van Kampen and S. Baauw, eds., *Proceedings of GALA 2003*, 401–408. Utrecht: LOT Publications.

Roeper, T., and W. Snyder. 2005. Language learnability and the forms of recursion. In A. M. Di Sciullo, ed., *UG and external systems*, 155–169. Amsterdam: John Benjamins.

Roeper, T., U. Strauss, and B. Z. Pearson. 2006. The acquisition path of the determiner quantifier *every*: Two kinds of spreading. In T. Heizmann, ed., *Papers in language acquisition*. Amherst: University of Massachusetts, Graduate Linguistics Student Association.

Sachs, J. 1983. Talking about the there and then: The emergence of displaced reference in parent–child discourse. In K. E. Nelson, ed., *Children's language*, vol. 4, 1–28. Hillsdale, N.J.: Lawrence Erlbaum.

Sauerland, U. 2003. Presupposition in plurals. Paper presented at the Workshop on Quantification, University of Amherst, Massachusetts, May.

Sauerland, U., J. Anderssen, and K. Yatsushiro. 2005. The plural is semantically unmarked. www-unix.oit.umass.edu/~janderss/work.

Schafer, R., and J. de Villiers. 2000. Imagining articles: What "a" and "the" can tell us about the emergence of DP. In S. C. Howell, S. A. Fish, and T. Keith-Lucas, eds., *BUCLD 24: Proceedings of the 24th annual Boston University Conference on Language Development*, vol. 2, 609–620. Somerville, Mass.: Cascadilla Press.

Schafer, R., and T. Roeper. 2000. The role of the expletive in the acquisition of a discourse anaphor. In S. C. Howell, S. A. Fish, and T. Keith-Lucas, eds., *BUCLD 24: Proceedings of the 24th annual Boston University Conference on Language Development*, vol. 2, 621–632. Somerville, Mass.: Cascadilla Press.

Schmiedtova, B. 2004. *At the same time . . . The expression of simultaneity in learner varieties*. Max-Planck-Institut für Psycholinguistik & Radboud Universiteit Nijmegen.

Searle, J. 1969. *Speech acts*. Cambridge: Cambridge University Press.

Searle, J. 1995. *The construction of social reality*. New York: Free Press.

Searle, J. 2005. Consciousness: What we still don't know. Review of *The quest for consciousness* by Christof Koch in *New York Review of Books*, January 13. www.nybooks .com/archives/.

*Seymour, H., and B. Z. Pearson, eds. 2004. *Evaluating language variation: Distinguishing dialect and development from disorder. Seminars in Speech and Language* 25(1).

*Seymour, H., T. Roeper, and J. de Villiers. 2003. *Diagnostic Evaluation of Language Variation–Screening Test (DELV-ST)*. San Antonio, Tex.: Harcourt Assessments.

*Seymour, H., T. Roeper, and J. de Villiers. 2005. *Diagnostic Evaluation of Language Variation–Norm Referenced (DELV-NR)*. San Antonio, Tex.: Harcourt Assessments.

Seymour, H., T. Roeper, J. de Villiers, P. de Villiers, L. Ciolli, and B. Z. Pearson. 2002. Developmental milestones for AAE-speaking 4-, 5-, and 6-year-olds. Unpublished technical report for the National Institutes of Health, University of Massachusetts, Amherst.

Siegel, M. 2002. *Like*: The discourse particle and semantics. *Journal of Semantics* 19, 35–71.

Smits, E.-J., T. Roeper, and B. Hollebrandse. 2006. Set comparison in first language acquisition. *Or* Whether many children quantify like many adults. Ms., University of Groningen and University of Massachusetts, Amherst. To appear in *Aarlberg papers in linguistics*.

Snyder, W., and T. Roeper. 2004. Learnability and recursion across categories. In A. Brugos, L. Micciulla, and C. Smith, eds., *BUCLD 28: Proceedings of the 28th annual Boston University Conference on Language Development*, 543–552. Somerville, Mass.: Cascadilla Press.

Snyder, W., K. Wexler, and D. Das. 1995. The syntactic representation of degree and quantity: Perspectives from Japanese and Child English. In R. Aranovich et al., eds., *Papers from the 13th Meeting of the West Coast Conference on Formal Linguistics*. Stanford, Calif.: CSLI Publications.

Spelke, E. S. 2002. Developing knowledge of space: Core systems and new combinations. In A. Galaburda, S. M. Kosslyn, and Y. Christen, eds., *Languages of the brain*, 239–258. Cambridge, Mass.: Harvard University Press.

Spock, B. 1968. *Baby and child care*. New York: Hawthorn Books.

Steele, C. 1997. A threat in the air: How stereotypes shape the intellectual identities and performance of women and African-Americans. *American Psychologist* 52, 613–629.

Stickney, H. 2003. Investigations into children's acquisition of *most*. Ms., University of Massachusetts, Amherst.

Strauss, U. 2006. Acquisition of exhaustivity. In T. Heizmann, ed., *Language acquisition*. University of Massachusetts Occasional Papers in Linguistics 34. Amherst: University of Massachusetts, Graduate Linguistics Student Association.

Strauss, U., T. Roeper, B. Z. Pearson, and H. Seymour. 2003. Acquisition of universality in *wh*-questions. Paper presented at the Generative Linguistics in the Old World Conference (GLOW), Lund, Sweden, April.

Takahashi, M. 1991. Children's interpretation of sentences containing *every*. In T. L. Maxfield and B. Plunkett, eds., *Papers in the acquisition of WH*, 303–327. Amherst: University of Massachusetts, Graduate Linguistics Student Association.

Tanz, C. 1980. *Studies in the acquisition of deictic terms*. Cambridge: Cambridge University Press.

Tavakolian, S., ed. 1981. *Language acquisition and linguistic theory*. Cambridge, Mass.: MIT Press.

Terada, M. 1991. The acquisition of the passive of small clauses. In B. Plunkett, ed., *Issues in psycholinguistics*, 367–383. University of Massachusetts Occasional Papers in Linguistics 15. Amherst: University of Massachusetts, Graduate Linguistics Student Association.

Terry, J. M. 2004. On the articulation of aspectual meaning in African-American English. Doctoral dissertation, University of Massachusetts, Amherst.

Thornton, R., and K. Wexler. 1999. *Principle B, VP ellipsis and interpretation in child grammar*. Cambridge, Mass.: MIT Press.

Tomioka, S. 2001. On a certain scope asymmetry in VP ellipsis contexts. In C. Rohrer, A. Roßdeutscher, and H. Kamp, eds., *Linguistic form and its computation*, 183–204. Stanford, Calif.: CSLI Publications.

Vygotsky, L. 1962. *Thought and language*. Ed. and trans. by Eugenia Hanfmann and Gertrude Vakar. Cambridge, Mass.: MIT Press.

Weinberg, S. 2001. The future of science, and the universe. *New York Review of Books* 48, no. 18 (November 15).

Weissenborn, J., T. Roeper, and J. de Villiers. 1990. The acquisition of *wh*-movement in German and French. In T. L. Maxfield and B. Plunkett, eds., *Proceedings of the University of Massachusetts Roundtable*, 43–73. Amherst: University of Massachusetts, Graduate Linguistics Student Association.

Whorf, B. 1956. *Language, thought, and reality: Selected writings*. Cambridge, Mass.: MIT Press.

Wijnen, F., T. Roeper, and H. van der Meulen. 2004. Discourse binding: Does it begin with nominal ellipsis? In J. van Kampen and S. Baauw, eds., *Proceedings of GALA 2003*, 505–516. Utrecht: LOT Publications.

Wittgenstein, L. 1978. *Culture and value*. Oxford: Blackwell.

Wyatt, T. 1991. Linguistic constraints on copula production in Black English child speech. Doctoral dissertation, University of Massachusetts, Amherst.

Yang, C. 2003. *Knowledge and learning in natural language*. Oxford: Oxford University Press.

Explorations

Index

Italics indicates a discussion of the actual word.